Ita Wegman and Karl König

Ita Wegman and Karl König

Letters and Documents

Peter Selg

Floris Books

Karl König Archive, Volume 3
Subject: Karl König's Biography

Translated by Regina Erich

First published in German in 2007 under the title
Ita Wegman und Karl König. Eine biografische Dokumentation
by Natura Verlag am Goetheanum
First published in English by Floris Books in 2008

British Library CIP Data available

ISBN 978-086315-661-8

Printed in Great Britain
by Athenaeum Press, Gateshead

Contents

Be assured that I will always remain connected to your work.

Ita Wegman to Karl König, January 18, 1940

Preface

> At six o'clock the message arrives that Dr Wegman has passed away. Rarely felt such immediate grief. Feel like broken apart.
>
> *Karl König, Diary, March 4, 1943*

The great life and work of Karl König (1902–66) leading to the development of the Camphill movement and to the formation of a holistic and humane curative educational initiative based on esoteric Christianity was, from the beginning, supported by Ita Wegman with emphasis, care and foresight. Soon after Rudolf Steiner's death König entrusted himself to Wegman with great respect and the highest regard for the Medical Section and its leadership at the Goetheanum. Karl König held Ita Wegman and her spiritual mission as Rudolf Steiner's associate and 'representative' in the field of anthroposophical medicine in the highest esteem — and he was not to be disappointed. Soon after making their acquaintance Ita Wegman clearly saw Karl König's spiritual abilities and his medical and social intentions, but also his one-sidedness and vulnerabilities. She was one of the few people by whom König felt understood and recognized. From Ita Wegman, Karl König gratefully accepted advice, encouragement and correction, and for a time became her medical and scientific assistant at the clinic in Arlesheim. The Clinical Therapeutical Institute had been founded in 1921. For König the essence of the clinic was and remained for all times inseparably interwoven with Rudolf Steiner's medical initiative. It was in Arlesheim, at the Sonnenhof, where in December 1927 he found the mission to which he would dedicate his entire life and work. Karl König's stay in Arlesheim lasted from November 1927 to summer 1928. He never resumed work there at any stage of his life, though several times, after moving east to Pilgramshain, König wanted to return to the clinic in Arlesheim. However, his relationship to Ita Wegman and the Medical Section at the Goetheanum was continuous from 1925.

Evidently Ita Wegman (1876–1943) had an intuitive understanding for the specific mission of König's life and destiny. Wegman knew what kind of social environment and space for development König needed. She understood his special potential as a doctor and scientist, his outstanding will-power and morality, but obviously she also knew that he relied on appropriate conditions and feedback, and needed time in order not to rush through his work or alter it impetuously. From the beginning Ita Wegman gave Karl König intense support, and shortly after making his acquaintance asked him to hold major lectures on behalf of the Medical Section. She helped him when his position within the Anthroposophical Society and curative educational movement turned out to be complex and difficult; her support involved frequent talks with other anthroposophists and on many occasions she acted as a mediator for him. She was also there for him when in 1938 König's life was under threat because of his Jewish origin. She played an active part in his emigration to Scotland and, as a result, also in the beginnings of the Camphill community in Kirkton House. From a distance she watched König's initiative in Scotland until her earthly parting at the beginning of March 1943.

Documentary evidence from that time shows that Ita Wegman led Karl König in a certain way: this was not leadership using determining or imperative force; instead it was a liberating way of guidance focusing on a person's individuality and destiny.

This was obviously a result of a spiritual dimension within Ita Wegman's being which Siegfried Pickert had experienced in May 1925, shortly after Rudolf Steiner's death, and which he later described in the words: 'This is the spiritual dimension of Rudolf Steiner which acts within and through Ita Wegman.'[1] Throughout his life Karl König was unable to accept this kind of advice, assistance and encouragement from anyone but Ita Wegman, which was probably due to her relationship to Rudolf Steiner.

★

My special thanks for all the personal and practical support I received while working on this documentation go to Gunhild Pörksen, Felicitas Graf and Ruth Andrea (Arlesheim/Dornach, Switzerland), Stefan Geider, David Coe, Friedwart and Nora Bock (Camphill, Scotland), Christof-Andreas and Norma Lindenberg (Beaver Run, Pennsylvania), Margit Engel, Simone Wantz and Hannes Weigert (Vidaråsen, Norway), Brigitte Köber (Rüttihubelbad, Switzerland), Johanna Spalinger (Humanus Haus, Switzerland), Erika von Arnim and Richard Steel (Föhrenbühl, Germany), Rike and Nils Ehmcke and Tony Foskett (Königsmühle, Germany).

Regarding the contents of this book I extend my sincerest gratitude to the doctor and curative teacher Hans Müller-Wiedemann (1924–97). In 1992 his profound biography of Karl König highlighted for the first time the importance of Ita Wegman in König's life and work. This book, therefore, is dedicated to the memory of Hans Müller-Wiedemann.

Peter Selg
Ita Wegman Institute
Arlesheim, Michaelmas 2006

1

The Relationship between Karl König and Ita Wegman

> This is what Rudolf Steiner placed as a task on the Medical Section, namely to form a community of people through the Section who, for the sake of the art of healing and its related fields, were willing to esoterically deepen themselves within this work. Sadly Dr Steiner left us and so this most sacred task remained only in our hearts like a longing. In my opinion this longing expressed itself in people who sensed it and who stood together out of the deepest profundity of their being.
>
> *Ita Wegman, 1934*[1]

> This community [of doctors] is possible. This community must be practiced in the hearts of those who genuinely want to connect themselves with the healing practice of the Goetheanum. ... Through a certain consciousness, it must connect those who want to work as doctors in an anthroposophical sense with the source of this work here at the Goetheanum. To strive for such a source of work for the medical movement is the purpose and aspiration of Dr Wegman's and my working together here at the Goetheanum.
>
> *Rudolf Steiner, September 18, 1924*[2]

Karl König turned to Rudolf Steiner's anthroposophy at the age of twenty-two while studying medicine in Vienna with keenest interest, with his own understanding and questions, but also with a distinctive social reserve.[3] König was a highly gifted, critical and withdrawn person. Even as a medical student he successfully treated patients. As an assistant at the University's Institute for Embryology he researched the efficacy of homeopathic substances, and also studied Ernst Haeckel's evolutionary theory and Rudolf Steiner's Christological theory of evolution. Long before discovering Steiner's systematic editions of Goethe's scientific writings and his qualitative understanding of nature, König had already found his own connection and understanding of them. Hence his astonishment when meeting anthroposophy ('I was overjoyed when I found my ideas brought to expression in an entire movement'[4]). In 1924, for the first time and with increasing conviction, Karl König took part in an anthroposophical study group led by Norbert and Maria Glas who were only a few years his senior. But even during the time immediately following König still did not feel completely comfortable within the anthroposophical sphere and, in a melancholic sort of way, remained distant — at the same time becoming increasingly confident that he had 'adopted the right path of knowledge.'[5] Karl König could have attended Rudolf Steiner's public lectures in Vienna at the beginning of the 1920s, for instance during the East-West-Congress at Whitsun 1922, but had avoided them ('My studies, a measure of youthful arrogance and also phlegma stood in my way'[6]). On March 23, 1925 as a result of a definite decision after overcoming considerable inner difficulties, König became a member of the General Anthroposophical Society which Rudolf Steiner had re-founded sixteen months earlier in Dornach.[7] Just seven days after Karl König had joined the Society the great spiritual mentor died at the Goetheanum, the new School of Spiritual Science — 'The news shook me to the roots of my being.'[8]

★

On May 5, 1925, five weeks after Rudolf Steiner's death, Karl König wrote for the first time to Ita Wegman, Steiner's assistant and personal physician for many years, who had treated her mentor and friend every day during the last six months of his life. In a formal letter Karl König asked Ita Wegman for an 'interim membership' of the Medical Section 'so that I can study Dr Steiner's lecture courses in the company of the members here.'[9] At this time Karl König had been a member of the General Anthroposophical Society for just over a month — nowhere near the two years of membership required for entering the School of Spiritual Science and its Medical Section in

Dornach; therefore he did not meet the requirements for entry. But Norbert Glas, who chaired the study group in Vienna and belonged to the Esoteric Core of the Medical Section, supported König's application to Ita Wegman: 'I believe that his entry to the Medical Section even at this early stage would be of advantage for everyone involved.'[10] Ita Wegman agreed and advised her assistant Dr Eberhard Schickler, who also belonged to the Esoteric Core of the Medical Section, to reply to Norbert Glas:

> As to your recommendation of Mr König whose application arrived here today; Frau Doctor [Wegman] would like to let you know that he can be regarded as an interim colleague at the Medical Section and also that he can gradually be included in the courses provided that you agree to take responsibility for him. Until he meets the requirements for full membership of the Class he is, therefore, colleague at the Section (subject to revocation regarding the literature).[11]

Shortly after this, in summer 1925, Karl König travelled for the first time to the Goetheanum, the place where Rudolf Steiner had worked and died. Here he felt as if he had found his 'home'; ' it left a profound and lasting impression on me.'[12]

Despite his immediate affinity for the Goetheanum König still had difficulties with the anthroposophical social sphere, even after summer 1925. In his view there was no social commitment and interest in current affairs whatsoever; he experienced (and suffered) the tendency of spiritual science with its cultural aspects to become increasingly bourgeois and the lack of a 'full awakening' to the actual challenges.

★

For the first time in February 1926 Norbert Glas sent one of Karl König's essays to Arlesheim, to Margarete Bockholt, a doctor, curative educator, eurythmist and member of the Esoteric Core who was the editor of the journal *Natura.* Norbert Glas asked her to consider for publication by the Medical Section König's embryological study about the etheric formative forces which shape the human nose.[13] Scientific publications were the responsibility of the Esoteric Core of the Medical Section, so Glas wrote to Bockholt:

> Enclosed I also send you a short study on embryology by one of our doctors. It is still quite scientific but well thought through and perhaps even suitable for being published in *Natura.* I have already talked to [Hilma] Walter about it.[14]

When Norbert Glas was left with no reply for more than three months Karl König himself wrote once more to Ita Wegman — exactly a year after his 'interim membership' application. He informed Wegman that Guenther Wachsmuth, head of the Natural Science Section, had asked him for a contribution to an almanac and suggested publishing his work there ('only if no other arrangements for printing have already been made'). However, Ita Wegman actually attached importance to its publication and through her assistant Margarete Bockholt told König that *Natura* would publish the study 'in the near future,' which (for reasons unknown) never happened.[15]

Nevertheless half a year later, at the end of November 1926, Karl König sent another study on embryology, this time to Ita Wegman personally. He offered the study for publication in the *Natura,* told about his work in Vienna and about the introductory courses in anthroposophy focusing on embryology which he had held together with Maria Glas and which had given him new insights. König also mentioned that he could send follow-up studies on embryology if desired by Ita Wegman. ('In case you, dear Doctor Wegman, as a result of this submitted essay, would agree to receiving more studies on biogenesis I would kindly ask you to notify me accordingly.') Within a week Karl König had Ita Wegman's reply in his hands — the first, albeit typed, letter he received from her. She accepted his essay on embryology for publication in *Natura* and encouraged him to continue his work: 'I would also be pleased if you were to continue working in this direction, and if you could soon send us more contributions.'

Shortly before Christmas 1926 Karl König once again wrote to Ita Wegman, this time by express letter because he thought he had found a serious error of content in his study ('I feel very guilty having done such a thing because something wrong would be put into the world, and I hope it is still possible to correct the mistake'). He was reassured by Arlesheim that the article was not in print yet and, apart from that, the proof-reading was always done with great care.

★

In March 1927, immediately after finishing his medical studies, Karl König — now in his twenty-fifth year — again turned to Ita Wegman. He wanted, so he informed her, to come to Dornach soon for a visit and introduce himself to her, the head of the Medical Section at the Goetheanum; he also planned to apply for official acceptance to the Section after two years of membership in the Society. He wanted to discuss with her the possibility of working at the clinic in Arlesheim as an assistant and to present a book project on embryology which he had started and for which he sought advice. He did not receive Ita Wegman's reply; during the second half of May, however, König already wrote his next letter. He did not send it from Vienna, however, where he had obtained a doctor's degree in April but had refused a position at the Institute of Embryology on the grounds that there was no academic freedom regarding anthroposophical issues. Instead he wrote in his position as medical assistant at the hospital in Klosterneuburg, site of the historic Cistercian monastery. Again he asked Ita Wegman for admission to the Medical Section of the School of Spiritual Science at the Goetheanum.[16] He mentioned that, as a result of the practical medical work he had started, he felt the 'deep desire to make steps in moral development':

> I therefore sincerely ask you to admit me to the Medical Section and to the First Class of the School [of Spiritual Science] so that I can begin with meditative work on the meditations given by Dr Steiner. This need is intense and continuous.

Concerning the acceptance to the first Class of the School of Spiritual Science he would, so König continued, contact Count Polzer-Hoditz as soon as he was back in Vienna; but he asked Wegman for acceptance to the Medical Section. Ita Wegman then supported König's request and advised him to contact Count Polzer quickly.

★

Although a few months later (in September 1927) Karl König was supposed to be accepted into the School and the Medical Section, he still had not met Ita Wegman in person — he had never attended her lectures nor had he ever spoken to her. In July 1927, on receiving a letter in Klosterneuburg from Norbert Glas, informing him that Ita Wegman had suggested him for the position of assistant surgeon at the private clinic of the anthroposophical doctor Viktor Wehrle in Salzburg, he was surprised, pleased and at the same time slightly disconcerted. It does not seem very likely that he felt sufficiently prepared for the position as a surgeon in Salzburg or that he would have aspired to it on his own initiative; but König took the recommendation, or rather the intent, of the head of the Section absolutely seriously and inquiringly wrote to Ita Wegman, asking for clarification:

> I now would like to ask you what kind of preparations for this position you have in mind. The reason for this is

> that I think I definitely need to gather experience through observation at the clinic in Arlesheim beforehand. But I do not know whether a position of assistant at your clinic is possible at present.
>
> Further I would like to ask you if there is the possibility that you would consider somebody else from the Medical Section as being more suited for this position than me.
>
> Before I write to Dr Wehrle I want to contact you first, Frau Doctor, in order to avoid doing something that might go against the plans of the Medical Section.
>
> I would be very grateful, Frau Doctor, if you could possibly give me some concrete information regarding this issue.
>
> Finally I would like to emphasize again that I place myself completely at the disposal of the Medical Section and that I await your decision.

Just two weeks later, on July 18, 1927, Ita Wegman replied that at the moment and in autumn too assistance at her clinic in Arlesheim would not really be feasible, due to overstaffing — and she continued:

> Therefore I would like to advise you just to make a start with Dr Wehrle and to try to get into the work with true anthroposophical resolve. It will surely work out, even without having been here beforehand, particularly as you cannot be properly trained here for surgical work.

Wegman advised König to cooperate closely with Maria Glas in Vienna until taking up his post in Salzburg and to take advantage of her therapeutic experience, and offered a placement as assistant at her clinic at a later time. 'And then, after having worked with Dr Wehrle for a while, it might be possible that you come here for a short stay; certainly your benefit will then be even greater.' Obviously she wanted to encourage this young Viennese doctor and at the same time wanted to prevent him from having unreasonable expectations of Arlesheim while not rejecting him, hence at the end of her letter and in an unexpected turn Ita Wegman did offer a placement in autumn, even if she did not recommend it:

> If it is of such importance for you to have been here beforehand, you are of course welcome in September, though you will not find the opportunities you have in mind and which I would like to see for you.

In late summer and autumn 1927, however, things turned out completely different. After Karl König had spoken to Wehrle personally and had found that Wehrle did not have sufficient funds available to pay a salary for an assistant doctor, he started doing his clinical training at a big children's hospital in a suburb of Vienna before the end of the summer. In October König took part for the first time in a public conference of the Anthroposophical Society in Vienna. On October 15 he gave his first anthroposophical lecture on Haeckel and the evolution of organisms and the biogenetic law. There the anthroposophical psychiatrist and Goetheanist, Friedrich Husemann, who had come from Freiburg to the conference in Vienna and also held lectures there, offered König a position as an assistant at his private psychiatric sanatorium in Freiburg-Günterstal which he had founded two years before, still with approval from Rudolf Steiner.[17] Before Karl König (obviously very pleased with Husemann's spur-of-the-moment proposal) gave a positive answer, he contacted the head of the Medical Section in Arlesheim again:

> I now would like to ask you, dear Frau Doctor, whether you would agree if I went to Dr Husemann. I would be very glad to work with him. ...
>
> I would be very grateful if you, dear Frau Doctor, could advise me in writing whether you approve of my working with Doctor Husemann or not; also whether you regard me as a member of the Section.

It is possible that Ita Wegman received Karl König's letter while still in Arlesheim and before travelling to Vienna to the funeral of Rudolf Steiner's sister Leopoldine who had died in the Waldviertel district of Vienna on November 1, a day before König had written his letter.[18] However, König definitely did not receive a written reply to his enquiry, but unexpectedly met Ita Wegman just a few days later in Vienna:

> I stood on the railway platform, reserved and uncomfortable, because with a few friends I had been delegated to welcome Dr Ita Wegman who was coming to Vienna. She was to attend the funeral of Rudolf Steiner's only sister. Along with a few others, I was asked to greet Dr Wegman. I had never met her before and constantly asked myself why it was necessary for me to wait for someone I did not know. I was at the time rather young and shy and did not like to be too much among people.
>
> At last the train pulled into the station and Dr Wegman alighted, greeting the welcoming party. I was introduced to her, we shook hands and all was quickly over. I left the station and went home, not knowing what it all meant.[19]

But a short time later König met Ita Wegman once more in Vienna and talked to her in a private, forward-looking conversation, which he described in an autobiographical essay:

> I felt quite at ease when I sat opposite her and she asked me a few questions about my life and work, and then suggested that I join her Clinic in Arlesheim. I was astonished at this offer but happy at the prospect of being introduced so closely to the wellspring of anthroposophical therapeutics. So I asked her when she would expect me to go, thinking that this might be some few months ahead after I would have concluded my

> clinical year in Vienna. Dr Wegman looked at me with a gracious smile and suggested that I go to Arlesheim in a couple of weeks. I had a slight shock and said that this was out of the question. But she would not give in and so we agreed that I would be in Arlesheim at the beginning of November. I then left her, inspired by her great personality which I had immediately recognized. On the 7th of November, 1927, I arrived in Arlesheim.[20]

Whether Karl König was mistaken about the date of his start at the Arlesheim clinic when writing later is not known; but it does not seem very likely, given that he must have based his essay on his own detailed and extraordinarily accurate diary entries. If, however, he did in fact arrive at Arlesheim on November 7, 1927 and started work there, he had stayed only a few days in Vienna after this decisive conversation with Ita Wegman.[21]

★

> The Clinical Therapeutic Institute in Arlesheim was not particularly striking nor notably big. But when you entered it and lived there for months and years, as I had the opportunity to do, you felt like at a prince's court. Hundreds of people came and went, there were telephone calls from all over the world, telegrams, letters, patients, attachés, attendants. It was very lively with comings and goings, but permeated by a deep sense of humanity. As a young person you were trustingly included, and you felt accepted as a friend.[22]

Although Ita Wegman was not present at his arrival in Arlesheim, for which reason his start at the clinic was not altogether easy, Karl König obviously settled there quickly and felt at home perhaps as never before: 'you felt accepted as a friend.' König felt immensely attracted by the warm, most lively, cosmo-

Karl König in Arlesheim, 1927/28.

politan and intellectually interesting atmosphere of the Clinical Therapeutic Institute. Apart from Ita Wegman, whose therapeutic charisma wove through the Institute and imbued it with light, warmth and life like a sun, the doctors, Hilma Walter and Margarete Bockholt, as well as many nurses had experienced Rudolf Steiner in his therapeutic work. In addition some young doctors who were close to Madeleine van Deventer and Gerhard Suchantke worked here or came on occasional visits; they belonged to the core of the former young doctors group and were able to give König an account of the esoteric courses held by Rudolf Steiner in January and April 1924. There was a pharmacist, Oskar Schmiedel, who already for a decade had been making innovative anthroposophical remedies and was of vital importance to the new medical movement. There were also artists and art therapists as well as a considerable number of accomplished scientists connected with the Natural Science Section at the Goetheanum who were working on studies and publications. At the end of November 1927 — only a few weeks after König's arrival — Ita Wegman wrote to the editor of the *Zeitschrift für experimentelle Medizin* asking for an off-print of a study König had published there in order to reprint it in *Natura* — 'since Mr König is one of our colleagues.'[23]

In the Clinical Therapeutic Institute Karl König worked temporarily in the laboratory, treated individual patients and joined eurythmy and curative eurythmy courses, but then — probably at the end of November or beginning of December — Ita Wegman took him to the Sonnenhof, a newly founded centre for curative education near the cathedral in Arlesheim, only a few minutes walk away from the Clinic. This visit, accompanied and led by Ita Wegman, was to set the course of life and destiny for Karl König, who had gathered first experience in pediatrics in Vienna and during his studies had attended lectures on curative education.[24]

> She acquainted me with her special charges and problem children and asked me if I would be interested in this kind of work. I was certainly taken by surprise by this question. Dr Wegman was an impulsive personality, and often acted out of immediate inspirations and ideas. I was faced with a completely new world here. I had encountered the problems of these children only twice before and both times they had made an impression on me — although not to the extent that a destiny-determining impulse had grown in me.
>
> ... But here at the Sonnenhof, there were about thirty smaller and bigger children with enormous or tiny heads, with paralysed limbs; some with an empty gaze;

> others traumatized by fits. But all of them were children! They laughed and cried; they were joyful and suffered pain like all other children. I was struck deeply and immediately by two things: The 'humanity' in each single one of these odd souls and the host of morphological deformations and flaws of nature that confronted me. 'Through these imperfections,' I said to myself, 'you will be able to research the hidden mysteries of development in the human form.'
>
> Consequently, when Dr Wegman asked me if I would be prepared to spend a part of my day working at the Sonnenhof as a doctor, I willingly agreed. I was instantly drawn to these children and they quickly became very dear to me. And so I spent many hours with them, learning to dress and undress them, to clean them, to play with them, to calm or encourage them, and to be their friend.[25]

Karl König came from Vienna, from his Goetheanistic-embryological research, with a Christological approach and with exceptional gifts of wonder, compassion and conscience, and an emphatic will to heal.[26] With this he started work at the Sonnenhof (alongside his responsibilities at the clinic), and together with the Sonnenhof children experienced in December the Advent festivities:

> The first Advent Sunday soon arrived, a festival that had been completely unknown to me in Catholic Vienna, and one I had never before celebrated. In the afternoon I went to the Sonnenhof to be with the children and there I found a group of co-workers and children gathered together. They sat along the walls in the biggest room in the house. In the middle of the space there was a small mound made out of green moss and earth and a candle was burning on top of it. A spiral

> marked out with moss lead to the small mound. Every child was given an apple upon which a small candle was fixed. Advent and Christmas songs were sung and one child after another attempted — alone or with help — to walk through the moss spiral to reach the central mound so that they could light their own candle from the main candle. I was profoundly surprised to behold the earnestness and joy with which each child approached the task. There was the great candle! Each small candle attached to an 'apple of sin' had to be lit from this 'proclaiming' Christmas light! And suddenly I knew: Yes, this is my future task! To awaken in each one of these children their own spirit light which would lead them to their humanity: yes, that is what I want to do! I am no longer able to say whether my decision was particularly conscious that Advent Sunday but my heart felt so fulfilled that tears just poured from my eyes and I had to leave the hall.[27]

★

At the beginning of December, about a month after König's arrival in Arlesheim, Ita Wegman asked him to hold a keynote lecture on behalf of the Medical Section at the Christmas conference of the Anthroposophical Society:

> A few weeks before Christmas Ita Wegman came to me and said, 'König, I think you should hold a keynote lecture at the Goetheanum.'
>
> I replied, 'But Frau Doctor, I have never held a lecture before.'
>
> And she said, 'But you will be able to do it, you will be able to do it.'[28]

Although König had already spoken in public in Vienna,

speaking at the Goetheanum — which he deeply respected as the place where Rudolf Steiner had worked and taught — was completely new to him. In addition König was totally unknown in Dornach — a twenty-five-year-old man of small build and Jewish origin who had only just completed his medical study course, without any anthroposophical background or patronage and therefore fundamentally different from prominent doctors and lecturers such as Friedrich Husemann, Felix Peipers or Ludwig Noll. But Ita Wegman defused König's doubts and hesitation with the confidence and leadership qualities of her typical 'sun-like' personality:

> She told me, 'I will accompany you to the lecture, take you to the room, show you the lectern from where you will speak and will sit in front of you, and everything will be fine.'
>
> And with the protection of her presence it all went very well.[29]

In fact that Christmas König lectured in the carpentry-shop to an audience of over one thousand and it was indeed a big success. He was thoroughly prepared and spoke about the human embryonic development, reaching as far as the Sistine Madonna.[30] One of the listeners, Fritz Götte, decades later wrote about the 'tremendous' impression König's presentation had left in people's souls,[31] and Ita Wegman too expressed in a letter of January 5, 1928 that she was happy and proud of her new colleague at the Section and the Clinic: 'Our Dr König had unexpectedly a great success with his lecture and was warmly applauded by the audience.'[32]

König's presentation on embryology at Christmas time was the start of his activities as an anthroposophical lecturer. From the beginning of the year 1928 he frequently went on lecture tours to Germany where he got to know the pioneers of anthroposophical curative education in Jena (especially Franz Löffler). König always discussed the topics and intentions of his lectures with Ita Wegman, whose supporting spiritual presence he experienced many times in difficult situations, also beyond his lecturing activities.[33]

★

During these months Ita Wegman expressed her wish that Karl König would stay in Arlesheim for a limited term and then take on the post of medical director at the convalescent home in Gnadenwald, a sizeable sanatorium in Tyrol which Ita Wegman had successfully established a short time before. At the end of the first week of April 1928 Wegman wrote to a colleague: 'Doctor König will stay with us for while in order ... to go to Gnadenwald later.'[34] Also in letters to Gnadenwald — for instance to Elisabeth Dank who was in charge of the organization and finances of the sanatorium — Ita Wegman emphasized that König would work in a responsible position in the near future. But Karl König's destiny took a different course, and Ita Wegman who, in Hans Müller-Wiedemann's words, felt 'understanding and love for the impulses of people of independence,'[35] not only accepted this change, but supported Karl König on his new course.

Using Karl König's autobiographical notes Hans Müller-Wiedemann described in detail König's visit to Tilla Maasberg, a young nurse, during a lecture tour to Breslau in spring 1928. In November 1927, on the same day as König, Tilla Maasberg had arrived in Arlesheim to receive therapeutic training for the institute for curative education she had recently established in Silesia. Because of her sister's illness she had had to leave Arlesheim shortly after Christmas and return home; but during the following weeks she had asked Karl König to come for a visit, to advise her regarding her sister's illness and to see the children's home which was just in its pioneering stage. When König travelled to Breslau and Gnadenfrei he encountered the tradition of the Herrnhuter, the Moravian Brotherhood, which had a

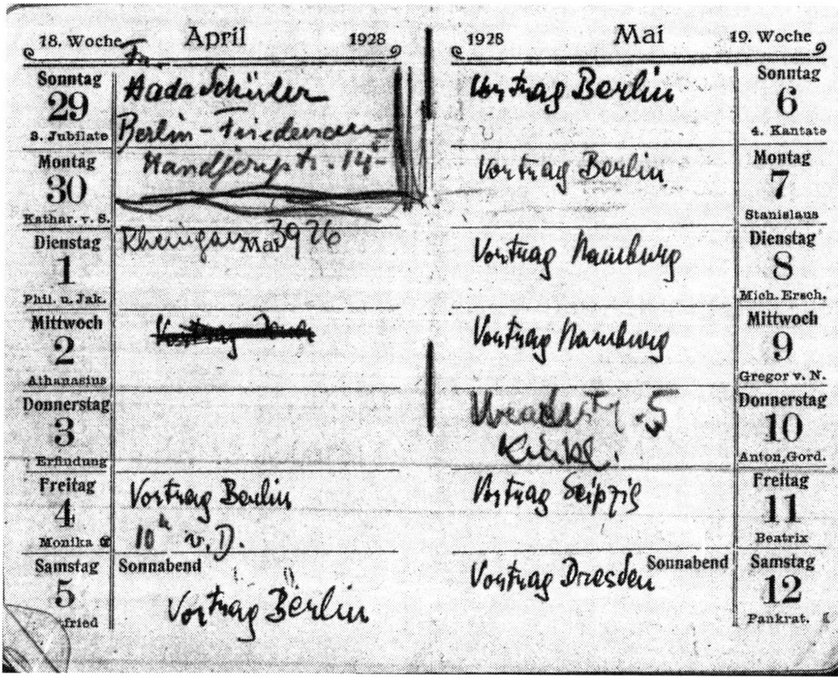

Karl König's Notebook. April/May 1928

deep effect on his destiny. Immediately he promised to contribute to the foundation of a more extensive children's home in Schloss Pilgramshain.[36] At the same time the relationship between König and Tilla Maasberg began to grow and both realized that joint tasks and responsibilities lay ahead. After his return to Arlesheim he wrote to her:

> When we were together I felt for the first time in my life that it — can be resolved. It was like a first thawing of the innermost ice-crust of my heart when we were with one another. The deeply Christian nature of your soul and the profound spirituality of the surrounding landscape made this possible.[37]

During the first half of the year 1928 Karl König accompanied Ita Wegman on some journeys; for instance to the Netherlands for the opening of Willem Zeylmans van Emmichoven's clinic where he held a lecture, and to the big World Conference of Spiritual Science and its Practical Applications in England. There König lectured again on the human embryonic development in continuation of his studies in Arlesheim. During the last few months these studies had enabled König to enhance the topic Christologically and in regard to the Logos Mysteries of Ephesus.

The conference in London was his first experience with the English-speaking world; he had to leave early, however, bade farewell to Ita Wegman and travelled via Vienna to Pilgramshain where he started work in August 1928.[38]

★

For the next few years Karl König mainly focussed on expanding his medical and curative work and on more lecturing. As always he stayed in close communication with Ita Wegman by mail and intermittently had conversations with her at various meetings in Dornach/Arlesheim, Berlin and Pilgramshain. At the end of October 1928, shortly before travelling to Pilgramshain ('to organize work there properly'), Ita Wegman wrote to Albert Steffen about the recently opened home.[39] At that time about 60 children lived in the home; apart from Tilla Maasberg and Karl König, Albrecht Strohschein had also contributed to its development. He was a curative teacher who also cooperated closely with Wegman. Because of social difficulties he had left the Lauenstein, the first centre for anthroposophic curative education.[40]

In October 1928 Wegman travelled to Jena, Breslau (where she gave a Class Lesson) and Pilgramshain, and visited the curative homes. After her return she wrote in a letter:

Monday, July 23
Anthropsophy or Spiritual Science

10.15 A.M. LARGE HALL. **Rudolf Steiner's Anthroposophy, the spiritual message to present Humanity.** DR. ING. CARL UNGER. (In German. Synopsis in English).

2 P.M. ROOM 7 and 8. Explanations of the Educational Exhibits.

3 P.M. LARGE HALL. **The Crisis of Philosophy and its Revival.** MRS. V. E. PLINCKE.

3 P.M. RUDOLF STEINER HALL. Demonstration of Educational Eurhythmy by the children of the New School, Streatham Hill and the Priory School, Kings Langley.

4.30 P.M. LARGE HALL. **The School of Chartres.** THE MARQUIS DE CASA FUERTE (France). (In French. Synopsis in English).

8.15 P.M. LARGE HALL. **Practical Aspects of Eastern and Western Folk-Psychology.** DR. H. HAHN (Germany). (In German. English translation by G. Kaufmann, M.A.).

Tuesday, July 24
Anthroposophical Therapy and Medical Science

10.15 A.M. LARGE HALL. **Anthroposophical Principles of the Art of Healing.** ITA WEGMAN, M.D. (Zurich). Leader of the Medical Section of the Goetheanum, and Head of the Clinical and Therapeutical Institute, Arlesheim, Switzerland.

11.30 A.M. ROOM 9. **The Treatment of Cancer.** DR. GALJART (Holland) and DR. E. SCHICKLER (Germany).

2.15 P.M. LARGE HALL. **The Origin of Man, the evolution of the embryo.** DR. KONIG, M.D. (Vienna). (In German. English translation by G. Kaufmann, M.A.).

4 P.M. Addresses by Dr. E. KOLISKO (Vienna), followed by Demonstrations on the following :—
Curative Eurhythmy (Frl. Dr. Bockholt and others).
Music as a part of therapeutical treatment, and Curative Education, demonstrated by means of special musical instruments (Herr Pracht), and by a special method of singing (Frau Valborg Svärdström-Werbeck and her choir).

8.15 P.M. LARGE HALL. **The Human Soul in connection with Sleeping, Dreaming, and Waking.** F. W. ZEYLMANS VAN EMMICHOVEN, M.D. (Amsterdam).

8.15 P.M. RUDOLF STEINER HALL.
Demonstration of Eurhythmy by Artistes of the Geotheanum School of Eurhythmy, Dornach.

394

Programme of the 'World Conference of Spiritual Science and its Practical Applications.' London, July 23/24, 1928

> My visit to Breslau-Jena has been really good. I had the chance to give a lot of input, and I believe that the curative work takes a big step forward, if you really keep doing what you intend to do.[41]

Apart from her practical therapeutic work and the further development of several training courses, Ita Wegman was intensely concerned during these months with presenting anthroposophy and its social-therapeutic implications to the public. She had established an association, Social Support, and together with her curative teachers and some other colleagues and friends had built contacts to the authorities for social welfare. Ita Wegman also organized many public lectures for the Medical Section and included Karl König as a possible lecturer. However, in January 1929 she asked Eugen Kolisko to step in for Willem Zeylmans van Emmichoven in Berlin, and categorically refused to consider Karl König as an alternative ('König is not at all suitable'[42]). Quite obviously Karl König had gone too far in previous lectures and had spoken with unbridled imagination and perhaps also with missionary zeal. Wegman replied to similar criticism expressed by Werner Pache, who at the end of February reported back to Margarete Bockholt about a series of lectures held by König in Berlin:

> I was concerned by what you ... wrote about Dr König. If it was really as bad as you say then perhaps you should have told him, or even called some people together who also thought it was bad, to make sure that this is not continued without letting the Medical Section know. It is not right to wait, as you write in your letter to Dr Bockholt, until the damage is done, until nobody turns up any more, before Dr König begins to see reason. In the meantime we have disgraced ourselves. If you are sure that people generally cannot accept König's way of

Heil- und Erziehungsinstitut
für seelenpflege-bedürftige Kinder
Schloss Pilgramshain e.V

Fernsprecher 384

Post Striegau Land
Schlesien

Zwischen

dem Heil- und Erziehungsinstitut für seelenpflege-bedürftige Kinder
Schloß Pilgramshain e. V.

und

dem Dr. med. Karl König, ebenfalls zu Pilgramshain ansässig, wir nachstehender

Anstellungsvertrag

geschlossen:

Herr Dr. König übernimmt die ärztliche Betreuung der im obengenannten Institut untergebrachten Kinder. Er erhält dafür freie Wohnung und Verpflegung, eventl. ein kleines Taschengeld. Auch sollen seine Angehörigen, sofern er sich verheiraten sollte, freie Wohnung und Verpflegung haben. Es wird Herrn Dr. König freigestellt private Praxis auszuüben, jedoch mit der Maßgabe, daß die Interessen des Institutes nicht beeinträchtigt werden. Der Vertrag beginnt am 1. September 1928 und läuft bis 31. Dezember 1932. Er kann durch gegenseitiges Einvernehmen auf fünf Jahre verlängert werden durch einfachen Zusatz an diesem Anstellungsvertrag. Der Vertrag wird in 2 Ausfertigungen ausgestellt, wovon ein Exemplar das Institut und ein Exemplar Herr Dr. König bekommt.

Schloß Pilgramshain, den 30. August 1928

Dr Karl König   Albrecht Strohschein

Karl König's employment contract at Pilgramshain

> lecturing then of course there is reason for intervening. So I would like to ask you now for detailed information which should be sent directly to me, so that I can do what is actually required for the progress of our work.[43]

Karl König's lectures in winter 1928/29 in Berlin were not initiated by Ita Wegman or the Medical Section but by König himself, which prompted her astonishment.[44] Ita Wegman, too, knew that König's way of lecturing — after being initially very successful — was now met with criticism in some anthroposophical circles. These objections, however valid they may have been, did not affect Wegman's esteem for her young and extraordinarily talented colleague; at the same time she realized that she must continue task to accompany König's path conscientiously. There were other friends of Karl König who occasionally made similar attempts. Gerhard Suchantke for instance, who also worked as an assistant doctor with Ita Wegman in Arlesheim, wrote in a long letter in summer 1928 to König in Pilgramshain:

> Now one more thing because I am concerned. After the lecture on Friday I had a long conversation with Wachsmuth. For some time we also spoke about you. He started with the question whether I had noticed that you, after having made a statement, made frequent remarks such as: Well, you cannot prove that, it was an intuition directly from the spiritual world. Several people had approached him and had expressed their astonishment. He himself had heard you giving a similar statement in the context of explanations about the Fifth Gospel during your lecture at Easter; unfortunately a couple of days before he had read the same sentence almost word for word in Dr Steiner's Fifth Gospel. Well this cannot be proved, but these facts are the result of spiritual research. Steffen, too, was annoyed by these comments from such a young person at an Annual General

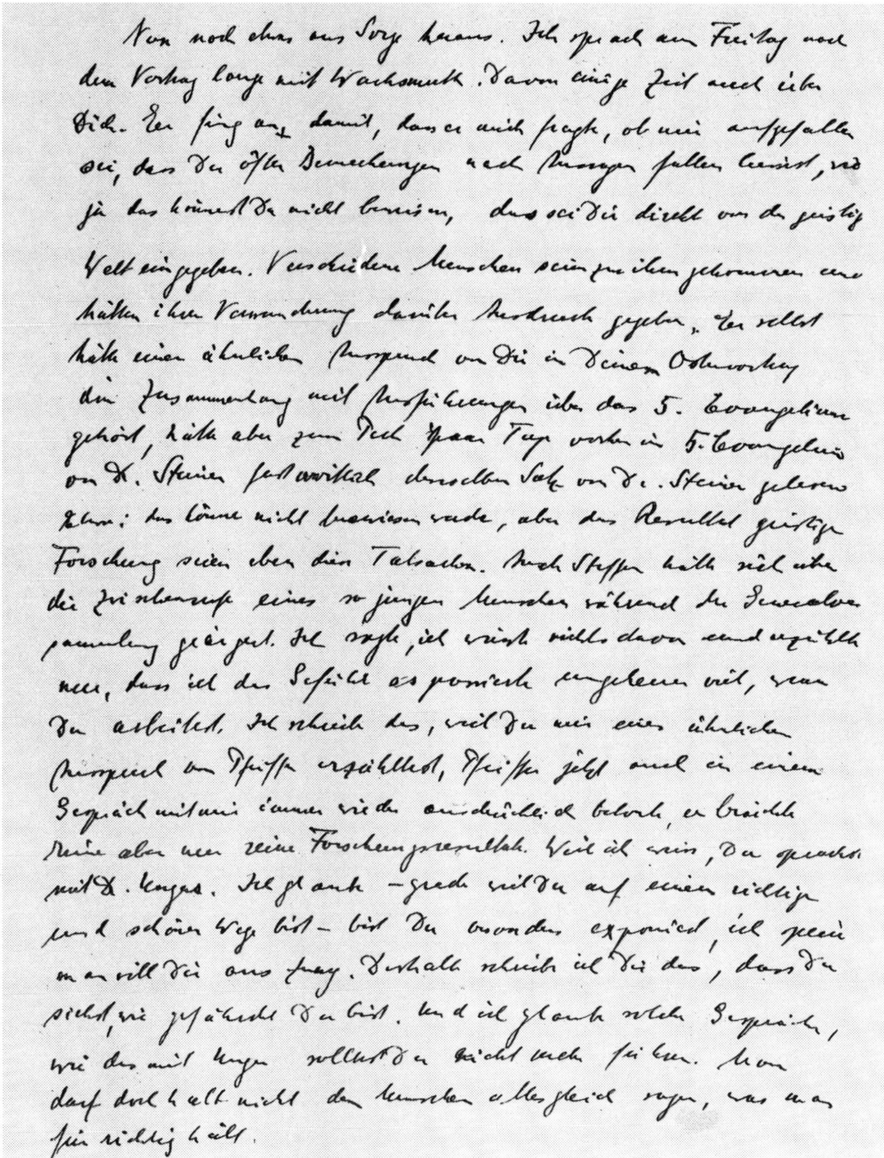
Nun noch etwas aus Sorge heraus. Ich sprach am Freitag nach dem Vortrag lange mit Wachsmuth. Davon einige Zeit auch über Dich. Er fing an damit, dass er mich fragte, ob mir aufgefallen sei, dass Du öfter Bemerkungen nach Vorträgen fallen liessest, wo ja das könntest Du nicht beweisen, das sei Dir direkt von der geistigen Welt eingegeben. Verschiedene Menschen seien zu ihm gekommen und hätten ihrer Verwunderung darüber Ausdruck gegeben. Er selbst hätte einen ähnlichen Ausspruch von Dir in Deinem Ostervortrag im Zusammenhang mit Ausführungen über das 5. Evangelium gehört, hätte aber zum Teil paar Tage vorher im 5. Evangelium von Dr. Steiner fast wörtlich denselben Satz von Dr. Steiner gelesen haben: das könne nicht bewiesen werden, aber das Resultat geistiger Forschung seien eben diese Tatsachen. Auch Steffen hätte sich über die Zurschaustellung eines so jungen Menschen während der Generalversammlung geäussert. Ich sagte, ich wüsste nichts davon und erzählte nur, dass ich das Gefühl so persönlich umgeben hatte, wenn Du arbeitest. Ich schreibe das, weil Du mir einen ähnlichen Ausspruch von Pfeiffer erzähltest, Pfeiffer gibt auch in einem Gespräch mit mir immer wieder ausdrücklich betont, er brächte keine aber nur reine Forschungsresultate. Weil ich weiss, Du sprachst mit Dr. Unger. Ich glaube – gerade weil Du auf einem richtigen und schönen Wege bist – bist Du besonders exponiert, ich spüre man will Dir ans Zeug. Deshalb schreibe ich Dir das, dass Du siehst, wie gefährdet Du bist. Und ich glaube solche Gespräche, wie das mit Unger solltest Du nicht mehr führen. Man darf doch halt nicht den Menschen alles gleich sagen, was man für richtig hält.

The second page Gerhard Suchantke's letter to Karl König.
August 12, 1928

> Meeting. I replied that I did not know anything about it and could only say that I felt that an incredible amount was happening when you work. I write this because you told me about a similar statement from Pfeiffer, and now Pfeiffer also has repeatedly emphasized during a conversation with me that he brought new scientific results, but only his own ones. Because I know that you have spoken to Dr [Carl] Unger. I think — especially because you are on a right and good way — that you are particularly exposed; I think that they are having a go at you. I write this to you so that you can see in what danger you are. And I think you should avoid conversations like that with Unger. You don't always need to tell people everything you think to be right.[45]

★

While in Dornach sentiments against Karl König began to grow Ita Wegman discussed her concerns with him in private. Being a skilled leader she did this with her usual tact and wisdom. In the following years Karl König became one of her most important and successful public speakers for the Social Support Association. With Ita Wegman's explicit support he also spoke together with lecturers from the Christian Community, like Emil Bock. During this time and after a conversation with Karl König she wrote in a letter to Siegfried Palmer, another colleague from the Social Support Association:

> Take ... immediate initiative and organize ... a conference initiated by Social Support together with Dr Feldner, Christian Community, curative teachers and doctors; a conference addressing all aspects of social issues and demonstrating how we, with our anthroposophical background, can contribute to social work. It is not

> appropriate to look at this issue just from the viewpoint of the priests, neither to consider it solely from the viewpoint of curative education nor solely from a medical standpoint, instead all of them need to work together to present the issue in a way that could have an extraordinary public effect. And as we have noticed often enough recently, an audience only responds if there is evidence of positive achievements; in particular if the achievements of the institutions and of the doctors working within the institutions ... can be presented as facts in the light of anthroposophy, then we will achieve great success.[46]

Especially Karl König, who joined the Social Support Association board on Wegman's request, soon won the hearts and minds of many socially interested people outside the anthroposophical movement, and at a time already feeling the influence of the shadow cast by growing social Darwinism and the threat of euthanasia. König tackled these urgent tasks thoroughly and with intensity. In November 1929, after his lectures and seminars in Hamburg and Berlin had again been well attended, he wrote to Ita Wegman:

> During my whole journey I had the strong impression that everything I have been talking about is guided by the spiritual world, so that the Social Support Association can establish itself within the wider context you have always wished for. ... I hope that there will thus be a broad base of consent so that all those wanting to work socially on the basis of spiritual and intellectual freedom can join together.

Three months later Ita Wegman wrote in a letter to König:

> We will certainly discuss the Social Support Association later. But what is important now is that we try to interest

SONNTAG, DEN 24. NOVEMBER 1929

Brüdervereinshaus
Kurfürstenstr. 115-16

Vormittags 11^{30} Uhr:

Demonstration von

heil-eurythmischen Übungen u. rhythm. Spielen von Kindern

Musik auf neuen für Heilzwecke gebauten Instrumenten

Erklärende Ausführungen von
Dr. med. **Grete Bockholt,** Klin.-therap. Institut
Arlesheim bei Basel

Nachm. ab 15 Uhr:

wird wieder die

Ausstellung

geöffnet sein

15^{15} Uhr:

Hermann Kirchner, Heil- und Erziehungsinstitut
Schloß Pilgramshain bei Striegau (Schlesien)

Künstlerische Betätigung als Heilfaktor für das geschädigte Großstadtkind

an Hand- von Kinderarbeiten

17 Uhr:

Siegfried Pickert, Heil- und Erziehungsinstitut
Lauenstein-Zwätzen (Jena)

Charakteristische Typen

des seelenpflege-bedürftigen Kindes

Abends 20 Uhr:

Dr. med. **Karl König,** Heil- und Erziehungsinstitut
Schloß Pilgramshain bei Striegau (Schlesien)

Die Bedeutung der anthroposophischen Heilkunst für die sozialen Probleme unserer Zeit

Lecture programme. Berlin, November 24, 1929

> many people in joining, particularly outsiders. This campaign should not be conducted by writing letters or sending advertising pamphlets but really by meeting people face to face, by kindling people's interest wherever you go.

On her visits to Pilgramshain, but also during regular meetings in Berlin, Arlesheim and Dornach, König continued to discuss the topics and priorities of his lectures with Ita Wegman and orientated himself according to her ideas ('also in this regard I will await your decision'); apart from this he conducted training courses in Arlesheim (for instance, for the nursing staff) and often asked Ita Wegman for advice. At the end of a letter dated February 18, 1930 he wrote:

> I have a deep need to talk to you again in detail, dear Frau Doctor, about a lot of things on my mind. To diffuse some doubts and gain fresh momentum.

★

In Pilgramshain König established a broad general practitioner's surgery and systematically developed methods of diagnostics and therapy for the children who were entrusted to him with developmental problems. König's notes taken in Pilgramshain show the detailed aspects and insights into the nature of the human being that he had gained and developed from his understanding of Rudolf Steiner.[47] Surviving documents also show that Ita Wegman helped with support, advice and reassurance. In April 1929 she answered a letter of König's which unfortunately has been lost. In her answer she expanded on an important issue:

> I have received your letter of April 16 in which you ask me about X-ray therapy for mental deficiency in

> children. This is a serious issue. Elsewhere there have been frequent initial improvements and yet it turned out later that there were bad side effects. What is happening in these things cannot without further ado be done by ourselves. The successful improvements which have been achieved by using this X-ray therapy, for instance with Down's syndrome children, have, as you describe in your letter, given these children a reasonably normal soul life. We do achieve the same effect but through the children's own individuality, whereas I feel that by using this X-ray therapy the individuality is forced out by the impact and possibly something subhuman is put into these children's bodies. The same thing that happens, but in a different way, when animal glands are transplanted into human bodies. From my point of view I can never agree that at an institute operating according to Dr Steiner's instructions such experiments are being done on issues which are still unclear. Otherwise we stray off the safe path which in every respect is meant to bring down the child's supersensible being, to do everything so that the child can embrace his karma, and if this fails, to do everything so that a normal body can be formed in the next incarnation. Such an X-ray intervention is not, and I know this from Dr Steiner himself, something that will get us any further.

Wegman's clear and decisive words were no doubt directing and significant for the young, just twenty-six-year-old König, who at the time he received the letter had worked in Pilgramshain for only nine months. These words encouraged him to follow the chosen path consistently and to work therapeutically and innovatively according to the intentions indicated; the path of anthroposophical medicine and curative education, 'which in every respect is meant to bring down the child's supersensible being, to do everything so that the child can embrace his karma,

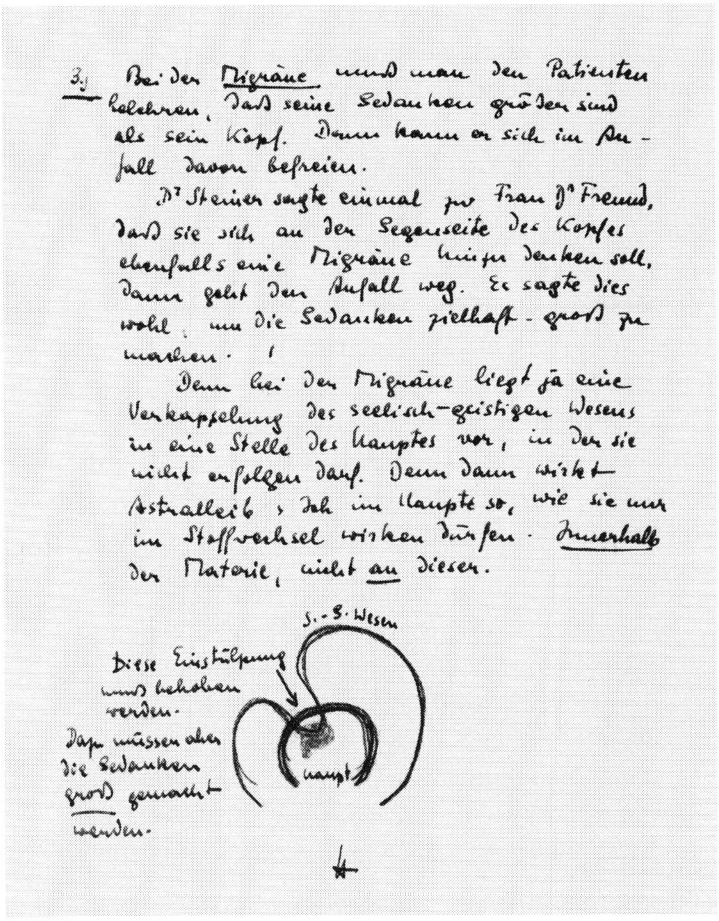
3.) Bei der Migräne muß man den Patienten belehren, daß seine Gedanken größer sind als sein Kopf. Dann kann er sich im Anfall davon befreien.

Dr Steiner sagte einmal zu Frau Dr Freund, daß sie sich an der Gegenseite des Kopfes ebenfalls eine Migräne hinzu denken soll, dann geht der Anfall weg. Er sagte dies wohl, um die Gedanken zielhaft-groß zu machen.

Denn bei der Migräne liegt ja eine Verkapselung des seelisch-geistigen Wesens in eine Stelle des Hauptes vor, in der sie nicht erfolgen darf. Denn dann wirkt Astralleib u. Ich im Haupte so, wie sie nur im Stoffwechsel wirken dürfen. Innerhalb der Materie, nicht an dieser.

Notebook entry of Karl König. Pilgramshain, 1932

and if this fails, to do everything so that a normal body can be formed in the next incarnation.'

But on the other hand Ita Wegman knew how skilled König already was in his medical care for children, in staff training and in representing the Institute. She supported his involvement in establishing further initiatives for curative education and tried to find more opportunities to keep him free for this kind of activity.

'We have been looking for an assistant doctor at Pilgramshain for some time already. If we were successful Dr König could of course be more flexible in his work.'[48]

Within a short period of time Karl König had become important, even vital, for the work and activities of the Medical Section at the Goetheanum, for the medical aspect of curative education but also for science and research. He brought interested doctors whom he met on his frequent travels to Ita Wegman's attention (for instance the young Werner Simonis in Hamburg) and, at Ita Wegman's request, contributed to the first edition of the Curative Education Course. He also became confidentially involved in some problems increasingly affecting Wegman's life and work in Dornach, which even included issues like the qualification for teaching curative eurythmy. Ita Wegman wrote to Karl König on March 3, 1930:

> If we do not set up a consistent system about the right to practice curative eurythmy and if we do not pay attention to what Dr Steiner has implemented — that is, curative eurythmy as part of the Medical Section — the resulting situation will soon be chaotic and everything Rudolf Steiner intended with the Christmas Conference will be lost at one blow. We should also discuss in detail all these fundamental questions.[49]

★

At the beginning of 1933, a year of culminating problems, Ita Wegman was again in Pilgramshain, the temperatures being almost –30°C (–20°F). After returning she wrote in an account of her journey:

> Pilgramshain is coming on well. There are also concurrent activities around the institution which is of course essential for Dr König because there is not

Kursus für Krankenschwestern, Fürsorgerinnen, Sozialbeamte

Schon vor längerer Zeit ist zu dem vom 6.—12. September 1931 in Arlesheim stattfindenden Kursus für

Krankenschwestern, Fürsorgerinnen, Sozialbeamte

eingeladen worden. Wir können Ihnen leider erst jetzt die endgültige Einladung mit dem Programm zuschicken, weil es durch die deutsche Notverordnung fraglich schien, ob es möglich sein würde, den Kurs hier abzuhalten. Da es aber auf Grund der früheren Einladung jeweils möglich sein wird, die Grenzgebühr erlassen zu bekommen, wird der Kursus nunmehr wie geplant stattfinden.

Die Einteilung wird etwa die folgende sein:

täglich morgens 9 Uhr: Vorlesung aus Vorträgen Rudolf Steiners über Pädagogik und soziale Fragen.

11 Uhr: Dr. K. König: „Anthroposophische Menschenkunde".

nachm. ½6—7 Uhr: Kursus von Dr. R. Hauschka: „Gesichtspunkte für rationelle Ernährung mit Beispielen".

In den Nachmittagsstunden vorher wird die Möglichkeit sein, einen Einblick in die verschiedenen Gebiete der künstlerischen Therapie zu bekommen wie z. B. Heileurythmie, Heilmusik und anderes mit Übstunden.

An den Abenden: Referate und Diskussionen über „Soziale Gegenwartsprobleme und die Ideen Rudolf Steiners über die Dreigliederung des sozialen Organismus".

Diese Abende werden eingeleitet durch einen Vortrag Dr. W. J. Steins über „Soziale Gesinnung in der heutigen Weltkrise auf Grundlage deutschen Geisteslebens".

Wir hoffen, dass trotz der schwierigen Lage eine zahlreiche Beteiligung möglich sein wird.

Die Medizinische Sektion:
Dr. Ita Wegmann.

Für billige Verpflegung und Unterkunft sind wir gern bereit, Sorge zu tragen. Anmeldungen sind bis zum 1. September an das Klinisch-Therapeutische Institut erbeten. Der Kursbeitrag beträgt Fr. 15.—.

Invitation from Ita Wegman for a course for nurses, carers and social workers, September 1931

> enough work for him in Pilgramshain alone. Otherwise things have settled nicely in Pilgramshain. I was also able to give a Class Lesson, and thus I will try to work with staff at the various institutes in such a way that esoteric aspects will not be lacking.[50]

When faced with the impending takeover by the National Socialists under Adolf Hitler in January 1933 Ita Wegman discussed necessary security measures and resistance strategies with Karl König. She told König, a Jew by birth, that she was planning a key meeting for a number of friends. She sent him an invitation at the beginning of the second week of March containing the following:

> Because of the extraordinarily difficult situation it is necessary that those of us who care for the worldwide success of anthroposophical work gather to discuss seriously what steps should be taken and how people can support each other in order to continue this work without disruption. During my visits to England and the Netherlands I could encourage a number of friends to hold regular meetings for discussing the continuation of our work. This is even more necessary because, firstly, in the current situation the relationships within the different countries must be properly upheld, and secondly, because in these difficult times the work in the various activities must be supported by mutual understanding and help. In this difficult time there needs to be intensive mutual support within the various teams and communities. And in order to promote this I have already started approaching some friends to arrange such a meeting.

Three weeks later Karl König travelled together with Albrecht Strohschein to the meeting taking place in Stuttgart which was meant to raise common awareness of the dangerous situation and to agree on possible supporting measures.[51]

During the first months of the year 1933 Ita Wegman repeatedly expressed her fears concerning some Jewish friends explicitly including Karl König, for instance in a letter of April 28 to the Dutch psychiatrist Willem Zeylmans van Emmichoven. How dangerous König's position and situation had actually over time become is illustrated by a report which Ita Wegman received by courier from her economic assistant Erich Kirchner six weeks later in the last week of June. Concerning Karl König it contained the following:

> In Pilgramsheim [Pilgramshain] there are numerous intrigues targeting Dr König and aiming at his deportation because of his Jewish and foreign origin. Actually he has already been denied the right to keep the title of Doctor because he obtained his doctor's degree abroad. The First President of the province has called for a report, which shows that the top authorities of the province are already concerned with him as a person and with Pilgramsheim [Pilgramshain]. Bert Keyserlingk told me that König has said that he would not be able to endure this witch-hunt against him for more than a few weeks and would prefer to leave. He called off a lecture in a neighbouring town because prior to this he had been told by the National Socialist side that the lecture would be disrupted in the middle by Nat. Soc. and that he would be prevented from continuing. Even if in the current situation and with the contacts which can be made to the present government authorities in Silesia, König's continuance could perhaps be forced through, I still think that his activities will not be of much effect any more and that, apart from this, the Institute would very likely suffer considerably.[52]

Despite these tensions, however, König gave a course on embryology from the viewpoint of spiritual science in Arlesheim in August 1933. He lectured to a group of anthroposophically orientated medical students, a group of people who subsequently travelled with Ita Wegman to England. But for the time being Karl König stayed in Central Europe and, at Ita Wegman's invitation, held another lecture at the conference for doctors and priests at the Medical Section of the Goetheanum in October.

★

Even during the last months of the year 1933 there was no indication that König was prepared to leave Pilgramshain, as recommended by Hermann Kirchner. In fact, in November 1933 König asked Ita Wegman for a capable new member of staff as a replacement for the skilled curative teacher Vala Bérence who was going to leave Pilgramshain to start work, at Ita Wegman's request, in France. König had specially asked for the eurythmist who worked at the Sonnenhof [Miss Wilke]. Ita Wegman was not really in favour of letting her move to Pilgramshain, yet she agreed and commented on this in a letter written from London to Madeleine van Deventer, giving an interesting reason for her decision:

> Certainly it will be difficult without Miss Wilke but Pilgramshain needs support. If Dr König is left too much to his own devices he will become quite autonomous and that will probably not work out.[53]

Obviously Ita Wegman was still sceptical of König's all too potent 'autonomy.' So she tried to influence him in a positive way to cooperate. Three years earlier Ita Wegman had already dampened König's plans for an independent curative home in Prague, pointing out that a project like this would be premature in the current circumstances, although in principle it was a valid idea.[54]

Ita Wegman took it amiss that Karl König had agreed, without her knowledge, to hold a lecture at Elisabeth Vreede's Conference on the Ancient Mysteries at the Goetheanum at Christmas

Care course in Arlesheim with Karl König and Ita Wegman

1933. This meeting was organized by Vreede at a time when conflicts within the Executive Board of the General Anthroposophical Society had come to a hopeless tangle and had been planned in opposition to the official conference lectures in the Great Hall. When König was told about Wegman's discontent he feared that he would now be excluded from the Section. This prompted Ita Wegman to ask Margarete Bockholt to meet König in Berlin and calm him down. She contacted Bockholt on

January 12, 1934 to this effect, despite being unhappy with Elisabeth Vreede's initiative and that both Dr Zeylmans and Dr König, belonging to her own Section, had taken part without notifying her. Concerned that problems at the Executive Council would escalate, Wegman wrote:

> I would like to ask you to contact Dr König somehow. I heard that he is holding a course with [Emil] Bock. I found his letter here implying that he thinks I will ask him to leave the Section after what I said about the episode with Dr Vreede. You know of these comments. Well, as often happens, such comments were passed on to others in a way — it seems as if Strohschein did it — that they became distorted. So Dr König has the impression that I do not want him in the Section any more. I have already written to him that I by no means meant him to leave the Section; all I meant was that I thought his course of action a serious issue because he did not inform us; as a result we found ourselves in an awkward situation, and that was not really necessary. Well, you know how these things happen; often there are misunderstandings and it is therefore important for me that you talk to him personally.[55]

The respective letters of Wegman and König are not extant, but the ill feelings were at any rate only temporary.

★

The year 1934 was a difficult one for Ita Wegman. Efforts and arguments about the anthroposophical resistance to the National Socialist rule in Germany were exhausting. Conflicts in Dornach resulted in her expulsion from the Executive Council at the Goetheanum. And on top of that Wegman was affected by a life-threatening illness, which meant that the Annual General Meeting of the Anthroposophical Society at the end of March took place in her absence. Wegman was again fiercely criticized for the way she led the Medical Section. For the first time this criticism also focussed on Karl König's *Natura* essays.[56]

At the time of the Annual General Meeting Karl König was not in Dornach, but he was extremely concerned about Ita Wegman's state of health. Despite the criticism he had experienced he kept working. In a letter of April 30 to Margarete Bockholt he described his successful lectures in Berlin and added: 'Please tell Frau Doctor about it so that she knows that we will not give in, but continue the work undaunted.'[57]

König organized an impressive Whitsun Conference in Pilgramshain together with some colleagues: Eugen Kolisko, then school doctor of the first Waldorf School in Stuttgart, who, like König, was also under severe criticism; Karl Schubert,

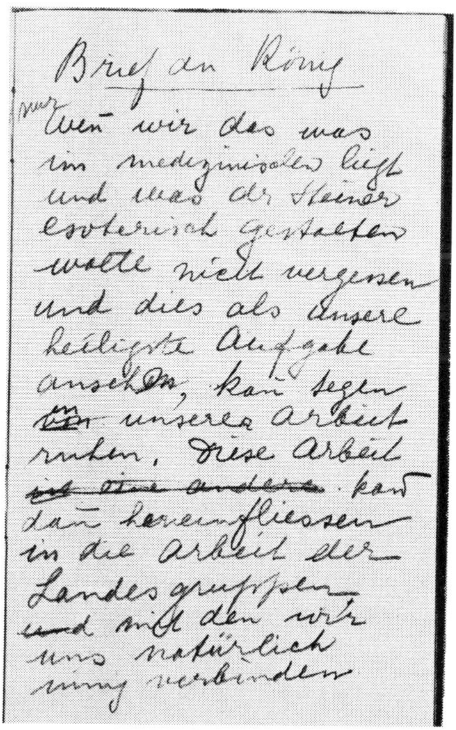
Brief an König
nur Wenn wir das was im medizinischen liegt und was Dr. Steiner esoterisch gestalten wollte nicht vergessen und dies als unsere heiligste Aufgabe ansehen, kann Segen in unserer Arbeit ruhen, diese Arbeit ~~ist eine andere~~ kann dann hereinfliessen in die Arbeit der Landesgruppen ~~und~~ mit den wir uns natürlich innig verbinden

Draft by Ita Wegman. Notebook. Hondrich, June 1934

curative teacher at the Stuttgart school and like König and Kolisko also from Vienna; Valborg Svardström-Werbeck, singer and music therapist. At this conference König brought curative education visibly into the foreground.[58] Meanwhile, after her health had slightly improved, Ita Wegman was brought for convalescence to Lake Thun where she slowly recovered during the following weeks and months.[59]

During those months in Hondrich and Wengen Ita Wegman reviewed her attitude towards the previous events and wrote diary notes and personal letters. Then in mid-June she wrote a remarkable letter to the curative institutes, a letter based on drafts she had sent to Karl König and Siegfried Pickert:

> Dear Friends
>
> On the tenth anniversary of Dr Steiner's visit to the Lauenstein, I would like to let the institutes, their leaders and co-workers know that I think of them warmly. With this tenth anniversary a certain seriousness has entered the memories of this day. Until now we succeeded in standing united. Despite the differences between the institutes and the different personalities in them we were able to cultivate a common form of curative education, to represent it and to aspire to common higher goals. These higher goals lived in our hearts and we strove to make them real; making real what Rudolf Steiner considered to be the esoteric medical element. This is what Rudolf Steiner gave as a task for the Medical Section, namely to form a community of people through the Section who, for the sake of the art of healing and its related fields, were willing to go deeper into the esoteric aspect of this work. Sadly Dr Steiner left us on our own and so this most sacred task remained only in our hearts like a longing. In my opinion this longing expressed itself by the people who sensed it standing together out of the greatest depth of their being.

Now this anniversary returns for the tenth time and this is most often an occasion for coming to a decision through trials of the soul. Therefore this day of remembrance is more important than were perhaps others before. Will we continue to remain united after the crisis in the [Anthroposophical] Society has brought so many difficulties towards us? Will the loyalty of the friends generate something new and will this be the moment for an esoteric breakthrough facilitated by intensified anthroposophical medical and curative work? If we resolve truly to intensify our work, acting in solidarity, keeping in mind the understanding of the higher goal which Dr Steiner set for the Medical Section, then no doubt we will be able to do new and productive work.

These thoughts have arisen in me, dear friends, in these days of mountain solitude. Although the world outside looks utterly gloomy, my heart beats joyfully at the thought of possibly returning to our circles in the foreseeable future in revived health, to work with you and to meet and embrace what is new.

May all of you be well!
With warm greetings
Yours
Ita Wegman MD[60]

The personal message from Ita Wegman to Karl König which accompanied this letter is lost. König received it in Carinthia where he was on holiday after having explored Burgenland, an area still steeped in mystery and goal of the journey of Gilgamesh. König replied to Ita Wegman immediately and extensively. He fully agreed to her intentions regarding the nature and spiritual goal of the Medical Section. But he also indicated the way in which — in his opinion — the Section should be organized in the future. He also explained from his viewpoint how difficult and socially deficient the practical work was at the different institutes and how little true cooperation took place. He was clearly correcting the statements which Wegman had expressed and questioning her intentions and hopes.

König wrote from his holiday:

> Dear Dr Wegman,
>
> Your dear letter which was forwarded to me here gave a deep and great joy. It tells me that you, dear Frau Doctor, are back in good health and are looking ahead with courage and strength. This means real hope and encouragement for all of us who are lonelier than ever in fighting the battle on earth for Rudolf Steiner.
>
> It was also very important for me to read about your ideas for the future and about your plans for our work. It is wonderful that you now want to put all your efforts into the esoteric processes; every truly aspiring student will be very grateful for that. We really need an intensification [of this work] and the sooner this happens the more grateful we will be. Hopefully you will soon be ready to lead us.
>
> What you say about the Section is something I also take for granted. I believe that all of us in the Section who want to serve the art of healing need to stay loyal, otherwise our work will lose its substance. However, at this point I would like to request something. Dear Frau Doctor, for the Section to work better you will have to lead the people there in a firmer and stricter way. You need to give us younger colleagues joint tasks and to work with us, particularly medically, in order to tackle them. And this relates to what you say about the institutes. You see, I do not think the institutes are *internally* prepared for the loyalty you suggest. What I see is that

each institute stands alone and completely isolated. There is absolutely no cooperation regarding curative educational problems. Personal relationships too are not as good as they should be. Only *you,* with your wide-ranging activities, can bring about change. [Expecting] solidarity at this time would be an illusion. I believe that especially the institutes could form an excellent and exemplary community if they wanted to. But they do not yet want to do this. Please help us make it happen. Then we will be able to meet our Mercurial commitments.

I consider it necessary for the national [Anthroposophical] Societies and the work group [*Arbeitsgemeinschaft*] to join together. We need to have the opportunity to accept members and we also need a base where we can meet. I believe that such a social community, initially loosely interconnected, can grow into something magnificent if energies can act freely within it. Of course particularly you and the Section need to be involved in this.

Dear Frau Doctor, because you, being put *afresh* into this life, are going to resume work I believe that the spiritual world is supporting us and that *true* anthroposophy shall continue on earth. We can take new courage from this rather than feel resignation. And I think that *you* have special responsibilities in two fields. Dear Frau Doctor, the *first* field is the art of healing; support it in all its aspects. The *second* field is esoteric anthroposophy; bring it into the newly forming work groups. But keep Section and Society separate. The Section is an esoteric being which should reach into all work groups, yet it is not a work group itself but a being which should act within the *body* of the work groups.

This is how I see your future work and I am happy that it will be there again. I hope that you trust in my

> faith and loyalty. Differences in some details do not really matter. As ever I am loyal to you as a person and I support you in your destiny as a servant of my own free will.
>
> All this I wanted to tell you. I hope you forgive my openness but I think it is better if things are openly expressed and you, too, always wanted it that way.
>
> Until the end of this week I am on holiday which I have spent walking in the Burgenland and in Upper Carinthia. In this wonderful country I made some fine discoveries of historical interest which I will tell you about another time. On Saturday and Sunday I shall be in Stuttgart, then again in Pilgramshain.
>
> I wish you, dear Frau Doctor, all the best. Get well soon so that you can lead and guide us in our work and commitment.
>
> With warmest regards and best wishes
> I remain faithfully and loyally
> yours
> Karl König

In this open and direct letter König sees and describes himself as Ita Wegman's 'servant of my own free will,' standing by her and supporting her task of destiny. König's reply not only reveals in which way he was disappointed and what he thought was essential for the Medical Section's future. 'For the Section to work better you will have to lead the people in a firmer and stricter way. You need to give us younger colleagues joint tasks and to work with us, particularly medically, in order to tackle them.' It also shows the degree of his frustration with the situation in Pilgramshain and with the anthroposophical curative movement. 'There is absolutely no cooperation regarding curative educational problems. Personal relationships too are not as good as they should be.'

Two months later, in August 1934, Karl König informed Ita Wegman in a letter that he wanted to leave Pilgramshain for a year to return to Arlesheim. From there he wanted to establish medical work in Vienna and Paris. He had done the same in Prague a few months earlier together with a large group of interested colleagues.[61] 'Dear Frau Doctor, this is *not* a plan I have; it is rather an inner vision which I put forward to you for assessment, asking you what you think about it.'

Karl König wanted to come to Arlesheim soon to discuss this project with Ita Wegman. She, however, was still on holiday; but still received Karl König's letter which had been forwarded to her in the south of Switzerland. She continued her journey to Italy and Palestine and did not return to Arlesheim until November. There is no evidence of Ita Wegman's reply to Karl König but she made a comment in a letter to Madeleine van Deventer, who was deputizing for her in Arlesheim: Wegman basically approved of König's project, although without notable enthusiasm.[62] But König's plan never materialized: whether the medical staff in Arlesheim objected to it or Karl König's intentions could not be put into practice for other reasons is not known.

The year 1935 was also difficult, complicated and wearisome for Wegman and Karl König. König had attended Ita Wegman's first Christmas workshop in Arlesheim after her return from Palestine.[63] Wegman then visited Pilgramshain during the first weeks of March and all in all was very satisfied with the situation there.[64] In April she was excluded from the Executive Council in Dornach and from leadership of the Medical Section by decision of the Annual General Meeting. Karl König was excluded from the Anthroposophical Society. For years König's lectures and essays in *Natura* had been the subject of vehement criticism by Friedrich Husemann and several other doctors. They demanded she publish critical reviews which Wegman had refused. Other prominent people, too — first and foremost Marie Steiner — also found König's speeches and writings almost intolerable.[65] In

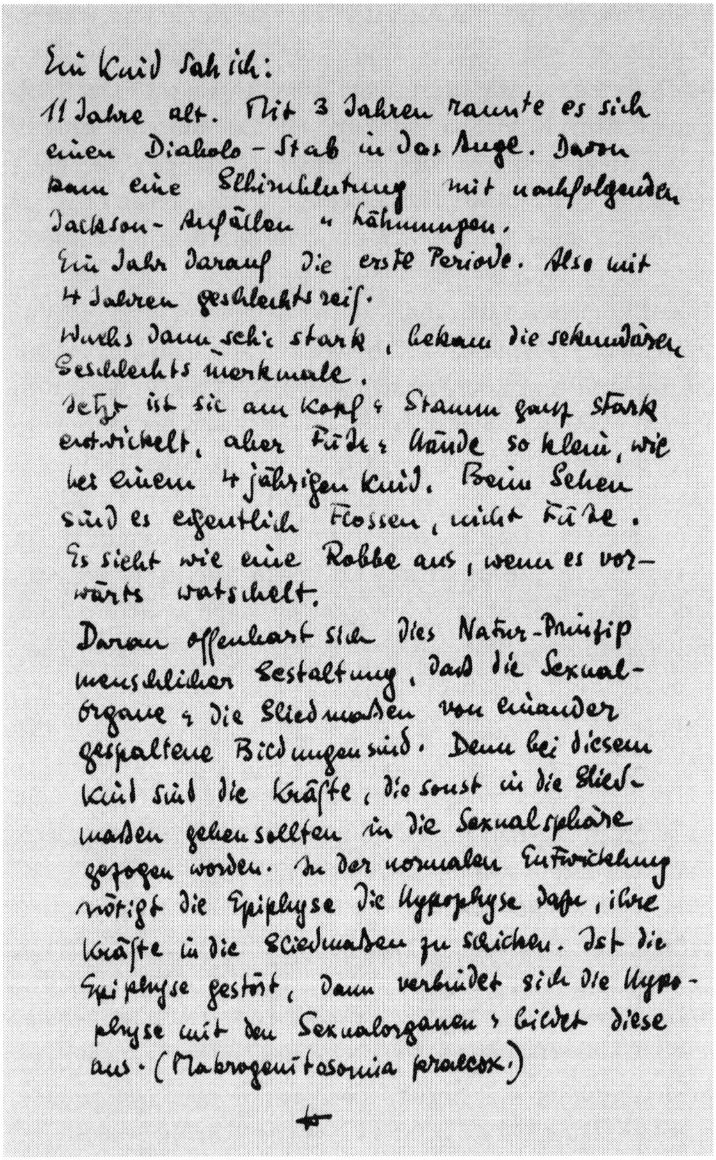

Ein Kind sah ich:
11 Jahre alt. Mit 3 Jahren rannte es sich einen Diabolo-Stab in das Auge. Davon kam eine Gehirnblutung mit nachfolgenden Jackson-Anfällen u. Lähmungen.
Ein Jahr darauf die erste Periode. Also mit 4 Jahren geschlechtsreif.
Wuchs dann sehr stark, bekam die sekundären Geschlechtsmerkmale.
Jetzt ist sie am Kopf u. Stamm ganz stark entwickelt, aber Füße u. Hände so klein, wie bei einem 4 jährigen Kind. Beim Gehen sind es eigentlich Flossen, nicht Füße.
Es sieht wie eine Robbe aus, wenn es vorwärts watschelt.
Daran offenbart sich dies Natur-Prinzip menschlicher Gestaltung, daß die Sexualorgane u. die Gliedmaßen von einander gespaltene Bildungen sind. Denn bei diesem Kind sind die Kräfte, die sonst in die Gliedmaßen gehen sollten in die Sexualsphäre gezogen worden. In der normalen Entwicklung nötigt die Epiphyse die Hypophyse dazu, ihre Kräfte in die Gliedmaßen zu schicken. Ist die Epiphyse gestört, dann verbindet sich die Hypophyse mit den Sexualorganen u. bildet diese aus. (Makrogenitosomia praecox.)

Notebook entry by Karl König. Pilgramshain, end of 1934

mid-February, after controversies and attacks had been going on for years, Karl König sharply criticized Curt Englert-Faye (one of Ita Wegman's fiercest opponents) and Albert Steffen in an open letter in the Society's weekly publication, *Das Goetheanum.*[66] As a result the mood at the biased and strategically emotionalized Annual General Meeting was ripe for his exclusion. In the end the exclusion was brought about by Friedrich Husemann's final proposal. Dr Miloš Brabínek's counter-proposal against the exclusion and his reference to König's important medical work in Prague did not change anything.[67]

Subsequently Karl König's position in Pilgramshain and Silesia became increasingly difficult — in many places he was regarded as an undesirable person, a Jew and now an outcast from the Anthroposophical Society. Slander and denouncement (which found its way into medical journals) from a large part of the Anthroposophical Society caused disruption even to his work with the doctors in Prague. König's work was damaged to such a degree that in May 1935 Ita Wegman had to step in. She firmly asked particular doctors in Prague and the Weleda company to support König in public.[68] Although even Ita Wegman was not altogether delighted with every lecture, essay or course of action by Karl König, or of his 'open letter' to Albert Steffen, she continued to support him as a matter of course and with greatest concern. But even Wegman could not make König's difficult situation in Pilgramshain any easier or better. Since his journey to Greece in spring 1935 König considered leaving and possibly returning to Vienna to open a medical practice there. By the end of January 1935 at the latest Ita Wegman knew about König's plans. On December 13 she made a passing remark in one of her letters (to Elisabeth Dank): 'Dr König actually wants to practice in Vienna and I think this is quite a good idea because this way many good things could be brought about.'[69]

⋆

In a remarkable letter on February 26, 1936, the eve of the seventy-fifth anniversary of Rudolf Steiner's birth, Karl König finally resigned not only from Pilgramshain but also from the anthroposophical curative movement, bluntly pointing to the fact that he was leaving 'forced by various internal and external events.' König's extensive medical practice had become a burden for the curative educational institute ('when I had to leave Pilgramshain in 1936 ... I reviewed my patient records and realized that during these seven years I had treated some 40,000 patients'[70]). He announced that during the next few months he would be working intensively with a larger group of doctors in Czechoslovakia. After that, by August 1, he wanted to open a medical practice in Vienna. In his letter, also copied to Ita Wegman, he looked back to seven and a half years of work at Pilgramshain:

> Building up the institute in Pilgramshain has been part of my life's work. Looking back, these years were my apprenticeship and I hope that I can now move on as a journeyman. These years of apprenticeship were full of the happiest and also most painful experiences. The rise of the curative educational work, the big conferences in Hamburg, Berlin and London are unforgettable. All the activities with hundereds of people who had an innermost interest in our work belong among good memories. The times of devotion when caring medically for the children are the dearest. Painful are the more 'internal' experiences: a repeated failure of community at the institute and between institutes, my own and my friends' complacency and the often blinkered view of the outside world in our ranks. And now the loss of everything that, until a few months ago, was the core of my life.
>
> But above all there is the great leadership that has brought us together, the spiritual momentum which made us start and develop all the work. There are the

> great breakthroughs shared by a community of friends and giving an immediate experience of the workings of the spiritual world. All this will stay steadfastly with us and in our community.

König's retrospect was complex, subtle and genuine — even when hinting at his desolation or rather the insufficient support he experienced when suffering antisemitic attacks and being insulted by other anthroposophists. As in his letter to Ita Wegman in early summer 1934 König also indicated in his farewell letter from Pilgramshain that there were severe shortfalls at the institute and between the institutes ('a repeated failure of community at the institute and between institutes'). But first and foremost he specifically included himself in those who failed ('my own and my friends' complacency') and the curative educational projects which were not yet really successful.[71] König expected the anthroposophical curative movement to be a much broader, more public orientated and Michaelic movement, believing that it should be prepared to work decisively and positively into the world's affairs through the strength of sound communities. In Pilgramshain and at other institutes, however, nobody shared his view ('the often blinkered view of the outside world in our ranks'). Despite all this König summed up those years of his work — which had begun with his introduction to the Sonnenhof by Ita Wegman — in positive terms:

> But above all there is the great leadership that has brought us together, the spiritual momentum which made us start and develop all the work. There are the great breakthroughs shared by a community of friends and giving an immediate experience of the workings of the spiritual world. All this will stay steadfastly with us and in our community.[72]

Karl König's farewell celebration at Pilgramshain was festive and joyful. Ita Wegman could not be there, but read about

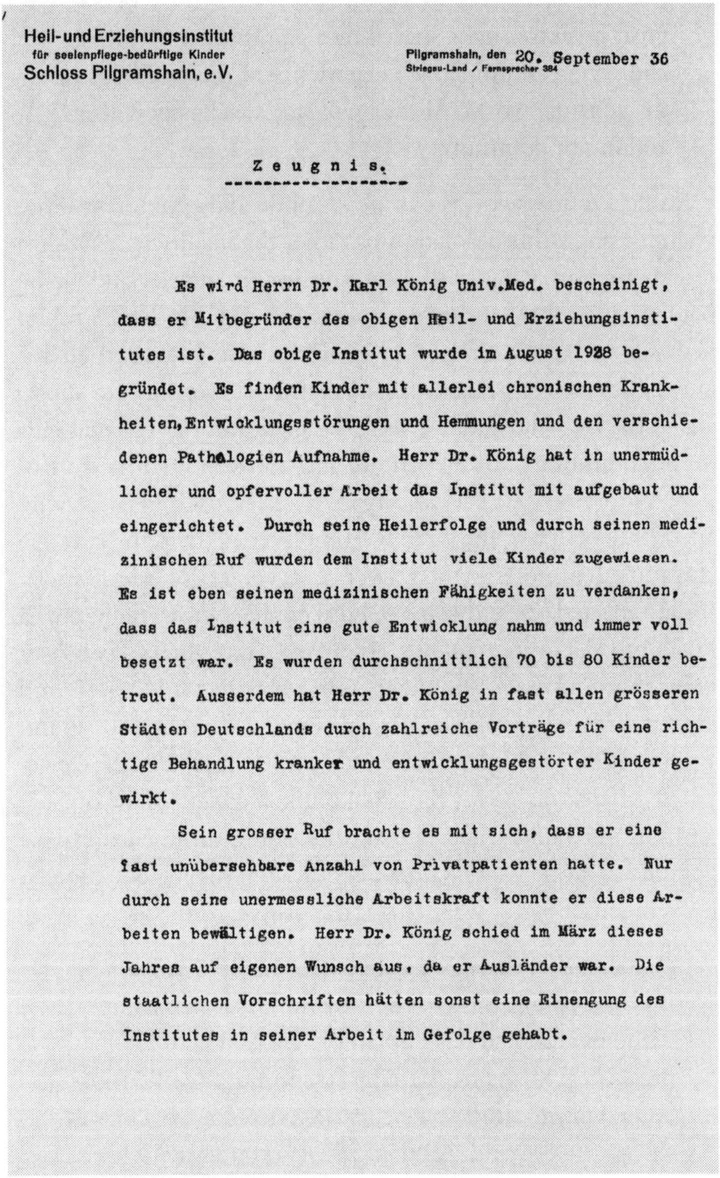

Heil- und Erziehungsinstitut
für seelenpflege-bedürftige Kinder
Schloss Pilgramshain, e.V.

Pilgramshain, den 20. September 36
Striegau-Land / Fernsprecher 384

Z e u g n i s.

Es wird Herrn Dr. Karl König Univ.Med. bescheinigt, dass er Mitbegründer des obigen Heil- und Erziehungsinstitutes ist. Das obige Institut wurde im August 1928 begründet. Es finden Kinder mit allerlei chronischen Krankheiten, Entwicklungsstörungen und Hemmungen und den verschiedenen Pathalogien Aufnahme. Herr Dr. König hat in unermüdlicher und opfervoller Arbeit das Institut mit aufgebaut und eingerichtet. Durch seine Heilerfolge und durch seinen medizinischen Ruf wurden dem Institut viele Kinder zugewiesen. Es ist eben seinen medizinischen Fähigkeiten zu verdanken, dass das Institut eine gute Entwicklung nahm und immer voll besetzt war. Es wurden durchschnittlich 70 bis 80 Kinder betreut. Ausserdem hat Herr Dr. König in fast allen grösseren Städten Deutschlands durch zahlreiche Vorträge für eine richtige Behandlung kranker und entwicklungsgestörter Kinder gewirkt.

Sein grosser Ruf brachte es mit sich, dass er eine fast unübersehbare Anzahl von Privatpatienten hatte. Nur durch seine unermessliche Arbeitskraft konnte er diese Arbeiten bewältigen. Herr Dr. König schied im März dieses Jahres auf eigenen Wunsch aus, da er Ausländer war. Die staatlichen Vorschriften hätten sonst eine Einengung des Institutes in seiner Arbeit im Gefolge gehabt.

Report and reference of Karl König's work in Pilgramshain, September 20, 1936

Nur mit dem allergrössten Bedauern sahen wir Herrn Dr. König scheiden. Für die Entwicklung des Institutes bedeutet es einen grossen Einschnitt. Trotzdem ein tüchtiger Arzt seine Stelle ersetzte, ist die Einbusse, die wir an medizinischem Ruf durch sein Fortgehen erhalten haben, noch nicht ausgeglichen.

Wir schulden Herrn Dr. König den grössten Dank und werden uns auch dessen stets bewusst bleiben.

A. Strohschein,

Direktor

it in letters and also told others 'how nice it all was and how everyone is committed to Pilgramshain with all their strength.'[73] At the end of the first week of March she wrote that König was currently staying at the country home of a Czech doctor and was looking around for opportunities; a young doctor, Alexander Rust, had succeeded to König's post. On the whole Ita Wegman was very happy with these developments although it resulted in König leaving the curative movement. She made a comment about his prospective work in Prague and Vienna:

> I think that although it will be hard for Dr König at the start he will do a lot of good work in the East, and am convinced that he can reach many people. I also hope that this will pave my way to the East because I am very close to Dr König.[74]

★

On May 1, 1936 Karl König was in Vienna and started work at his medical practice. He was thirty-three years old and at a difficult turning point of his life. Together with his wife and three children he had returned to his birthplace. They had left a large community which he and Tilla Maasberg helped to build. Even though this therapeutic community had been deficient in many ways it had been real. Now König had to make a completely new start, and reflected on this intense crisis in his life.[75] He arrived as an unknown stranger, relying only on his own resources and politically under threat. 'Pilgramshain, the large and faithful circle of patients, the lecturing activities — all had come to an end. I was alone and reliant only upon myself.'[76] What remained, however, was the close relationship to Ita Wegman and to the Medical Section of the Goetheanum. König continued to inform Wegman regularly about his work which, after the first difficult months, soon expanded: both the constantly growing medical practice and wide-ranging lecture tours.[77] He often visited Ita Wegman in Arlesheim and helped to organize conferences. Before the opening of his practice in summer 1936 medical students from Vienna met König at a conference in Arlesheim and had started to arrange regular meetings with him. This group of students, who found it difficult to get on with the Anthroposophical Society, and another circle of young questing people became closer to Karl König after he had moved to Vienna. Together with him they studied anthroposophy. From the start this positive working group was in line with the spiritual intentions of Wegman and her Section: 'This community is possible. This community must be practiced in the hearts of those who want honestly to join the healing practice at the Goetheanum' (Rudolf Steiner[78]).

Ita Wegman was delighted with König's rapid progress in Vienna, the city where Rudolf Steiner had studied. She kept Karl König regularly informed about relevant developments at the Clinical Therapeutic Institute and also told him about the death of Helene von Grunelius who had initiated the courses for young doctors in January and April 1924. She wrote to him in March 1937, three months after the death of Grunelius:

> It was a great joy to me that you have started a youth group which is doing good work, as you write in your letter. That you are successful and will continue to be, dear Dr König, does not surprise me because there is something about Austria, and you feel the same, which is certainly important for promoting spirituality. That Dr Steiner was born and used to live there, that he felt so close to the Burgenland, is indeed a fact which contributes to the success of spiritual work. The soul-needs and the hardships of everyday life can bring out something which does not arise in life's abundance.

In May 1937 when Karl König was thirty-five he received the sacrament of Baptism in the Christian Community from Josef Kral, the priest in Vienna.[79] Ita Wegman continued to advise him in difficult situations. One of these problems was an apology to Albert Steffen. König had considered this for a while for moral reasons but also because of his relationship to the Anthroposophical Society in Vienna. But Ita Wegman who knew Albert Steffen well and who believed that König's objections were basically justified, advised against an apology although she too attached some importance to a prospective understanding with Dornach. Regarding this issue Wegman wrote in her letter of March 1937:

> Your conflict with Mr Steffen needs to be considered differently from a personal insult. You wanted to defend yourself because you thought you had been treated unfairly by Mr Steffen. Of course it is unfortunate that you made your case against unfair treatment in an inappropriate way. However, you really cannot take back now what you have expressed earlier. Nor can you tell Steffen that you are sticking to what you said but feel that the way you said it was not right because it was insulting to him. You put yourself in a difficult situation when trying to do things so they appear to be right on both sides. Steffen will never accept half an apology only addressing the manner in which you expressed yourself. And surely you cannot, as a man over thirty, change your mind now all of a sudden and have a different opinion than you had three years ago. Doing something just for the sake of pacifying a few people in Austria who otherwise will not want to work with you cannot be right either.
>
> If you ask me what I would do if I were in your place, I think I would just accept that I indeed acted

> clumsily but that I did so because of my sense of fairness. Of course you have fallen into disgrace and have to deal with some unpleasantness because of this. However, there is nothing else you can do about it than accept this and, for the next time, remember to use your sense of fairness in a way that does not personally offend the other person. Otherwise the person who has acted unfairly can claim to have been deeply insulted; he can pretend that he is completely innocent, that he had been insulted for no reason and that everybody else has made themselves guilty. It is not quite right to support this kind of attitude because everything goes in the wrong direction without proper understanding.
>
> It will be enough if you have a good idea of what happened at that time because you certainly will act differently next time and will still be keen to defend fairness. These things do have an effect in the moral world. We should not care whether others approve or disapprove. Judgment is only done in higher worlds.
>
> If you still wish to write that letter, dear Dr König, then my message should not prevent you from doing so. Deep in your soul, there may still be other reasons urging you to act, reasons which cannot be fully understood by a third party.[80]

★

As can be seen from the correspondence between Karl König and Ita Wegman, König's medium-term plan was to establish a clinic and a children's home near Vienna. For the moment, however, this plan remained only an idea. Patients in need of treatment he usually sent to Arlesheim and discussed their treatment plans with Ita Wegman. In summer 1938 König travelled to the Black Sea — as Wegman did a year later — and studied the ancient mysteries of the area. He continued the anthroposophical work with his circle of friends and students. This circle grew closer together and looked towards the future with interest, vigilance and determination.[81] In February 1938, in one of her letters, Ita Wegman hinted for the first time that she needed staff for her curative educational initiative in France; at the same time in London Eugen Kolisko already planned to organize the emigration of Karl König and his family. On April 2, 1938 Karl Nunhöfer wrote from London to Wegman: 'I think Dr Kolisko's plan to bring König and his wife over to England with the help of Dame Florence is very daring.'[82]

Indeed — despite all hesitation — it was high time for quick and decisive action. In March 1938, a few weeks prior to Nunhöfer's comment, Hitler's troops had annexed Austria. In April the first antisemitic waves of arrests started. In this extremely difficult and life-threatening situation, of which Kolisko was well aware, Karl König hoped for support from Arlesheim or at least for a 'word of sympathy.' In mid June, after Ita Wegman had written him a letter no longer extant, he asked her if he could come to Arlesheim in the near future for a year to do work in the Clinic and on scientific publications. He also wanted to prepare the emigration of his Viennese friends who, despite the difficult circumstances, had decided to start a curative educational project in Ireland or Cyprus. One by one they fled Vienna after the National Socialists had occupied the city.[83] König wrote to Ita Wegman asking the same question regarding Arlesheim he had put in summer 1934:

> It is now ten years since I left that place [Arlesheim]. During this time I have seen many patients and have learnt quite a lot and I think I have reached

> a certain standard in diagnostics: I would like to discuss all this in depth with friends. During these ten years I have been rather alone with my ideas and have gathered so much knowledge that I would like to share this with others. In addition a lot of patients have recently come to me from west Switzerland, so that I have thought perhaps I could oversee and develop the outpatients' department of the clinic. It would be most important for me, however, to work once again with the friends and under your guidance. I would also like to watch from Arlesheim how the other projects are doing, particularly the one in Ireland.

Karl König emphasized that he only needed food and accommodation but no money, and concluded his letter with the words:

> I wanted to ask you now, dear Frau Doctor, if you think that there is such an opportunity, if you consider it a good idea to include me again for a while in the clinic community. I really would like to work for a year in peace and to write down and communicate much of what is on my mind.

Ita Wegman replied to König — after a delay of almost four weeks — that she would gladly like to let him stay in Arlesheim but that she had to seek approval of the authorities first. 'I shall write to you as soon as we know. Should it be possible we shall all be very pleased for you to rejoin us.' König's possible emigration to England was also on Ita Wegman's mind as can be seen from her correspondence during these weeks.[84]

By mid August 1938 König had to leave Vienna in great haste without waiting for an answer from Arlesheim.[85]

The young community surrounding Karl König was still resolved to turn its intentions into reality, even if the lives of

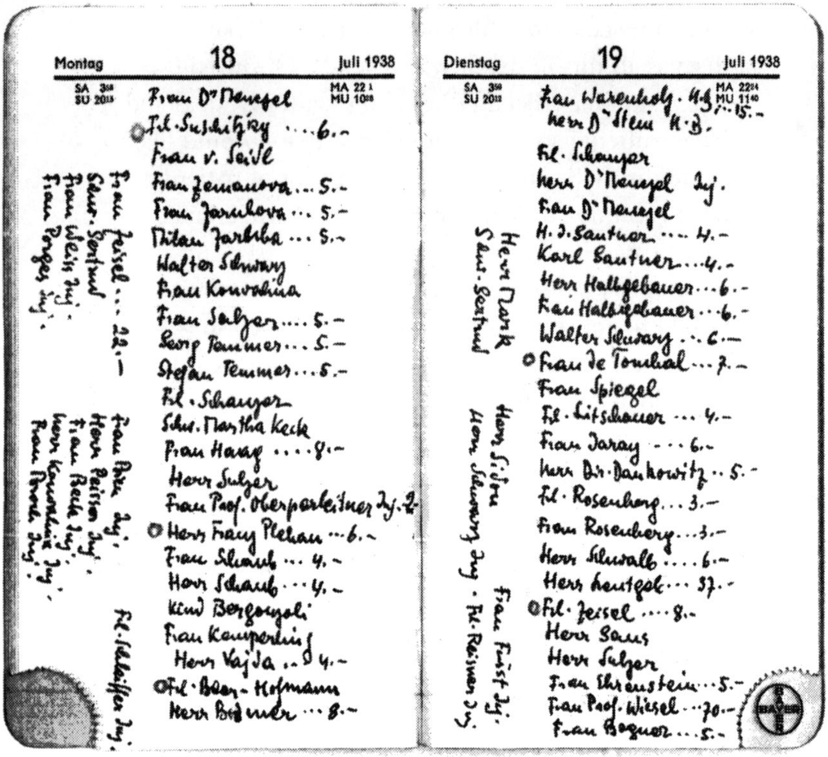

Unpaid accounts of patients, Vienna, July 1938

individual members were at risk because most of them were Jewish. ('The soul-needs and the hardships of everyday life can bring out something which does not arise in life's abundance,' Wegman wrote.) After he had managed to leave Austria König stayed for a few days in Italy and then went to Switzerland where he unsuccessfully applied for a post as scientific assistant at an epilepsy clinic near Lake Thun.

> As I had already been developing new ideas for the treatment of epilepsy for quite some time, and empirical proof and confirmation were still needed, I thought this

> would be a productive use of the time given to me. Soon after their initial agreement, however, I was informed that there was no interest in my inadequately substantiated statements.

At the same time and to his deep regret König learnt that he was not actually welcomed in Arlesheim either:

> I was received warmly by Dr Wegman but with the greatest reserve by the workers at the clinic and at the Sonnenhof. I realized that it would be impossible to stay there for any length of time.[86]

Already in August 1934 because of the general mood it had obviously been difficult for Ita Wegman to include König in the clinic in a positive way. Although in June 1938 the authority's regulations Wegman had mentioned were an important reason for her cautious reply to König's enquiry, König felt in Arlesheim that there were strong reservations against his work and himself. The Clinical Therapeutical Institute was a small building and staffed with a number of rather headstrong people; therefore it was only partly suited for including another highly dynamic, intensive and not altogether uncomplicated person like Karl König (for this reason he had prudently applied for a post at the outpatients' department). It can also be assumed that the majority of Ita Wegman's medical staff strongly objected to König's *Natura* essays which were in parts highly speculative. They also may have objected to his open letter to Albert Steffen and to more of his actions during the previous years, especially since they knew that König's words and conduct had reflected badly on Ita Wegman and the Medical Section. It had indeed caused damage to Ita Wegman and further undermined her reputation at the Goetheanum.[87]

Additionally König had left the curative movement on his own initiative in February 1936 and probably sent his final statement to every institute ('a repeated failure of community at the institute and between institutes'). So a friendly welcome for Karl König would have been surprising. However, in face of the dangerous political situation it should have been seen as an absolute necessity. Most people in Arlesheim were unaware that König had meanwhile taken a critical position on his early *Natura* essays and on the style of his letter to Albert Steffen — but this probably would not have significantly changed their opinion of Karl König.

★

Ita Wegman not only continued to stand steadfastly by König, she also helped and supported him as much as she could. She asked him to teach at her nurses' school, to give lectures on spiritual embryology in the therapy house at the clinic, to give public lectures in Basle (arranged by Ernst Marti who was working closely with her) and, last but not least, to help with her curative educational initiative in France. In September 1938 König stayed, with Wegman's support, in Paris at the small curative education centre in the Rue de l'Assomption. The project in France had started here and now Vala Bérence and the children in her care had relocated to a castle near Versailles. On September 28, the eve of Michaelmas and twice seven years after Rudolf Steiner's last address, Karl König wrote a first letter from Paris to his friends giving a detailed outlook on the project in France:

> Friends here want an institute and a farm to be established and will help towards this coming about, and the official possibilities are extraordinary. To be sure, residence permits are not easily obtained for Paris; but this is an easy matter in the countryside. There are several hundred properties which can be rented for little money, and what we are looking for

> is unique to France. Some Parisian doctors have promised their help, and I now have the following plan: I shall return to Switzerland for a while (from three to four weeks) so as to make a start with the preparations in Paris at the beginning of November. There is a house here in Rue de l'Assomption where I can live. ... and I shall have the opportunity from here to get to know many people, to work with the resident doctor here, Dr Clary, and to assist in Courcelles itself ... I should also like to make a connection with a solicitor who will look for suitable property for us. With any luck such a property will have been found by February or March, and then I should like to begin with the work on the land.[88]

König hoped that the friends from Vienna would gradually follow him to France, and he vividly described France and its spirit:

> It is a strange country. I believe that in the coming decades it will have a further great significance, for everything speaks for its becoming the place for the spiritual rebirth of Central Europe. Much that is holy and healing can be found here. The old stream of Mary wisdom lives strongly here, and the grace which issues from it can be felt everywhere. True motherhood is still at home here. And yet this motherhood is sad, like Herzeloide when Parzival rode away from her. He left his mother to seek the path to the Holy Grail. An image of the *Pietà* also rises up in one's soul when one searches for *'La France.'* I think that you should take this image of the Mother weeping for her Son into your hearts; it will help us on our way. Then perhaps we may come to be able to comfort this grieving mother. ... Please make efforts to start learning French. Please also read, as far as

Karl König

> is possible, the legends of Parzival, especially the versions by Wolfram von Eschenbach. There lives 'Notre-Dame.'[89]

★

Two months later, on November 27, Karl König celebrated the first Advent Sunday with the children at the castle of La Courcelles. In the meantime, however, he had learned how difficult it would actually be to found something in France. He reported this to Ita Wegman in a letter which is no longer extant. In her reply of November 28, one day after the Advent celebrations, Wegman suggested asking Jules Sauerwein for help regarding the authorities and stated:

> You wrote that you were a bit disappointed with the French. This is a valid point of view but it would be a pity if spiritual work could not be carried out in France. In that case the situation in France would deteriorate rapidly and Europe too will perish because I have no trust ... that England will then help Europe. I rather have the feeling that a close alliance between England and America will form, and that this will be the end of Europe.

Wegman's comparatively matter-of-fact words at the end of November 1938 show that even she at that time was still hoping for possibilities in France regarding König's curative community project, and was ever hopeful about the political situation in Europe and its global implications.

However, chances in France became bleaker and bleaker. After he had received the entry and work permits, Ita Wegman herself emphatically supported König's emigration to Britain.

> I discussed everything with Dr Wegman and she was of the opinion that I should immediately respond to this helping hand stretched out towards me. Previously she had told me about friends living near to Aberdeen who were prepared to provide assistance to a group of refugees. She considered it vital that curative work should begin in Scotland, thereby fruitfully complementing the work that had already started in England. She also promised to give us as much help as possible.[90]

Karl König's entry permit for Britain was granted on October 2, and König received it in the middle of October (although he did not receive permission for further medical studies and for a future occupation as a doctor until the end of November).[91] However, the approving and encouraging conversation with Ita Wegman which König mentioned probably did not take place before the end of November or the beginning of December 1938, after König's return from France and a realistic review of the experiences made there and when he had received permission from the Home Office.[92]

On December 8, 1938 König finally arrived in London with a letter of reference from Ita Wegman to Mr and Mrs Haughton. They had been Wegman's patients and belonged to the anthroposophical friends of the clinic in Arlesheim. Wegman herself had visited them on the Williamston Estate in Scotland earlier in 1938.

France was attacked and occupied by the German army only seventeen months later. In autumn 1942 a close colleague of Vala Bérence, Hanna Lissau from Vienna, originally a member of König's youth group and of Jewish origin, was deported from the children's home and died in Auschwitz, a fate which Karl König had narrowly escaped.

★

Any communication on the subject of this letter should be addressed to:—

THE UNDER SECRETARY OF STATE,
HOME OFFICE
(ALIENS DEPARTMENT),
STANLEY HOUSE,
MARSHAM STREET
LONDON, S.W.1,

and the following number quoted:—

K 12858

HOME OFFICE,
STANLEY HOUSE,
MARSHAM STREET,
LONDON, S.W.1.

18th November, 1938.

Sir,

With reference to Dr. Karl Koenig's application for permission to establish himself in medical practice in the United Kingdom, I am directed by the Secretary of State to say that he decided, subject to confirmation by the British Consul General of Dr. Koenig's suitability for medical practice in the United Kingdom, to raise no objection to his proceeding to this country with his wife and children in order to study for a British medical qualification. When he has been placed on the British Medical Register, after a period of not less than two years' study, the Secretary of State will be prepared to consider sympathetically an application for him to establish himself in medical practice in this country.

A communication was sent to the British Consul General at Zurich on the 3rd October.

I am, Sir,
Your obedient Servant,

C B McAlpine

The Secretary,
German Jewish Aid Committee,
Woburn House,
Upper Woburn Place,
W.C.1.

Letter from the Home Office (Karl König Archive).

Just a few days after his arrival in London König visited Mr and Mrs Haughton in Scotland and was offered an old vicarage as a place where he and his friends could start their work. In his next letter to Ita Wegman (also no longer extant) he must have described the situation there; again she replied with approval and encouragement:

> I have read it all with great interest and think that it is definitely the right thing to do, the way you want to go about it now. Since the Haughtons take so much interest in medicine and have shown so much good will you should not reject this course of destiny. I have seen the house next to the church myself, it certainly has potential for something good. Hopefully you will find enough young people for the work because of course this is what needs to be done first.
>
> Of course I feel very sorry that you cannot commit yourself to the project in Paris, but after all people in Paris are becoming increasingly narrow-minded and nobody knows what will happen there, whereas Scotland's island location provides more safety.

Ita Wegman was pleased when König wrote to her that he was prepared to keep an eye on the curative project in France — 'That you are going to come to Paris for a visit in February and also that you are going to come here will be a great joy for us. I can well imagine that the projects in Scotland and in France will be able to support each other effectively.' But she advised him to focus on the British Isles and the opportunities there. For many years and with increasing intensity since Hitler's takeover in spring 1933 Wegman had worked for and encouraged the expansion of anthroposophy in Great Britain. Rudolf Steiner had emphasized the importance of developments which could take place there, especially in the pedagogical field, and he had visited Margaret MacMillan's educational, curative educational and medical projects in a poor district of London.[93] König's friends

Kirkton House

Eugen Kolisko and Walter Johannes Stein, his former 'teachers' and comrades-in-arms from Vienna who both were founder members of the Waldorf School in Stuttgart, had emigrated to England in order to develop significant anthroposophical projects. Kolisko who was very close to Karl König and, like him was troubled by the traumatic situation of the Society in Dornach, had helped König to emigrate and supported him in many ways during his first time in England. In summer 1928, ten years before leaving Central Europe, König had attended parts of the World Conference for Spiritual Science and its Practical Applications in London, and in December 1938 may have remembered the wording of the letter in which Gerhard Suchantke had told him how the conference had ended with seven concluding comments: 'It was overwhelming: Rittelmeyer spoke about England's mission, how it would be ruined if it did not recognize ... the golden ships of spirituality which were now coming up to its shores.'

Now König himself had arrived in Britain and Ita Wegman trusted him with his project despite — or perhaps because of —

the fact that her own many efforts and medical-therapeutical intentions had never taken sufficient effect there. She advised König to set his priorities on pursuing his studies in Britain and on obtaining full medical qualifications and approbation (something the doctors Nunhöfer and Engel had been unable to achieve) and not yet on trying to commit himself to the project in France. In her letter of January 11, 1939 she concluded: 'But perhaps your activities can bring some of the work back to life and your powerful energies can inspire others to work harder. Most often the cause for failure is a lack of effort.'

As a result König's activities developed quickly, and — surprisingly — with the support and good will of the authorities.[94]

★

From 1939 onwards the correspondence between Ita Wegman and Karl König became noticeably less frequent. This was the time when the community at Kirkton House formed, when the actual work with the children started, with all its problems and responsibilities, and particularly the time of a threatening and eventually real world war.

Karl König's friends from Vienna successively arrived in Britain, some of them via the Sonnenhof in Arlesheim and with Ita Wegman's support. Margarete Bockholt, doctor at the clinic in Arlesheim, met König at the Scottish Summer School in spring 1939; Wegman, too, had planned to come to Scotland but then decided to stay in Arlesheim. In early summer she travelled to the Black Sea, her last journey before the start of the Second World War. After her return on August 19 Ita Wegman wrote in detail to Karl König about her experiences, obviously in the knowledge of König's understanding of Eastern Europe and the responsibilities there. None of the numerous people she wrote to received a description of her journey to the Balkans as extensive and detailed as in her letter to König. In a letter three years previously she had expressed

The early group at Kirkton House in 1939

her hope that König would pave her 'path' to the East; now she wrote to him:

> On my journey to the East — I went to the Black Sea — I passed through Vienna. This Vienna was a very sorry sight to see. It was as if people were unable to recover from the blow they had been dealt. The people on the street did not seem to be quite there and those who were a bit more cheerful were foreigners or Germans. On the whole you had the impression of a culture that was already dead, independently of what Hitler had done.
>
> Further East it was a different picture. There was a sense of something youthful, vigorous, which had not yet taken shape. How important it would be to bring

anthroposophy to these places in the East and to empower people there. Just now they are looking around, at one time they believe that strength and support will come from England, another time they desperately look towards Germany or Russia, or even Turkey, because they do not feel spiritually strong enough to withstand the brunt of those forces.

Yugoslavia is mostly Roman Catholic and Bulgaria is mostly Greek Catholic [Orthodox]. The latter has something of Russia, of Russian spirituality I mean, very appealing and very spiritual. At the Black Sea I could experience much of importance, giving me a clear idea of historical events which took place there. Visiting historical sites definitely helps one to understand many things which happened in the past.

I was also in Germany, and something strange is going on there: a decline and at the same time a steep rise in spirituality. Many people are ready for anthroposophy and actively involved in it. There is a lot of understanding for spirituality, yet not a calm, contemplative understanding. It is rather reckless and thrives on demolishing and knocking over everything, although there are no achievements of their own whatsoever. They demonstrate their powers by pushing over everything, knocking down many buildings and replacing them with new ones which are no different; they are not built in a new architectural style which would indicate some progress. Nothing changes but there is a lot of stir, and this stir is expressed by the demolishing of whole streets and quarters. You can talk to some of them and point out to them the effects of spirituality which can be found everywhere; then they might listen, agree to some points and demonstrate

> briskness and a thirst for action. What is overly structured in England is still completely lacking in shape in the East; and in Central Europe they are breaking the old structures without having anything new to build.
>
> That is how the world looks. If the leading powers were any wiser they would understand it and would reach out to each other and a lot would happen for the benefit of mankind. Unfortunately ignorance prevails, not the intention to be a bit more tolerant towards others. As a result we are in a very difficult situation, and any moment this tension can trigger an outburst. Europe will then be lost. Even so I am still hopeful that it will not come to that. England should be very watchful and look eastwards because the greatest danger will certainly come from there. If they do not succeed in sorting out the East, it will act as a bridge for the Mongols coming over to Europe; this again will be another, perhaps equally great danger.
>
> Well, in Scotland perhaps you will be able to work in peace. Mr and Mrs Haughton have always said that if there is any war it will not reach the North of Britain. So now you have the opportunity to work intensively and constructively.

★

On New Year's Eve 1939 Karl König wrote another letter to Ita Wegman (no longer extant) telling her about the intensive pioneering work during the past months, and informing her about his plans to leave Kirkton House because of difficult circumstances.[95] In his letter König also wanted to know about Wegman's health — probably because he had heard that she had fallen and been in hospital immediately after the start of the war. He also asked her if she could come to Scotland for a visit. In addition König enquired if there were opportunities to continue and expand anthroposophy in America and asked Wegman if she could support such a project. In all likelihood he did not know at this time that Wegman herself had thought about moving to Canada and establishing a clinic there just before the war.

In her reply of January 18, 1940 Ita Wegman expressed her regret that König was planning to leave Kirkton House and that disagreements with the Haughtons had arisen. She frankly told König about her concerns: 'I really hope there will be no breakup with Williamston, that would a be real pity because we rely on each other for our progress.' However, in a letter to Frances Melland which she wrote (in English) having received the latest letter sent by the Haughtons, she expressed her views in even more unequivocal terms:

> There is no understanding between Dr König's group and herself [Mrs. Haughton] and her husband, I think they are too strange for one another. Mrs Haughton is always willing to help, but she likes also to manage, and Dr König has the same tendency. But König is the stranger and should understand the circumstances and he must be thankful for the help he received.[96] That matters are not going as they should makes me very sad for it will all be reflected back on Anthroposophy. Dr König has altered the house, which the Haughtons let him have free, without first consulting them, but told them after that it was done. It will not be good if such things are done. So you see that in Scotland there are always difficulties and dissension has crept it. I tell you this, dear Miss Melland, that you may understand the situation of Mr and Mrs Haughton, and perhabs [*sic*] it will be good and my advice is that people do not just 'worship' Dr König, but that he understand, he cannot

> take liberties in a strange land where he is receiving hospitality. For me, I have nothing against Dr König, but would only *warn* against a repetition of the situation of adoration of Stein and Kolisko and now König, it is not good for you all nor for König.

Despite her own concerns regarding König's departure from Kirkton House, Ita Wegman wished him luck for finding a suitable property: 'I hope you will find something good.'

In her letter of January 18, 1940 Ita Wegman also described her own position and the general situation at the clinic five months after the start of the war. She indicated that she was including into her considerations the Casa Andrea Cristoforo in Ascona where she had first been for a longer stay in November 1939, just when König's friend Kolisko had unexpectedly died in London. In this context and referring to König's enquiry regarding America, she wrote:

> It is a question whether America at the present time stands open to us; I do not think that this is the case. It is also the human issue which plays a part. Kolisko's death has left a huge gap because I always hoped he would be the right person for America. I do not see real opportunities in America, although I have some friends there who would gladly help if something could be done. I have also often thought of British Columbia, I even had a kind of vision of the actual house (a nice clinic on a hill). But that may have been pure imagination.

At the end of her letter Ita Wegman finally replied to König's complaint that she had given him too little advice and supportive direction during the past year. It is possible that in 1939 König had written several times (the letters are not extant) from Kirkton House to Arlesheim expressing his concerns, worries and doubts. But Ita Wegman was not really aware of owing him an answer — and explained to König in a few sentences how she was planning to support his social work:

> You accuse me of not sending any messages or advice or instructions for the hard work you are doing there. But dear Dr König, how could I possibly do so? That is something which cannot be done from here. In new situations like this when you have to build relationships with people you do not know very well, things keep changing rapidly. The situation today can have completely changed by tomorrow. I rather had the feeling that you should be left to get on with things because you have always been considerate and tactful enough to solve any difficult situations. So please do not begrudge me for not having written very often. Be assured that I will always remain connected to your work. I am also very closely connected to everyone who is with you now. The clinic is also very connected with you and the work you are doing over there.

Ita Wegman supported Dr König, his colleagues and their plans although she knew that König — like Kolisko and Stein — would continue to go along his own path, a path that to some extent had led him away from anthroposophical circles. Wegman viewed this with regret, particularly regarding the curative education movement, because the consistent coordination of the movement had since 1925 been her deep-felt concern. But at the same time she recognized König's great individuality and the indisputable moral integrity of his intentions, and kept in touch with him.

⋆

From the last three years of Ita Wegman's life, only two letters and a telegram from Karl König and one letter of reply from Wegman are extant. Given the difficult and dangerous mailing-route during the war and also the general spiritual situation it seems likely that there was not much more correspondence during this time anyway. In spring 1940 König informed Wegman that Susanne Lissau, a qualified music therapist and curative educator whose move to König's project had been confirmed, had decided to stay at the Sonnenhof after all — much to König's annoyance. He sent the letter in which Lissau had informed him of her decision to Ita Wegman, vehemently protesting against it. König knew that Susanne Lissau wanted to stay at the Sonnenhof and that Wegman approved of this but had not actually suggested it.[97] In this situation he emphatically complained to Wegman, addressing her in her role as the spiritual leader of the Medical Section at the Goetheanum with an overall social responsibility, and also as the director of the Sonnenhof. König felt 'let down,' and in his letter of April 14, 1940 he also clearly stated how vital curative eurythmy in his opinion was for curative education and how serious he was about Susanne Lissau (or an adequate replacement for her):

> We are in most urgent need of a curative eurythmist, and you know how vital curative eurythmy is for curative education. I am not keen on doing things like in Clent where they have been working year after year without curative eurythmy.

★

In the same letter — and in a more settled tone — Karl König informed Ita Wegman that the community would soon be moving to Camphill, and described the new property; at the end of his letter he referred again to curative eurythmy:

> It is a big house and two smaller ones with four rooms each in the middle of 22-acre grounds with a beautiful

> fruit and vegetable garden, two fields and a number of stables and outhouses. They are ideal for setting up everything we need for our work. I am really glad that this progress could be made within a year and am quite surprised — as I mentioned before — about the interest which even the authorities are taking in our work. That means there are excellent opportunities and on the other hand equally great challenges, and in this regard I do not want to miss anything. Regarding curative eurythmy I would ask you again not to leave us out in the cold, and hope you will be able to find a replacement.

In this letter — before the actual move — König made clear his intentions for Camphill to continue developing contact to the general public as well as cooperating with the authorities: 'and am quite surprised — as I mentioned before — about the interest which even the authorities are taking in our work.' This had been his intention for many years when working with the authorities and with the Social Support Association to mutual benefit. Although König had started his life in Scotland in a small enclave of Jewish immigrants, he insisted on exclusive use of the English language in Kirkton House. He made every effort to build and keep good relationships to the local community. In this respect too he was very close to Ita Wegman and her cosmopolitan, Michaelic approach. But he disagreed with many in the curative movement who worked rather introvertedly — 'the often blinkered view of the outside world in our ranks.'

The move to Camphill was planned for early summer 1940. At that time Ita Wegman had gone to the Casa Andrea Cristoforo. There she soon heard that Karl König and the men of the community had been interned on the Isle of Man as 'enemy aliens.' She also heard that, despite this, the women and children had moved to Camphill Estate at the end of May. Later she was informed of the men's gradual release, starting with Karl

König who returned to Camphill from the internment camp on October 4.

At Christmas 1940, during the first anthroposophical Christmas celebrations at Casa Andrea Cristoforo, Ita Wegman received a telegram in English:

> All good wishes and heartiest thoughts for a bright Xmas to you all friends
> Dr König and Camphill

Shortly after this Ita Wegman wrote Countess to von Bonstetten:

> I have just received a telegram from Dr König in England telling me that he and his family are well. I am really glad about this news.[98]

★

Six months later, on June 9, 1941, Ita Wegman wrote after a long time, asking about König, his work and his colleagues. Wegman wrote in English after reading about König's activities in the anthroposophical *News Sheet* published in Britain. She wanted to know how he and his friends were doing, about his family and her godchild Renate, and described the current state of their communication and relationship:

> The News Sheet speaks of the work but cannot of course give the details one would so gladly hear and in any case it is not possible in these times to write of those things which lie deep at heart. So you must understand in the same way when you do not hear so often from me for it does not in any way mean that you are not, all of you, frequently in my thoughts, and I long for the time when all the present[-]time barriers are away and we may again have free intercourse with each other.

CAMPHILL

MILLTIMBER

ABERDEENSHIRE

Telephone: Culter 214.
Station: Culter and Aberdeen.

Principal: Karl König, M.D.
Matron: Mrs. T. König.

Camphill House

For boys and girls from 2-14 years of age, with all kinds of difficulty and backwardness, and those who are not able to be placed in a regular school.

Camphill Cottage

For a small number of boys over 14 years of age who are not able to find a place in the social order.

First Camphill prospectus, page 2

Ita Wegman obviously kept the most important issues to herself ('it is not possible in these times to write of those things which lie deep at heart') and during the last three years of her life she kept up only very little of the wide-ranging correspondence she had had before. She was certainly aware that König had been waiting a long time for her enquiries, attention and interest, for a 'word of sympathy.' There is every indication that Karl König, after waiting long and in vain, had almost stopped writing to

Arlesheim. Wegman's unexpected letter of June 9, 1941, however, was a great joy and relief for him, as it informed him about her own situation in Ascona and confirmed her continued interest in his efforts and those of the community. He began his reply with the sentence 'Dear Dr Wegman, you can hardly imagine what joy we all felt when your letter arrived.' König had just returned from lectures he had held at the Annual General Meeting of the Anthroposophical Society in London where he had heard good news of Ita Wegman and her situation in Ascona, when Wegman's letter arrived. Now he was even more pleased to read these personal, unexpected words from her. In his reply to Wegman's letter — their last exchange of letters — König described in detail and cheerfully the situation in Camphill; he concluded his letter of July 15, 1941 with words addressing Ita Wegman and the community at Casa Andrea Cristoforo:

> Please give our kindest regards to all your friends and helpers, and we all send you our love and confidence and inmost feeling with you and your work.
>
> With heartiest greetings,
> I am, yours ever,
> Karl König

⋆

In the early evening of March 4, 1943 Dr König was informed by way of telegram that Ita Wegman had unexpectedly died in her house in Arlesheim during the morning. Emotionally devastated by the news — 'rarely felt such immediate grief; feel broken apart' — König decided to read Rudolf Steiner's Christological lecture of July 28, 1923 for Wegman and, that same evening, held a memorial celebration with his friends in Camphill. On the following day, late at night on March 5, when many people had already said their farewells to Ita Wegman who was lying in state in her house in Arlesheim, he wrote in his diary:

Now this good and great woman has gone into the spiritual world. Perhaps Rudolf Steiner's best friend. The friend who cared for him day and night during his illness, the central figure in the new medicine, the new curative education. Doctor, helper, adviser for many, many people. The helper and motherly friend is no more. For me, it is as if a living nerve has been severed. I can hardly believe I will never see her again here on earth. How empty it suddenly is around me.

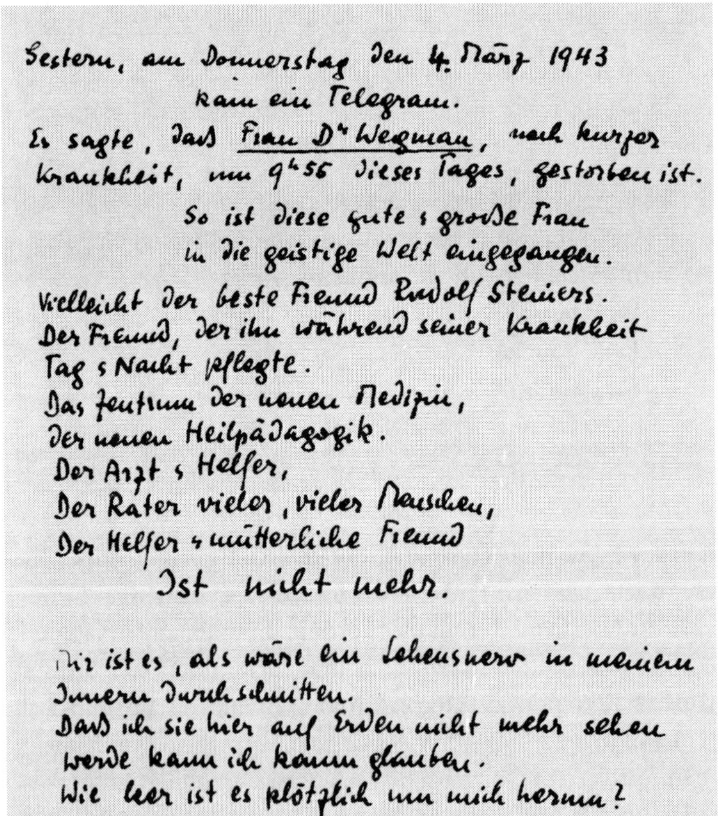

Gestern, am Donnerstag den 4. März 1943
kam ein Telegram.
Es sagte, dass Frau Dr Wegman, nach kurzer
Krankheit, um 9h56 dieses Tages, gestorben ist.
So ist diese gute & grosse Frau
in die geistige Welt eingegangen.
Vielleicht der beste Freund Rudolf Steiners.
Der Freund, der ihn während seiner Krankheit
Tag & Nacht pflegte.
Das Zentrum der neuen Medizin,
der neuen Heilpädagogik.
Der Arzt & Helfer,
Der Rater vieler, vieler Menschen,
Der Helfer & mütterliche Freund
Ist nicht mehr.

Mir ist es, als wäre ein Lebensnerv in meinem
Innern durchschnitten.
Dass ich sie hier auf Erden nicht mehr sehen
werde kann ich kaum glauben.
Wie leer ist es plötzlich um mich herum?

Karl König's diary of March 5, 1943

Ita Wegman (Ascona 1942)

> Up in the morning, but totally broken down. In infinite grief unable to do anything. ...
>
> Later I make a start writing the Kaspar Hauser story as a sort of requiem for Frau Doctor. It is slow going.[99]

On the day Ita Wegman died König put a photograph of her on his desk where it stayed from then onwards. It was her portrait taken in Ascona, which she had evidently sent him at the end of 1942, probably at Christmas. Until March 8, 1943, the day of Wegman's cremation in Basle and the bombing of the old part of Nuremberg, König worked on his Kaspar Hauser story. In the following months he concerned himself intensively with this subject in connection to the Isis-Osiris mystery and Ita Wegman; partly working together with Walter Johannes Stein.

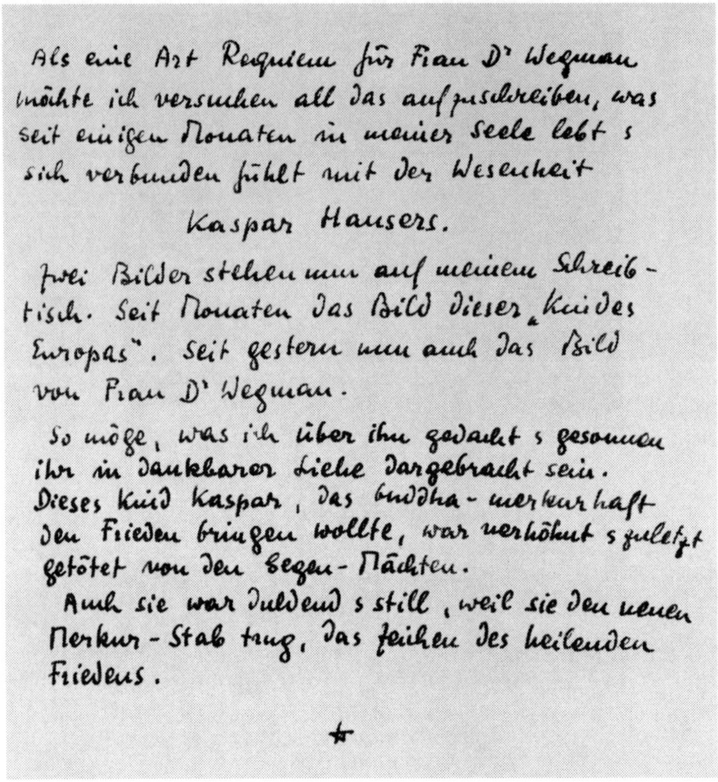

Als eine Art Requiem für Frau Dr Wegman
möchte ich versuchen all das aufzuschreiben, was
seit einigen Monaten in meiner Seele lebt u
sich verbunden fühlt mit der Wesenheit

Kaspar Hausers.

Zwei Bilder stehen nun auf meinem Schreib-
tisch. Seit Monaten das Bild dieses „Kindes
Europas". Seit gestern nun auch das Bild
von Frau Dr Wegman.

So möge, was ich über ihn gedacht u gesonnen
ihr in dankbarer Liebe dargebracht sein.
Dieses Kind Kaspar, das buddha-merkurhaft
den Frieden bringen wollte, war verhöhnt u zuletzt
getötet von den Gegen-Mächten.
Auch sie war duldend u still, weil sie den neuen
Merkur-Stab trug, das Zeichen des heilenden
Friedens.

★

First draft of König's 'Kaspar Hauser.' (March 1943)

On March 5 Karl König referred in his diary to Kaspar Hauser and the work on his story, which occupied him those first days after Ita Wegman's death.[100]

> This child Kaspar, who was to bring peace from out of the Mercury impulse of the Buddha, was ridiculed and ultimately murdered by the counter-forces. She too was patient and calm, because she bore the new staff of Mercury, the sign of healing peace.[101]

★

The still surviving diary entries and also some comments in his lectures during these two decades show that Karl König sought to relate to Ita Wegman's spiritual being for the rest of his life and experienced this as a reality in his Camphill work.[102] He understood himself as working and living within the 'Ephesus stream' represented by Wegman; he wanted to work in 'the spirit of her intentions' and saw even his late phase of initiatives at the Lake of Constance decidedly in this context.[103] Around St John's day 1964 König wrote to Erika von Arnim, the founder of the Camphill School Community at Föhrenbühl:

> I always sensed that what wants to come about at Lake Constance must be understood against the background of Ephesus ... There is already a strong destiny there pointing to the individuality of Ita Wegman, and we must try to raise it more and more into consciousness.[104]

In September 1965, six months before his death, König spoke once more about Ita Wegman at the opening ceremony for the new house in Föhrenbühl near Heiligenberg at the Lake of Constance. He described her social charisma and her powerful Michaelic force of initiative which had helped the anthroposophical medical movement to achieve global significance. About her relationship to Rudolf Steiner he said:

> Dr Wegman was not only his personal physician but also his carer and accompanied him continuously throughout the last months and days of his life. She cared for him, she looked after him. He told her once that her whole life had actually been directed towards these six months together. It really needs to be considered that the anthroposophical medical movement originates from Rudolf Steiner himself becoming a patient and Ita Wegman his doctor.[105]

Since 1925 Karl König had experienced Rudolf Steiner's continuing intentions through Ita Wegman's life and work to which he had increasingly devoted his own work and creativity. Rudolf Steiner had once said that *he* would lead the Medical Section *through* Ita Wegman. König had experienced the spiritual reality of this statement in Ita Wegman but at the same time also in his own destiny with her as his guide and adviser.[106] For Karl König Camphill was part of the anthroposophical movement on earth, facilitated by and associated with Rudolf Steiner, which was also in accordance with Ita Wegman's words on December 23, 1933:

> What we do here always aims at forming a stronger and stronger connection to Rudolf Steiner. Despite all difficulties within the Society we aspire to this connection, and only thereby can we live and work here.[107]

2

The Correspondence Between Ita Wegman and Karl König (1926–41)

In every single group of people, be it at a school or at an institute, we face a special task. We either have to accomplish our task without compromise *or we* have to compromise *in order to preserve what has been accomplished. While the latter is certainly necessary, those who uphold the 'original intentions' of anthroposophy will break away from it in order to start something new together with the young generation who at present want an answer to the question 'Which way do we go?' It does not matter any longer* what *is being done but* how *it is being done.*

Karl König, 1934[1]

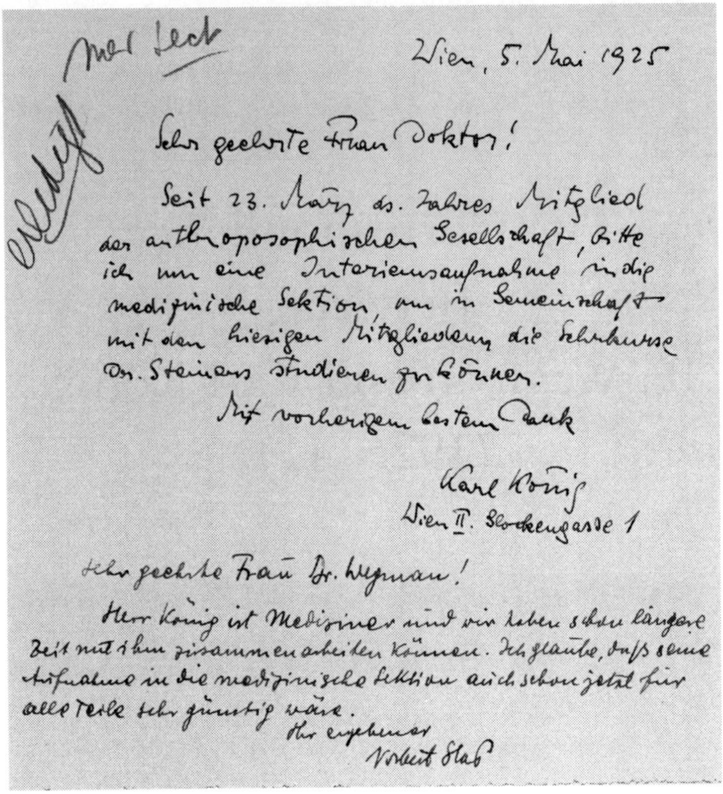

med Sekt

erledigt

Wien, 5. Mai 1925

Sehr geehrte Frau Doktor!

Seit 23. März ds. Jahres Mitglied der anthroposophischen Gesellschaft, bitte ich um eine Interimsaufnahme in die medizinische Sektion, um in Gemeinschaft mit den hiesigen Mitgliedern die Lehrkurse Dr. Steiners studieren zu können.

Mit vorherigem besten Dank

Karl König

Wien II. Glockengasse 1

Sehr geehrte Frau Dr. Wegman!

Herr König ist Mediziner und wir haben schon längere Zeit mit ihm zusammenarbeiten können. Ich glaube, dass seine Aufnahme in die medizinische Sektion auch schon jetzt für alle Teile sehr günstig wäre.

Ihr ergebener

Norbert Glas

Vienna, May 5, 1925

Dear Frau Doctor,

As a member of the Anthroposophical Society since May 23, of this year I hereby apply for acceptance as an interim member of the Medical Section so that I can study Dr Steiner's lecture courses in the company of the members here.

With many thanks in advance
Karl König
Wien II. Glockengasse 1

Dear Dr Wegman,

Mr König is a medical student and we have worked together for some time. I believe his entry to the Medical Section even at this early stage would be of advantage for everyone concerned.

Yours sincerely,
Norbert Glas

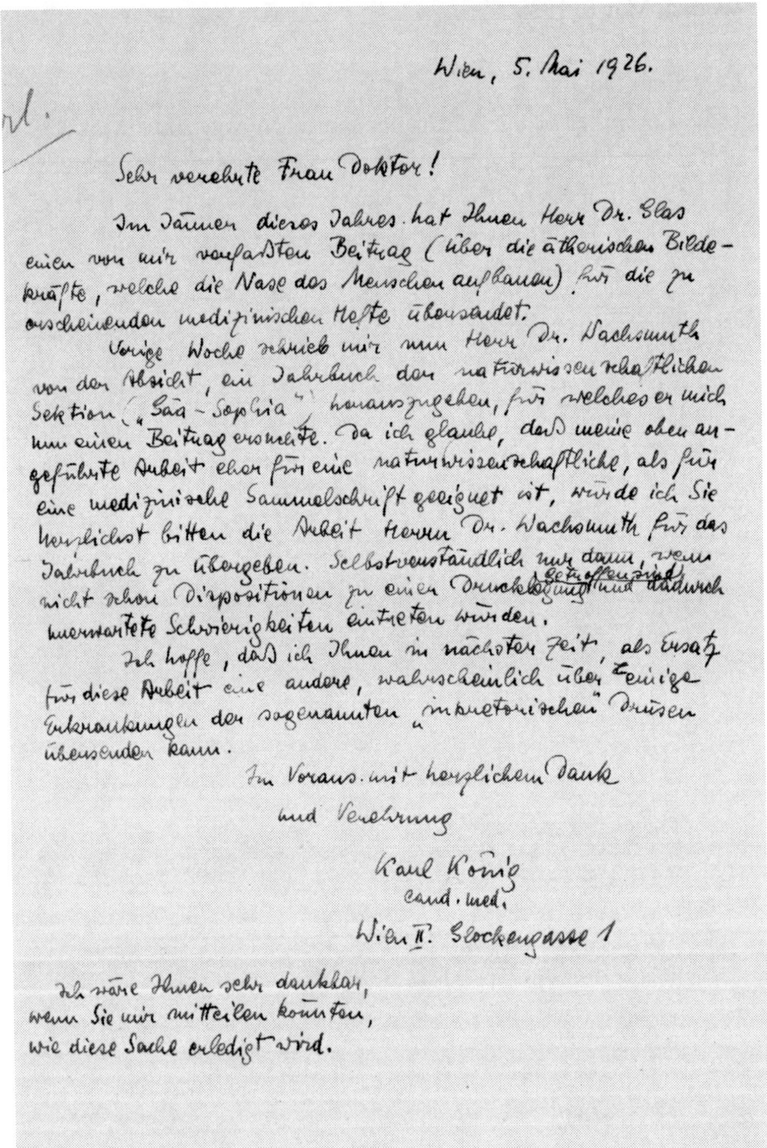

Wien, 5. Mai 1926.

Sehr verehrte Frau Doktor!

Im Jänner dieses Jahres hat Ihnen Herr Dr. Glas einen von mir verfaßten Beitrag (über die ätherischen Bildekräfte, welche die Nase des Menschen aufbauen) für die zu erscheinenden medizinischen Hefte übersandt.

Vorige Woche schrieb mir nun Herr Dr. Wachsmuth von der Absicht, ein Jahrbuch der naturwissenschaftlichen Sektion („Gäa-Sophia") herauszugeben, für welches er mich um einen Beitrag ersuchte. Da ich glaube, daß meine oben angeführte Arbeit eher für eine naturwissenschaftliche, als für eine medizinische Sammelschrift geeignet ist, würde ich Sie herzlichst bitten die Arbeit Herrn Dr. Wachsmuth für das Jahrbuch zu übergeben. Selbstverständlich nur dann, wenn nicht schon Dispositionen zu einer Drucklegung getroffen sind und dadurch unerwartete Schwierigkeiten eintreten würden.

Ich hoffe, daß ich Ihnen in nächster Zeit, als Ersatz für diese Arbeit eine andere, wahrscheinlich über einige Erkrankungen der sogenannten „inkretorischen" Drüsen übersenden kann.

Im Voraus mit herzlichem Dank
und Verehrung

Karl König
cand. med.

Wien II. Glockengasse 1

Ich wäre Ihnen sehr dankbar, wenn Sie mir mitteilen könnten, wie diese Sache erledigt wird.

Vienna, May 5, 1926

Dear Frau Doctor,

In January of this year Dr [Norbert] Glas sent you one of my articles (about the etheric forces shaping the human nose) for the medical journals which are to be published.

Last week Dr Wachsmuth wrote to me that he is planning to publish an almanac of the Natural Science Section *(Gäa-Sophia)* for which he asked me for a contribution. As I think that my above mentioned study is more suited for a scientific rather than for a medical anthology I would kindly ask you to give it to Dr Wachsmuth for the almanac. Of course only if other arrangements for printing have not yet been made and it would not cause any unexpected difficulties.

I hope I shall be able to send you another of my studies soon as a replacement for this one, probably about some conditions of the so-called 'incretory' glands.

Thank you very much in advance,
yours faithfully
Karl König
cand.med.
Wien II, Glockengasse 1

I would be very grateful if you could let me know how this matter is going to be handled.

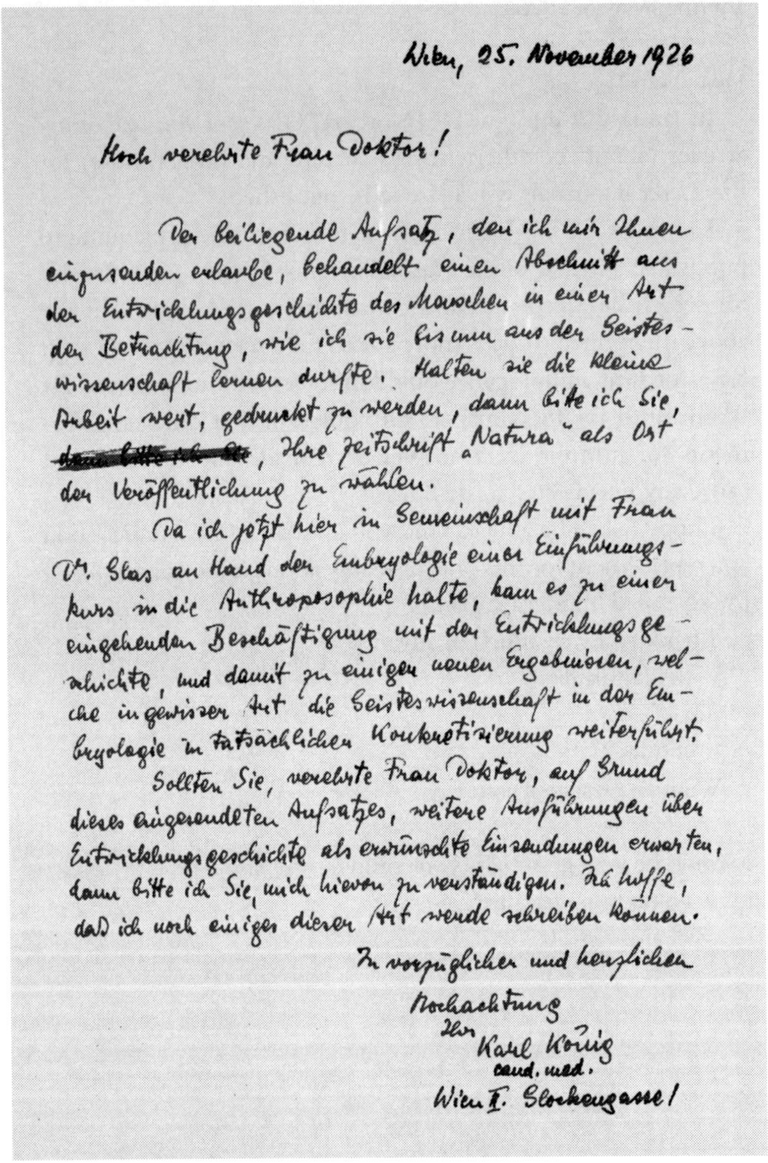

Wien, 25. November 1926

Hoch verehrte Frau Doktor!

Den beiliegenden Aufsatz, den ich mir Ihnen einzusenden erlaube, behandelt einen Abschnitt aus der Entwicklungsgeschichte des Menschen in einer Art der Betrachtung, wie ich sie bis nun aus der Geisteswissenschaft lernen durfte. Halten Sie die kleine Arbeit wert, gedruckt zu werden, dann bitte ich Sie, ~~dann bitte ich Sie~~, Ihre Zeitschrift „Natura" als Ort der Veröffentlichung zu wählen.

Da ich jetzt hier in Gemeinschaft mit Frau Dr. Glas an Hand der Embryologie einen Einführungskurs in die Anthroposophie halte, kam es zu einer eingehenden Beschäftigung mit der Entwicklungsgeschichte, und damit zu einigen neuen Ergebnissen, welche in gewisser Art die Geisteswissenschaft in der Embryologie in tatsächlichen Konkretisierung weiterführt.

Sollten Sie, verehrte Frau Doktor, auf Grund dieses eingesendeten Aufsatzes, weitere Ausführungen über Entwicklungsgeschichte als erwünschte Einsendungen erwarten, dann bitte ich Sie, mich hievon zu verständigen. Ich hoffe, daß ich noch einiges dieser Art werde schreiben können.

In vorzüglicher und herzlicher
Hochachtung
Ihr
Karl König
cand. med.
Wien II. Glockengasse 1

Vienna, November 25, 1926

Dear Frau Doctor,

The enclosed essay which I would like to submit to you is about a certain stage in human biogenesis and reflects this topic in a way I have learned through spiritual science. If you consider this little study worthy of printing I would like to ask you to publish it in your journal, *Natura*.

Since together with Dr [Maria] Glas I am here giving an introductory course based on embryology I made an intensive study of biogenesis; this led to some new insights which substantiate spiritual science factually in embryology and in a way develop it further.

In case you, dear Doctor Wegman, as a result of this submitted essay, would agree to receiving more studies on biogenesis I would kindly ask you to notify me accordingly. I hope that I will be able to write something more of this kind.

Yours sincerely and respectfully,
Karl König
cand.med.
Wien II, Glockengasse 1

Arlesheim, November 29, 1926

Dear Mr König,

I received your letter of November 25 and the enclosed essay, and would like to let you know that I will gladly include this essay in *Natura.* I would also be pleased if you were to continue working in this direction and could soon send us more contributions.

Yours sincerely,
Ita Wegman, MD

Vienna, December 22, 1926

Dear Frau Doctor,

During this week of contemplation before Christmas, while reviewing recently gained insights, I found a serious mistake in the essay I sent you about the four enveloping structures of the embryo, where the relationship of these four membranes to the higher archangels are discussed. It is not Michael who is weaving inside the chorion but Uriel, and Michael is the one working inside the allantois. The body-stalk reaching from the chorion to the yolk sac where the embryonic development will take place is like Michael's sword preparing the way for the blood stream from the cosmos (chorion) to the embryo. The words for the four membranes stay the same but should now read: 'And *Uriel* helps the incarnating self and says: I protect you. *Michael* enfolds the astral body, channels the blood to the embryo and says: I need to direct you.'

If the essay has already been printed I would like ask for an *erratum slip* amending these passages.

Please forgive me for requesting this alteration but I feel very guilty having done such a thing because something wrong would be put into the world, and I hope it is still possible to correct the mistake.

With best wishes for Christmas,
Yours faithfully and respectfully
Karl König
Wien II, Glockengasse 1

Arlesheim, December 29, 1926

Dear Mr König,

I have received your express letter and can inform you that we actually wanted to contact you about this error. Of course here too essays are all proof-read. And in the meantime you will have been reassured to see that the article has not yet been published.

Sincerely,

Ita Wegman, MD

Vienna, March 14, 1927

Dear Frau Doctor,

For a long time I have felt the deep need to introduce myself to you, the head of the Medical Section. Since in a few weeks I will have completed my medical studies at university, it is possible for me to come to Dornach during the first two weeks of April. My main reason for coming to Dornach is, as mentioned above, to introduce myself to you, so I would therefore like to ask whether you are in Dornach at that time, and would then be able to receive me.

At the same time I would like to apply for admission to the Medical Section and to ask whether it may be possible for me to come to your clinic for observation.

I would be very grateful if, on the same occasion, you would allow me to talk to you about some of my further medical studies; I would also like to seek your advice regarding a book project I have started which will put a rather detailed, new focus on embryology.

I would very much appreciate it if you could notify me about these matters.

Yours sincerely and respectfully,
Karl König
Wien II, Glockengasse 1

Klosterneuburg, May 10, 1927

Dear Frau Doctor,

My firm decision to come to Dornach soon in order to introduce myself to you has again been thwarted. Unexpectedly I have been offered a position as a guest student at a hospital in a small town near Vienna. I accepted immediately because the hospital is excellently managed and in addition I will have opportunity not only to learn internal medicine here but also surgery and obstetrics.

Because I am very busy out here, I am hardly able to keep up connections with Vienna and also in consequence with the anthroposophical movement.

On the other hand the intense practical medical work wakens in me a deep need to make steps in moral development.

I therefore sincerely ask you to admit me to the Medical Section and to the First Class of the School [of Spiritual Science] so that I can begin with meditative work on the meditations given by Dr Steiner. This need is intense and continuous. Since I have been a member of the Anthropos. Society for two years already I hope that you will grant this request.

Regarding my admission to the Class I will talk to Count Polzer as soon as he is in Vienna.

With greatest thanks in advance I remain
yours faithfully
Karl König

I would be very grateful if you could let me know whether you received the second essay I sent you for *Natura.*

Arlesheim, May 30, 1927

Dear Dr König,

I have received your letter of May 10. We are very pleased about this excellent study you sent to us. Its first part on embryology will already be published in the next issue of *Natura.* Hopefully you will enjoy the new work you have now started; but I also hope that some time you will be able to send us another one of your fine articles.

As for your other questions, there will not be any problems with your admission to the Medical Section as soon as you have been admitted to the Class and this too should be possible if you apply in writing. Count Polzer should also know about it and then recommend you.

Yours sincerely,
Dr Wegman

Klosterneuburg, July 5, 1927

Dear Frau Doctor,

A few days ago Dr [Maria] Glas told me that Dr Wehrle in Salzburg is looking for an assistant at his private surgical clinic.

Two days ago I received a letter from Dr [Norbert] Glas informing me that Dr Wehrle would like to appoint someone soon and that you, dear Doctor, thought of me as a person to be appointed to this post.

I now would like to ask you what kind of preparations for this position you have in mind. The reason is that I think I definitely need to gather experience through observation at the clinic in Arlesheim beforehand. But I do not know whether a position of assistant at your clinic is possible at present.

Further I would like to ask you whether you would consider somebody else from the Medical Section as being more suited for this position than me.

Before I write to Dr Wehrle I want to contact you first, Frau Doctor, in order to avoid doing something that might go against the plans of the Medical Section.

I would be very grateful, Frau Doctor, if you could possibly give me some concrete information regarding this issue.

Finally I would like to emphasize again that I place myself completely at the disposal of the Medical Section and that I await your decision.

With sincere admiration and respect,
Yours Dr Karl König
Klosterneuburg near Wien
General Hospital

Arlesheim, July 18, 1927

Dear Dr König,

I have received your letter of July 5. I also had a message from Dr [Maria] Glas suggesting that perhaps you, rather than she, should come here on September 1 for a month for observation. However, at present there are three other doctors here for observation. Therefore I would like to advise you just to make a start with Dr Wehrle and to try to get into the work with true anthroposophical resolve. It will surely work out, even without having been here beforehand, particularly as you cannot be properly trained here for surgical work. During the time you have available until then it would be good if you could work intensely with Mrs Glas so that she can tell you about therapies in anthroposophical medicine and practice. And then, after having worked with Dr Wehrle for a while, it might be possible that you come here for a short stay; certainly you will then profit even more. If it is of such importance for you to have been here beforehand, you are of course welcome in September, though you will not find the opportunities you have in mind and which I would like to see for you. If you now work intensively with Dr Glas you will certainly gain the help you will need when you start working, and I do hope that you will act accordingly.

Sincerely,

Dr I. Wegman

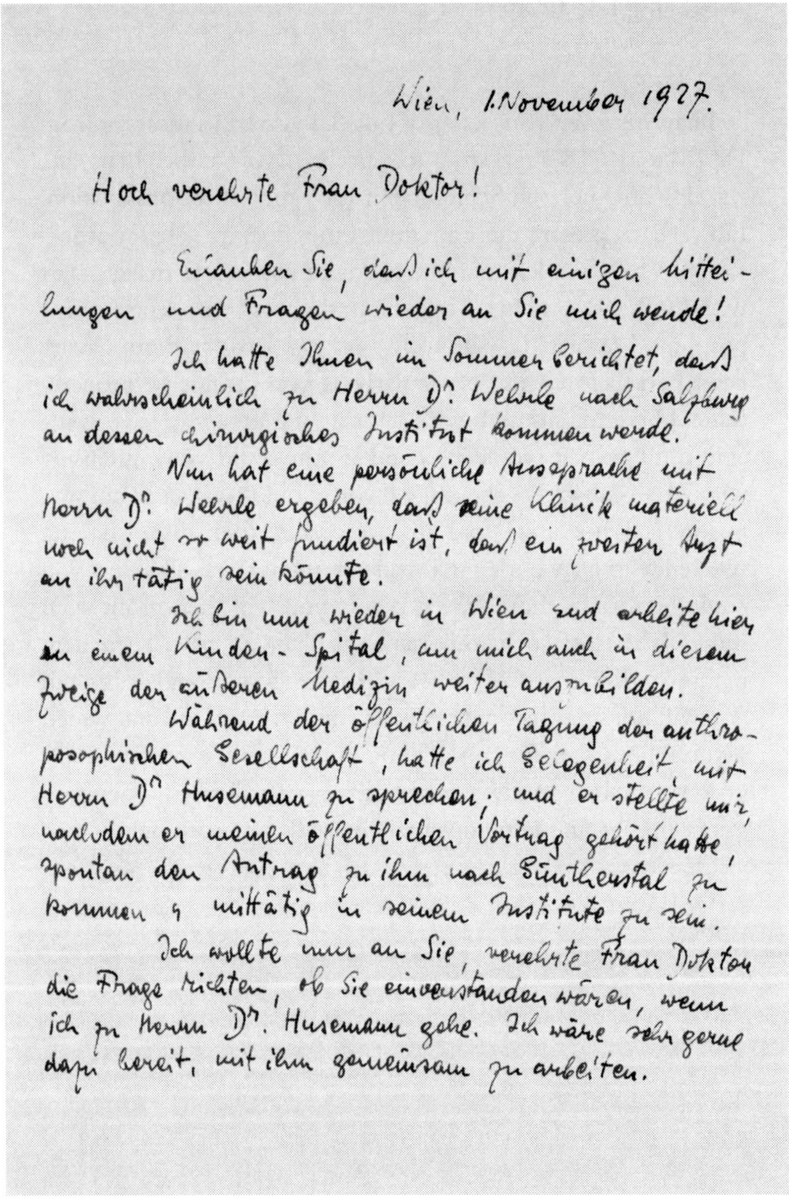

Wien, 1. November 1927.

Hoch verehrte Frau Doktor!

Erlauben Sie, daß ich mit einigen Mitteilungen und Fragen wieder an Sie mich wende!

Ich hatte Ihnen im Sommer berichtet, daß ich wahrscheinlich zu Herrn Dr. Wehrle nach Salzburg an dessen chirurgisches Institut kommen werde.

Nun hat eine persönliche Aussprache mit Herrn Dr. Wehrle ergeben, daß seine Klinik materiell noch nicht so weit fundiert ist, daß ein zweiter Arzt an ihr tätig sein könnte.

Ich bin nun wieder in Wien und arbeite hier in einem Kinder-Spital, um mich auch in diesem Zweige der äußeren Medizin weiter auszubilden.

Während der öffentlichen Tagung der anthroposophischen Gesellschaft, hatte ich Gelegenheit, mit Herrn Dr Husemann zu sprechen, und er stellte mir, nachdem er meinen öffentlichen Vortrag gehört hatte, spontan den Antrag zu ihm nach Güntherstal zu kommen u. mittätig in seinem Institute zu sein.

Ich wollte nun an Sie, verehrte Frau Doktor die Frage richten, ob Sie einverstanden wären, wenn ich zu Herrn Dr. Husemann gehe. Ich wäre sehr gerne dazu bereit, mit ihm gemeinsam zu arbeiten.

Weiters wollte ich mitteilen, daß ich seit September dieses Jahres Mitglied der I. Klasse geworden bin. Ich hoffe, daß Sie die Güte haben, mich auch als ordentliches Mitglied der medizinischen Sektion zu betrachten.

Aus dem heraus bitte ich auch, mir die Ärzte-Beiblätter der „Natura" zu senden, die ich bis nun noch nie erhalten habe. Vielleicht würden Sie einen derartigen Auftrag an die Administration der „Natura" geben.

Endlich bitte ich, meine Anmeldung für die Zusammenkunft der Mediziner vom 28. XII. 1927 entgegenzunehmen. Ich wäre für Quartiers-Beschaffung sehr dankbar.

Ich hoffe, daß ich bald ein grösseres Manuskript über die menschliche Embryonalentwicklung im Lichte der Geisteswissenschaft werde übersenden können.

Sehr dankbar wäre ich, wenn Sie, verehrte Frau Doktor mir schreiben würden, ob Sie für oder gegen mein Zusammenarbeiten mit Dr. Husemann sind, ebenso auch ob Sie mich als Mitglied der Sektion betrachten.

Ich verbleibe mit ergebenen Grüßen
in Verehrung u. Dankbarkeit
Ihr
Dr Karl König
Wien I. Glockengasse 1

Vienna, November 1, 1927

Dear Frau Doctor,

Please allow me to contact you again with some information and a few questions.

I told you in the summer that I will probably go to the surgical clinic of Dr Wehrle in Salzburg.

In a conversation with Dr Wehrle it emerged that his clinic is not yet financially so far as to allow another doctor to work there.

I am now back in Vienna and working at a local children's hospital to learn more about this field of external medicine.

During the public conference of the Anthroposophical Society I had opportunity to speak to Dr Husemann; after having listened to my public lecture he spontaneously invited me to come to Günthenstal to work at his institute.

I now would like to ask you, dear Frau Doctor, whether you would agree if I went to Dr Husemann. I would be very glad to work with him.

Furthermore I would like to tell you that as of September this year I am a member of the First Class. I hope you will be so kind also to regard me as a member of the Medical Section.

Therefore I would also like to ask for the medical supplements of *Natura* which I have not received up to now. Perhaps you could instruct the *Natura* management accordingly.

Finally I would like to ask you for acceptance of my registration for the doctors' meeting on December 28, 1927. I would be very grateful if accommodation could be arranged.

I hope I will soon be able to submit a more extensive manuscript about human embryonic development in the light of spiritual science.

I would be very grateful if you, dear Frau Doctor, could advise me in writing whether you approve of my working with Doctor Husemann or not; also whether you regard me as a member of the Section.

With appreciation I remain
yours respectfully and faithfully
Dr Karl König
Wien II. Glockengasse 1

Klinisch-Therapeutisches Institut, Arlesheim
Klinik, Erholungs- und Kinderheim

Abteilung der Allgem. Anthropos. Gesellschaft.
Telephon 200. Postscheck V 6487 · Telegr. Adr.: Clinic Arlesheim

Arlesheim, den 27. April 1939.

Lieber Dr. König!

Ihren Brief vom 18. April habe ich empfangen, in dem Sie mich fragen über die Röntgen-Therapie bei dem Schwachsinn der Kinder. Es ist dieses eine schwerwiegende Frage. Oft hat man zunächst bei Fällen in der Aussenwelt Besserungen gesehen und dann hat sich doch gezeigt, dass schlimme Nebenerscheinungen aufgetreten sind. Das was mit diesen Dingen geschieht, ist doch nicht das, was durch uns so ohne weiteres gemacht werden kann. Die Erfolge, die mit dieser Röntgen-Therapie erreicht worden sind, z. B. bei mongoloiden Kindern, haben, wie Sie schreiben, diese Kinder zu einem halbwegs normalen Seelenleben gebracht. Zu diesem Resultat bringen wir es auch und zwar mit der eigenen Individualität des Kindes, während ich das Gefühl habe, dass bei dieser Röntgentherapie durch Schockwirkungen die Individualität ganz herausgetrieben wird und eine Möglichkeit besteht, etwas Untermenschliches dann in diese Kinderkörper hereinzubringen; das Gleiche in einer anderen Art, was auch stattfindet bei der Transplantation der tierischen Drüsen in menschliche Körper. Ich kann von meinem Standpunkt aus niemals damit einig gehen, dass in einem Institut, was nach Angaben von Dr. Steiner geführt wird, solche Versuche gemacht werden von Dingen, die noch unklar sind. Wir verlassen sonst den ganz sicheren Weg, der eigentlich dahin geht, das Übersinnliche Wesen des Kindes in jeder Beziehung herunterzulocken,

Herrn Dr. König, Schloss Pilgramshain. II. 27. IV. 1930.

alles zu tun, dass es sein Karma bejaht und wenn dies dann nicht gelingt, alles zu tun, damit in der nächsten Inkarnation ein richtiger Körper aufgebaut werden kann. Solch ein Eingriff mit Röntgen ist, und das weiss ich ganz genau von Dr. Steiner selber, nicht dasjenige, womit wir weiterkommen können.

Ich wollte Ihnen noch sagen, dass ich zu Pfingsten Sie für einen Vortrag im Goetheanum angegeben habe. Hoffentlich haben Sie schon eine Einladung von Dr. Wachsmuth bekommen. - Dann ist auch Trummler hier gewesen, um zu fragen, ob Sie mitmachen wollten an einer Tagung in Finnland. Ich habe natürlich gar nichts dagegen, möchte aber auch sehr stark auf den Vordergrund setzen, dass wenn dieses geschieht, dass es dann auch ganz korrekt und grosszügig und ganz im Sinne Rudolf Steiners geschieht. Wir werden darüber noch eingehend dann sprechen, wenn Sie zu Pfingsten hierherkommen. Es sind dann auch verschiedene andere Fragen wegen der Arbeit in der Schwesternschule und der "Natura" zu beraten. Wir wollen vielleicht doch am besten aus der "Natura" eine dreimonatliche Zeitschrift machen, sobald dieser Jahrgang fertig ist, weil es doch den Anschein bekommt, dass eine monatliche Zeitschrift ein bischen schwer durchzuführen ist. Krankheit und recht viel Arbeit hier haben wieder einmal die "Natura" verzögert. Diesmal wird Allgemeines über die Signatur des Menschen kommen und ich hoffe, dass Sie es dann weiter fortsetzen können durch die Anatmomie-Aufsätze, die Sie vorhaben, uns zu geben. Auch habe ich eingeführt im Goetheanum jetzt alle Montag Abende einen von der Medizinischen Sektion ausgehenden Vortrag, was schon einen ganz guten Anfang genommen hat durch einen Vortrag von Dr. Glas über die Physiognomie des Ohres und Physiognomielehre im allgemeinen und jetzt von

Dr. Schickler, der den Anfang gemacht hat, die Entwicklung des Kindes vom hygienischen Standpunkt aus zu betrachten.

Ich höre, dass Sie bald heiraten werden. Man spricht hier, dass Sie sich schon verheiratet haben, lieber Dr. König. Wenn es wirklich so wäre, so ist es schade, dass wir den Tag nicht gewusst haben, sonst hätten wir Ihnen gern einen Gruss und gute Wünsche geschickt. Das tun wir jetzt nachträglich, und wenn es nur ein Gerede ist, so melden Sie uns doch einmal, wann dieser glückliche Tag sein wird.

Ich freue mich zu hören, dass es in Pilgramshain gut geht.

Seien Sie recht herzlich gegrüsst

Ihre Dr. I. Wegman

Arlesheim, April 27, 1929

Dear Dr König,

I have received your letter of April 16 in which you ask me about X-ray therapy for mental deficiency in children. This is a serious issue. Elsewhere there have been frequent initial improvements and yet it turned out later that there were bad side effects. What is happening in these things cannot without further ado be done by ourselves. The successful improvements which have been achieved by using this X-ray therapy, for instance with Down's syndrome children, have, as you describe in your letter, given these children a reasonably normal soul life. We do achieve the same effect but through the children's own individuality, whereas I feel that by using this X-ray therapy the individuality is forced out by the impact and possibly something subhuman is put into these children's bodies. The same thing that happens, but in a different way, when animal glands are transplanted into human bodies. From my point of view I can never agree that at an institute operating according to Dr Steiner's instructions such experiments are being done on issues which are still unclear. Otherwise we stray off the safe path which in every respect is meant to bring down the child's supersensible being, to do everything so that the child can embrace his karma, and if this fails, to do everything so that a normal body can be formed in the next incarnation. Such an X-ray intervention is not, and I know this from Dr Steiner himself, something that will get us any further.

I also wanted to tell you that I have put you on for a lecture at the Goetheanum at Whitsun. Hopefully you have already received an invitation from Dr Wachsmuth. Trummler has also been here to ask if you would like to join a conference in Finland. Of course I am not opposed to that but would like to emphasize that if this is going to happen then it needs to be done in an entirely correct and generous way and completely according to Rudolf Steiner's intentions. We will talk about this in detail when you come here at Whitsun. There are also various other questions to be discussed regarding the work at the nurse's school and *Natura.* Perhaps it will be best if we changed *Natura* into a quarterly publication as soon as this year's issues are complete because it seems as if a monthly journal is difficult to keep going. Illnesses and quite a lot of work here have again caused delay foı *Natura.* This time there will be some general information about the distinctive human character and I hope you will be able to continue this [topic] in the essays about anatomy which you are planning to send us. Furthermore I have initiated that every Monday evening a lecture is going to be held by the Medical Section at the Goetheanum. This has started off well with a lecture by Dr [Norbert] Glas on the physiognomy of the ear and the science of physiognomy in general and now by Dr Schickler who has started to look at child development from a hygienic viewpoint.

I hear you are soon going to get married. There is talk that you are actually married already, dear Dr König. If this was the case it is a pity we did not know the date because we would have been glad to send you regards and good wishes. We do this now belatedly, but if it is just talk then please let us know when this happy day is going to be.

I am pleased to hear that things go well in Pilgramshain.

With kindest regards,

Dr I. Wegman

Gnadenfrei, September 20, 1929

Dear Frau Doctor,

Countess Keyserlingk will already be in Arlesheim by the time you receive this letter. I just wanted to inform you in brief about my observations during the last two weeks concerning the Countess's illness. On September 2 and 3 the Countess suffered quite severe weakness with mild fever which seemed to be caused by the heart. The heart itself was very weak, pulse rate 110 to 120, easy to suppress, severe respiratory arrhythmia. The Countess' condition gave reason for concern because it seemed as if in a way she did not want to keep going. I gave Cardiodoron and Melissa essence internally and Arnica and Formica packs. On the following night of September 4, at about 2 AM I was suddenly called to Sasterhausen because the situation was serious. The fever had increased (38.7°C) and nausea, diarrhea and spasms of the limbs had set in. When I entered the patient's room I noticed a strange smell. It smelt like in the room of a woman in childbed. The Countess was very weak, a bit apathetic, and spoke only in a whispering voice. She said that she had closely escaped death, only the spiritual strength streaming to her from her son Berti had kept her alive. I had the impression of a genuine, severe bout of hysteria. The heart was so weak that you could hardly feel the pulse, severe arrhythmia with a heart rate of 120 to 130. I tried to think of a solution when I remembered the strange smell. And I said to the Countess: 'Countess, you have just given birth..' She sat up with a jolt and said: 'Yes, Doctor König, that is what it was.' At the same moment she was awake, the pulse was strong and regular, the crisis was over. After a few days diarrhea set in, the condition had developed into a mild enteritis which could soon be cured with a diet and Arsenic D6. When I saw the Countess five days ago she was out of bed, bright and lively and had decided to go to Arlesheim; to which I could only agree.

I still think the whole episode was a case of genuine hysteria probably brought on by unclear spiritual experiences. I hope, dear Frau Doctor, that my description gives you a good picture.

I am away from Pilgramshain for a week now taking some time off because I could not go on any longer. Dr Kroker is filling in for me and I hope it will work out.

In a few days I would like to write in detail about some issues regarding Pilgramshain and myself but before that would like to have a bit more time to think about it.

With very kind regards,
yours faithfully
Dr Karl König

Post Striegau, October 29, 1929

Dear Frau Doctor,

First of all I want to apologize for not having written for such a long time. But I have been in Vienna and therefore did not get around to it until today. In a long telephone conversation with Pache last night, he explained about the conference in Vienna and indeed we also discussed the title of my lecture. The course in Hamburg together with [Emil] Bock will start next week; you will probably have received the programme already. At the same time I was asked to hold an evening lecture at the branch there, which I shall gladly do. Unfortunately I do not have anything for *Natura* at the moment because I am busy working on a book about anatomy. As a title I am thinking of:

'Towards a Pure Anatomy of the Human Being.'

I have firstly differentiated between pure and practical anatomy and, as suggested by the title, am first treating pure anatomy. I imagine the book will be 400–450 pages long. Each organ and system within the human body will be described in a separate chapter. In addition I am now working on a spiritual-scientific anatomy of the 12 cranial nerves and have already made some progress. It will perhaps soon be possible to publish this study as an article. Apart from that I am cooperating with Mr Vögele regarding agricultural and physiological questions in relation to the human calcium metabolism. Finally I have an urgent request. I would be very grateful if you could send me Dr Steiner's lectures on hygiene and social hygiene by express mail because I need them *urgently* for preparing the lecture in Berlin. Mr Strohschein has probably told you in detail about issues regarding the institute. I am really looking forward to the conference in Berlin and would just like to express again how much we would appreciate it, if you could include a short visit here in your Berlin journey. We all would be immensely grateful.

With kindest regards,
yours respectfully and faithfully
Dr Karl König

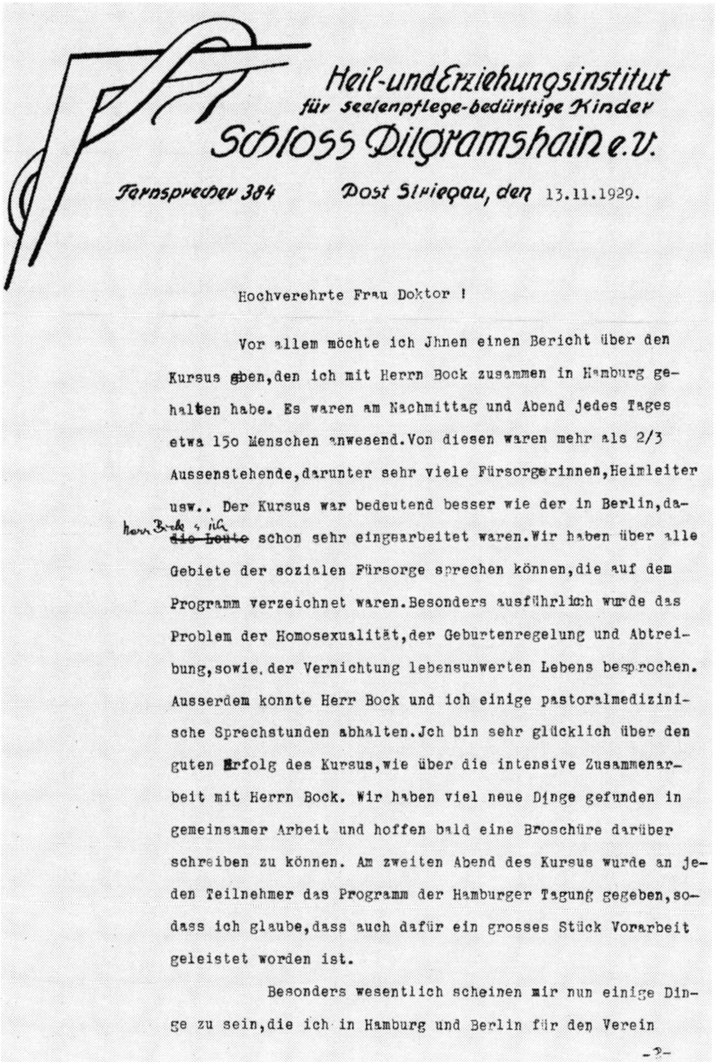

Heil- und Erziehungsinstitut
für seelenpflege-bedürftige Kinder
Schloss Pilgramshain e.V.

Fernsprecher 384 Post Striegau, den 13.11.1929.

Hochverehrte Frau Doktor !

Vor allem möchte ich Jhnen einen Bericht über den Kursus geben, den ich mit Herrn Bock zusammen in Hamburg gehalten habe. Es waren am Nachmittag und Abend jedes Tages etwa 15o Menschen anwesend. Von diesen waren mehr als 2/3 Aussenstehende, darunter sehr viele Fürsorgerinnen, Heimleiter usw.. Der Kursus war bedeutend besser wie der in Berlin, da ~~die Leute~~ Herr Bock u. ich schon sehr eingearbeitet waren. Wir haben über alle Gebiete der sozialen Fürsorge sprechen können, die auf dem Programm verzeichnet waren. Besonders ausführlich wurde das Problem der Homosexualität, der Geburtenregelung und Abtreibung, sowie der Vernichtung lebensunwerten Lebens besprochen. Ausserdem konnte Herr Bock und ich einige pastoralmedizinische Sprechstunden abhalten. Jch bin sehr glücklich über den guten Erfolg des Kursus, wie über die intensive Zusammenarbeit mit Herrn Bock. Wir haben viel neue Dinge gefunden in gemeinsamer Arbeit und hoffen bald eine Broschüre darüber schreiben zu können. Am zweiten Abend des Kursus wurde an jeden Teilnehmer das Programm der Hamburger Tagung gegeben, sodass ich glaube, dass auch dafür ein grosses Stück Vorarbeit geleistet worden ist.

Besonders wesentlich scheinen mir nun einige Dinge zu sein, die ich in Hamburg und Berlin für den Verein

-2-

-2-

Soziale Hilfe leisten konnte. Jch hoffe,dass Jhnen schon mitgeteilt worden ist,dass Jhrem Wunsche gemäss,den Sie ja öfter ausgesprochen haben,Herr Strohschein und ich in den Vorstand des Vereins übergegangen sind.Von den ersten Leistungen möchte ich Jhnen also jetzt erzählen. Jch traf in Hamburg eine sehr schwierige Situation der von Werbeck gegründeten philanthropischen Vereinigung.Jch hatte den Eindruck,dass sie keinen neuen Lebensinhalt bekommt und dass der Vorstand dieses Vereins nicht mehr recht weiss was er tun soll.Die ganze Arbeit leistet jetzt dorten die Jhnen wohlbekannte Frau Burdett mit grosser Hingabe,aber nicht sehr grossem modernem Verständnis.Jch sprach dann ausführlich mit Frau Werbeck über diese ganze Angelegenheit,und sie machte dann von selbst den Vorschlag,dass es wohl möglich wäre,den Philantropischen Verein der Sozialen Hilfe einzugliedern. Jch habe dann um eine Vorstandssitzung dieses Vereins gebeten und darin die ersten Vorbesprechungen für eine solche Eingliederung geführt.Alle waren sehr einverstanden mit meinen Vorschlägen,nur habe ich dann die letzten Besprechungen für die Zeit Jhres Aufenthalts zur Hamburger Tagung verschoben. Jch hoffe,dass wir dadurch eine grosse Zweiggruppe der Sozialen Hilfe in Hamburg haben werden.Ausserdem möchte ich vorschlagen,dass Sigfried Palmer doch die Arbeit in Hamburg weiterführen müsste.Es sind ja doch eine grosse Anzahl von Fürsorgerinnen und sozial interessierten Menschen da,die ein grosses Stück Arbeit leisten können, Ausserdem hat Herr Palmer ziemlich viel Fäden geknüpft,die m.E.sofort zerrissen werden würden,wenn er Hamburg verlassen würde. Die erste Arbeit der philantropischen Gesellschaft

3

-3-

wird die sein,dass zwei pastoralmedizinische Sprechstunden wöchentlich abgehalten werden,einerseits von Dr.Thylmann und Dr.Hemleben,andererseits durch Dr.Solti und Frau Garms. Die Patienten wird Frl.Dr.Feldner von ihrer Zentrale für private Wohltätigkeit zur Verfügung stellen.Ausserdem wird jetzt eine intensive Zusammenarbeit von Priestern,Aerzten und Fürsorgerinnen in Hamburg einsetzen.

Jn Berlin war die Sachlage so,dass Priester Palmer aus seinen Bedürfnissen heraus eine Vereinigung für freie Wohltätigkeit gegründet hat,in welcher eine grössere Zahl von Menschen mit Rang und Namen ihre Mitarbeit zugesagt haben.Herr Palmer denkt da vor allem an eine Hilfe für Menschen,die in der heutigen Grossstadt zerbrochen werden. Er steht auch bereits in Unterhandlung wegen eines grösseren Hauses mit Grundstück in der Nähe von Berlin,das frühere Besitztum des buddhischen Arztes Dr.Dahlke. Priester Palmer hat mir sofort,als ich ihm die neue Situation der Sozialen Hilfe dargestellt hatte,angeboten,seine Vereinigung ganz in den Rahmen der Sozialen Hilfe hinneinzugliedern.Auch da habe ich wieder die letzten Besprechungen für Jhre Anwesenheit in Berlin verschoben.Jch glaube,dass es äusserst günstig für die Entwickelung der Sozialen Hilfe sein wird, wenn auch diese Arbeit in ihren Rahmen hinneingegliedert wird Wir haben dadurch sofort eine starke Berliner Ortsgruppe. Weiters hatte Herr Palmer gerade Nachricht von dem Priester Stegmann aus Essen vorliegen,der seine neue Zeitschrift "Zur sozialen Frage" aus dem Kreis der Christengemeinschaft herausgliedern will.Jch habe nun gedacht,dass es wohl möglich wäre,diese Zeitschrift in Zusammenhang mit unserer So-

-4-

zialen Hilfe herauszugeben oder erscheinen zu lassen,sodass wir damit auch ein eigenes Organ hätten.Jch werde dazu ganz unverbindlich an Priester Stegmann schreiben. Weiter habe ich mir gedacht;dass im Anschluss an diese Zeitschrift eine Art Schriftenreihe "Zur sozialen Frage" erscheinen müsste,die näheren Aufschluss über unsere Bestrebungen gibt.

Jch hatte auf der ganzen Reise den tiefen Eindruck, dass diese ganzen Dinge,von denen ich jetzt gesprochen habe, von der geistigen Welt geführt werden,damit die Soziale Hilfe in den weiten Rahmen hinneinkommt,den Sie immer von ihr gewünscht haben.Jch hoffe,dass Sie selbst auch einverstanden sind mit all den Dingen,die sich da abgespielt haben. Jch habe die Hoffnung,dass so eine breite Plattform gefunden wird,auf der alle Menschen,die vom freien Geistesleben aus sozial wirken wollen,sich zusammenfinden können.Jch wäre sehr dankbar,wenn ich umgehend eine Nachricht darüber von Jhnen bekommen könnte.

Mit sehr herzlichen und ergebenen Grüssen

bin ich

Jhr getreuer

Dr Karl König

Post Striegau, November 13, 1929

Dear Frau Doctor,

First of all I would like to give you a report about the course I held together with Mr Bock in Hamburg. Every day in the afternoon and evening about 150 people attended. More than two thirds of them were outsiders, including many social workers, directors of children's homes etc. ... This course was a lot better than the one in Berlin because Mr Bock and I had already worked outselves in. We were able to talk about all areas of social work listed in the programme. We especially discussed in detail the problem of homosexuality, birth control, abortion and euthanasia — annihilation of unworthy life. Apart from that Mr Bock and I could hold a few pastoral-medical consultations. I am really happy about the good result of the course and the close cooperation with Mr Bock. Working together we gained many new insights and hope that we will soon be able to describe them in a pamphlet. On the second evening of the course every participant was given a programme of the Hamburg conference and I believe that a lot of preparatory work has thereby been done for this as well.

There are a few things I was able to achieve in Hamburg and Berlin for the Social Support Association which seem to me to be of special importance. I hope you have already been told that, following your repeated requests, Mr Strohschein and I have joined the board of the association. So now I would like to tell you about my first achievements. In Hamburg I found a very difficult situation in the Philanthropic Society founded by Werbeck. I got the impression that it is lacking in purpose and that its board is somewhat at a loss what to do. The whole work there is being done by Mrs Burdett — whom you probably know — with great devotion but not much advanced understanding. I then discussed the whole thing in detail with Mrs Werbeck and as a result she herself suggested that it would be feasible to incorporate the Philanthropic Society into the Social

Support Association. I then asked for a meeting of the board of this society during which we had a preliminarily discussion about the matter. Everyone broadly agreed to what I suggested but I postponed final discussions until your stay in Hamburg for the conference. I hope that with this we will have a strong Social Support branch in Hamburg. Apart from this, I would suggest that Siegfried Palmer must indeed continue working in Hamburg. There is a large number of social workers and socially interested people who can do a great deal of work. Moreover, Mr Palmer has made quite a lot of contacts which, in my view, would break off immediately if he left Hamburg. The first project of the Philanthropic Society will be two pastoral-medical consultations held weekly, once by Dr Thylman and Dr Hemleben and the other time by Dr Solti and Mrs Garms. The patients will come from Dr Feldner's centre for private charity. In addition there will be an close cooperation of priests, doctors and social workers in Hamburg.

The situation in Berlin was that the priest, Mr Palmer, felt the necessity of founding an independent charitable association, and a considerable number of important and influential people have agreed to support it. In particular Mr Palmer is thinking of help for people who cannot cope with modern urban life. He is already negotiating about a rather large house with grounds near Berlin formerly belonging to the Buddhist physician, Dr Dahlke. When I described the new situation of the Social Support Association to Mr Palmer he at once offered to integrate his whole association into the Social Support Association. In this case too I have postponed the final discussions until you are in Berlin. I believe the Social Support Association will greatly benefit if this project is also incorporated into it. With this we have straightaway a strong local group in Berlin. Furthermore Mr Palmer had a message from the priest, Mr Stegmann, in Essen, who wants to separate his new journal *Zur sozialen Frage* [the social issue] from the Christian Community. I am now thinking that it should be possible to issue this journal as part of our

Social Support so that we also have our own publication. I will write informally about this to Mr Stegmann. Furthermore, I thought that as a follow-up of this journal some kind of publication series about social issues should be published which provides more detailed information about what we are trying to do.

During my whole journey I had the strong impression that everything I have been talking about is guided by the spiritual world, so that the Social Support Association can establish itself within the wider context you have always wished for. Hopefully you will agree to everything which has happened. I hope that there will thus be a broad base of consent so that all those wanting to work socially on the basis of free spiritual life can join together. I would be very grateful if you could send me a message as soon as possible about this.

With kindest regards I remain
yours respectfully and faithfully
Dr Karl König

Arlesheim, January 6, 1930

Dear Dr König,

I have received your letter of December 23. Unfortunately I could not write to you earlier because I have actually been much occupied by all the Christmas events, the many people from outside and the patients. Strohschein already told of his and your journey to Prague during the Advent season, I heard a bit from the priest Mr Kral who told me about a few things in Prague. Of course it is very positive that people in Prague gradually show interest in the work of curative education. But it is still too early to start an institute because we do not have enough people available who are able to carry the curative educational work. We will otherwise not actually get the results Dr Steiner intended. You cannot have people working at the institutes who have not undergone training here; only if they have been taught the theory here and have afterwards been working at one of the institutes for a year or two, can you talk of an appropriate training. Otherwise you get a badly watered down version for which I cannot take responsibility. We simply cannot think about new foundations in the near future until enough people have been properly trained. There is a general lack of the right people. But I fully agree with you that in the future a fertile ground for curative education will certainly arise in Prague.

I feel very sorry that you cannot come here in January but I also understand that you do not want to go away again after travelling for so long. Work will now be divided between Suchantke, Bockholt and also Dr Schnurmann from Pforzheim who is very actively working with us on the nurses' courses. Perhaps it will be easier for you to come in February.

But there is still another question. We have agreed that from January 11 onwards — which is a Saturday — there will be regular lectures from the Medical Section in Berlin in the Meister Halls every two weeks until March 15 when this lecture series will conclude with a 1–2 day weekend. I do not really want to use the term 'conference' for this because I prefer to see it as a conclusion of the lecture series. The conference on nutrition which I had planned for March is postponed at the request of the farmers who would be able to be more involved if the event took place in autumn. So in March we will hold a smaller event than originally planned.* Now I would like to know if you could also in February hold one or two lectures in this context in Berlin. It would be much the same as we have done until now: study of the human being in relation to curative education as well as addressing social questions; actually an intensified version of what we have been lecturing about before. Dr Suchantke will make a start on January 11 with a lecture entitled, 'Soul Crises of Young People Today.' Two weeks later Dr Schickler will probably speak about the child at the age of seven and all related medical issues. Of course the lecture titles need to be phrased in an appealing way so that people are attracted. So much for now just in order to ask whether you would like to contribute to this project in Berlin.

Just now I am busy asking each institute to compile for me a list of people working in the institutes so that we have a general idea of the situation. There are so many enquiries that one needs to stay on top of things regarding all the people working at the institutes.

I really hope Mr Weiss will be able to come to Pilgramshain because I believe you probably still need support for the teaching staff.

I hope you could enjoy a good Christmas in Pilgramshain. We had a busy life here.

Kindest regards to you, dear Dr König,

Yours

Dr I. Wegman

* and later on in autumn the nutrition conference with the farmers in Berlin.

Arlesheim, den 6. Februar 1930.

Lieber Herr Dr. König!

Ich bin ja auch einverstanden, dass Sie die beiden Vorträge hintereinander halten. Dr. Bockholt wird von Berlin aus Ihnen telefonieren, für die Veranstaltung von Dr. Zeylmans, der in der Aula der Universität sprechen wird, und für den Vortrag von Pache nach Berlin gereist ist. Für Ende März finde ich es gut, dass Sie ohne den Namen "Eugenetischen Okkultismus" zu erwähnen über diese Dinge sprechen, (weil das doch vielleicht nicht gut wäre in einem öffentlichen Vortrag, und vielleicht einen Titel wählen würden wie z. B. "Vererbung und Volksgesundheit" oder "Wie können wir den Erbkörper verbessern?"

Wir haben gemeint, dass wohl Dr. Stein anfangen soll damit, im allgemeinen über Anthroposophie zu sprechen, indem er dann versuchen muss, die Reinkarnationslehre und Vererbung zu besprechen. Dann hoffen wir noch von Dr. Kolisko Vorträge zu bekommen, dann Pache, Dr. Zeylmans und von Ihnen, und dann wollen wir enden mit einem allgemeinen Tee Sonntag Nachmittag, während dann noch Dr. Schickler vorher über Ernährungsfragen gesprochen hat. So haben wir uns einigermassen das Programm gedacht. Dr. Steins Vortrag könnte z. B. so heissen "Die Reinkarnationslehre als Erkenntnisweg in die Gesetze der Vererbung", sodass dann Ihrem Vortrag vielleicht sehr schön vorgearbeitet ist. Dr. Zeylmans könnte dann von dem therapeutischen Okkultismus sprechen "Anthroposophie als Kraftquelle für wirksames Tun im sozialen Leben". Pache würde als Thema nehmen "Verzweiflung und Gewalttätigkeit in der heranwachsenden Generation als Notschrei nach einer zeitgemässen Weltanschauung." Man müsste eigentlich jetzt schon in Berlin das Programm fertigstellen, es wird dieses Dr. Bockholt auch versuchen zu tun. Sie wird nach Pilgramshain telephonieren.

Dann hätte ich noch einen grossen Wunsch, lieber Dr. König. Ob Sie nicht auch tüchtig mithelfen wollen bei unserer medizinischen Tagung, die wir jetzt im April im Goetheanum geben wollen, zu unterstützen? Ich rechne auf einen schönen Vortrag von Ihnen. Ich habe vor, gleich nach der Generalversammlung im Goetheanum, für alle Mitglieder zugänglich, eine medizinische Tagung zu veranstalten, die vom 14. - 17. April stattfinden wird. Am 11. April wird die Generalversammlung sein, zu der natürlich doch alle unsere Freunde unbedingt kommen müssen, weil da sicherlich wichtige Dinge zur Entscheidung kommen. Dann wollen wir nach der Generalversammlung zwei Tage einen kleinen Kurs über Heil-Eurythmie geben und dann am 14. April die medizinische Tagung anfangen. - Ueber die "Soziale Hilfe" werden wir wohl noch reden. Wichtig ist doch nun einmal erst jetzt, dass wir versuchen, viele Menschen zu interessieren, Mitglieder zu werden, und zwar Aussenstehende. Diese Werbearbeit soll aber nicht durch Briefe gemacht werden oder durch Herumschicken von Werbeschriften, sondern wirklich von Person zu Person gehen, überall wo man hinkommt, Menschen zu interessieren. Im Grunde genommen ist eigentlich gar keine Neuregelung getroffen, als dass man zu dem Vorstand noch einige Menschen dazugenommen hat und den Verwaltungsrat noch hat, in den alle diejenigen Menschen hineinkommen, die in den Instituten sind oder mit sonstigen Arbeiten in der Sozialen Hilfe beschäftigt sind. Die Arbeit in Berlin soll nun wie verabredet, intensiv eingesetzt werden, nur sollen die Dinge soviel wie möglich doch einheitlich gemacht werden. Das wird dann immer die Kraft sein, die uns zusammenhält.

Herrn Dr. König, Schloss Pilgramshain. Blatt II. 6. II. 1930.

Ich werde, wenn Sie in Berlin sind, zu einem Ihrer Vorträge auch versuchen, nach Berlin zu kommen. Dieses Mal muss ich noch nach Essen, um dort Klassenstunden zu halten.

Hoffentlich geht es Ihnen gut!

Seien Sie recht herzlich gegrüsst

gez. Ihre Dr. I. Wegman.

Arlesheim, February 6, 1930

Dear Dr König,

Of course I also agree to you holding both lectures successively. Dr Bockholt will call you from Berlin regarding the event of Dr Zeylmans who will speak in the university auditorium and is travelling to Berlin for Pache's lecture. Regarding your lecture at the end of March I think it would be a good idea not to mention 'Eugenic Occultism' when speaking about these issues (because this is probably not such a good idea for a public lecture) and perhaps choose a title like 'Genetics and Public Health' or 'How can the Genetic Makeup be Improved?'

In our opinion Dr Stein should probably begin by speaking on anthroposophy in general and trying to discuss the teaching of reincarnation and genetics. We also hope to arrange lectures by Dr Kolisko, Pache, Dr Zeylmans and yourself, and then we want to finish with tea on Sunday afternoon after Dr Schickler has spoken about nutrition. This is more or less what we have planned for the programme. The title of Dr Stein's lecture could be, for example, 'The Teaching of Reincarnation as a Way of Understanding the Laws of Genetics' which would perhaps nicely pave the way for your lecture. Dr Zeylmans could then speak about therapeutic occultism: 'Anthroposophy as a Source of Strength for Effective Social Work.' Pache could focus on the topic: 'Despair and Violence Among Young People as an Outcry for a View of the World Appropriate to our Time.' The programme must now actually be finalized in Berlin, and Dr Bockholt will try to do so. She will call you in Pilgramshain.

Then, dear Dr König, I would like to ask you a big favour. Could you perhaps help us by supporting our medical conference in April at the Goetheanum? I count on a fine lecture from you. I am planning to organize a medical conference for all members from April 14 to 17 straight after the Annual General Meeting at the Goetheanum. On April 11 the Annual General Meeting will take place, and of course all our friends definitely need to attend because no doubt important issues are going to be decided. After the Annual General Meeting we would like to hold a short course of curative eurythmy over two days and then start with the medical conference on April 14.

We will certainly discuss the Social Support Association later. But what is important now is that we try to interest many people in joining, particularly outsiders. This campaign should not be conducted by writing letters or sending advertising brochures but really by meeting people face to face, by kindling people's interest wherever you go. Basically nothing new has been agreed apart from accepting a few more people to the Executive Board; and there is still the administrative board for which everyone is eligible who works at the institutes or is involved in other projects of Social Support. As agreed intensive work in Berlin should go ahead now, but things should follow common standards as much as possible. This will act as a continuous force that will keep us united.

While you are in Berlin I will try to come to one of your lectures there. At present I still need to go to Essen to hold Class Lessons there.

I hope you are well,
With kind regards,
Dr I. Wegman

Heil- und Erziehungsinstitut
für seelenpflege-bedürftige Kinder
Schloss Pilgramshain e.V.

Fernsprecher 384 Post Striegau, den 18. VI. 30.

Hoch verehrte Frau Doktor!

Vor allem möchte ich um Entschuldigung bitten, dass mein Brief so lange auf sich warten ließ. Ich habe mich aber immer damit abgeplagt ein richtiges Thema für das Weekend in Berlin zu finden, ohne dass es mir richtig gelungen ist. Über das von Ihnen vorgeschlagene Thema „Vererbung u. Volksgesundheit" wage ich nicht zu sprechen, da ich das Empfinden habe, dass es meinen einstweiligen persönlichen Rahmen weit überschreitet. Vielleicht findet sich jemand, der doch schon darüber sprechen kann. Ich wage es wirklich nicht. Ich hätte nur einen Vorschlag, der immer wieder in mir aufgestiegen ist, nämlich über „Geburt und Tod" zu sprechen. Etwa „Geburt und Tod als völkerbestimmende Ereignisse" u. dabei auf das westliche u. östliche Volkstum zu sprechen zu kommen. Dazu möchte ich aber ganz u. gar Ihren Rat haben u. Ihre Zustimmung.

[margin: …egmans Schlag]

Für die medizinische Tagung im April bin ich sehr gerne bereit, einen Vortrag zu halten. Dabei würde ich gerne über ein Gebiet aus der Menschenkunde oder Metamorphosenlehre sprechen. Ich wollte nur fragen, ob es mehr medizinischen, oder allgemeinen Charakter haben soll. Wenn das Erstere der Fall ist, würde ich gern über Metamorphosen am Gehirn u. den Aufbau des Nervensystems sprechen, worüber ich in der letzten Zeit gearbeitet habe, oder über die inkretorischen Drüsen, an denen ich manche wichtige Neuerkenntnis errungen habe.

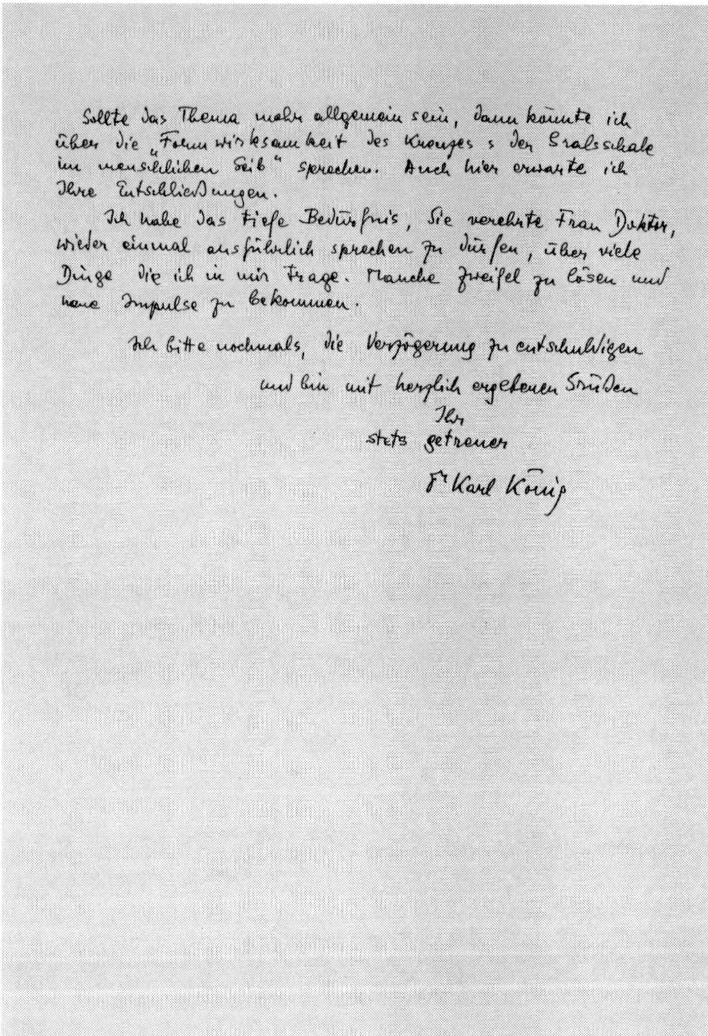

Sollte das Thema mehr allgemein sein, dann könnte ich über die „Formwirksamkeit des Kreuzes & der Gralsschale im menschlichen Leib" sprechen. Auch hier erwarte ich Ihre Entschließungen.

Ich habe das tiefe Bedürfnis, Sie verehrte Frau Doktor, wieder einmal ausführlich sprechen zu dürfen, über viele Dinge die ich in mir trage. Manche Zweifel zu lösen und neue Impulse zu bekommen.

Ich bitte nochmals, die Verzögerung zu entschuldigen

und bin mit herzlich ergebenen Grüßen

Ihr

stets getreuer

Dr Karl König

Post Striegau, February 18, 1930

Dear Frau Doctor,

First of all I want to apologize that my letter took so long. But I was struggling all the time to find a suitable topic for the weekend in Berlin, without really succeeding. I would not dare to speak about the topic you suggested, 'Genetics and Public Health,' because I feel it to be far beyond my own present expertise. Perhaps somebody else can be found who is able to speak about it. I really would not dare to. But I have another idea which time and again has been on my mind: I could speak about 'Birth and Death.' Something like 'Birth and Death as Events which Define Peoples' and in this context I could discuss western and eastern traditions. But on this I really need your advice and your approval.

I will gladly hold a lecture at the medical conference in April. On this occasion I would like to speak about a topic relating to the study of the human being or the teaching of metamorphosis. I just want to ask you whether it should be a more medical or a more general lecture. If the former I would like to speak about the metamorphosis of the brain and the structure of the nervous system which I have been working on recently, or the incretory glands whose study has given me some important new insights.

If it should be a more general topic I could speak about the 'Forming Effects of the Cross and the Grail in the Human Body.' Here too I await your decision.

I have a deep need to talk to you again in detail, dear Frau Doctor, about a lot of things on my mind. To diffuse some doubts and gain fresh momentum.

Again I apologize for the delay and remain with kindest regards,

your ever faithful

Dr Karl König

Arlesheim, den 3. März 1930.

Lieber Herr Dr. König!

Ich habe es sehr bedauert, dass ich nicht nach Berlin kommen konnte. Leider ist in der letzten Zeit meine ganze Arbeit ein bischen durcheinander gekommen durch die vielen Schwierigkeiten, die man mir gemacht hat, auch gerade in dieser Heileurythmie-Frage, und zuallerletzt bin ich dann noch krank geworden, sodass ich auch meine Reise nach England, die schon vorgesetzt war, habe verschieben müssen. Ich kann erst, glaube ich, jetzt den 10. März wieder da sein. Von dieser Zeit ab bin ich wohl wieder in Arlesheim und vielleicht wäre es doch gut, wenn Sie einmal in aller Ruhe hierherkommen könnten, um manches mit mir zu besprechen. Das Reisegeld werden wir Ihnen gern dazu zur Verfügung geben. Kündigen Sie aber vorher Ihr Kommen an, damit Sie mich ja zu Hause treffen.

Schwester Wally hat mir geschrieben, dass sie den Fortbildungskurs für Heileurythmie von Dr. Bockholt mitmachen möchte und dass sie gern dann nachher ihre Arbeit einmal so geregelt haben möchte, dass sie mit ihrem Mann zusammen an der gleichen Stelle arbeiten könnte. Ich kann das letztere natürlich gut verstehen, weiss aber auch, dass Sie dadurch in Pilgramshain, wenn die Schwester Wally weggeht, eine grosse Lücke haben werden und ich möchte doch zeitig daran denken, wenn es wirklich so weit kommt, dass sie weggehen will, dass man diese Lücke gut ausfüllt. Auch deshalb ist es gut, dass wir miteinander sprechen, und hauptsächlich die wahl einer Heileurythmistin ist momentan von der allergrössten Bedeutung. Wenn wir da nicht wirklich ein System aufbauen, wer das Recht hat, Heileurythmie zu geben, und dasjenige, was Dr. Steiner eingerichtet hat - ich meine, die Heileurythmie als Bestandteil der Medizinischen Sektion - ausser Acht lassen, werden wir bald chaotische Zustände haben und alles, was Rudolf Steiner mit der Weihnachtstagung gewollt hat, würde mit einem Schlag aus der Welt gebracht. Auch über all diese prinzipiellen Fragen müssten wir eingehend sprechen.

Mit freundlichem Gruss

[illegible] Ihre Dr. Wegman

Fräulein Dr. Bockholt teilt mir mit, dass sie wegen der Heileurythmistin schon mit Ihnen gesprochen hat und Frl.Wegener vorgeschlagen, die dann zusammen mit Frl. Maasberg arbeiten könnte. Ich glaube, dass dieses eine gute Regelung sein könnte.

gez. I.W.

Arlesheim, March 3, 1930

Dear Dr König,

I felt very sorry that I was not able to come to Berlin. Unfortunately all my work got a bit disrupted lately because things have been really difficult for me especially regarding this issue of curative eurythmy, and in the end I also fell ill so had to postpone my journey to England which had already been planned. I believe I can only be back again on March 10. From then onwards I will probably be back in Arlesheim and it might be a good idea if you quietly came here so that we have time to discuss a few things. We would gladly cover your travel expenses. But tell me in advance when you are going to arrive to make sure you find me at home.

Sister Wally has written to me that she would like to attend Dr Bockholt's training course for curative eurythmy. After that she would like to have her work organized so that she can be in the same place as her husband. I can understand this very well, of course, but also know that there will be a huge gap in Pilgramshain if Sister Wally leaves. If she really does want to leave I will have to think in good time about a suitable replacement for her. For this reason, too, it would be good if we could talk, especially as the choice of a curative eurythmist is at the moment of immense importance. If we do not set up a consistent system about the right to practice curative eurythmy and if we do not pay attention to what Dr Steiner has implemented — that is, curative eurythmy as part of the Medical Section — the resulting situation will soon be chaotic and everything Rudolf Steiner intended with the Christmas Conference will be lost at one blow. We should also discuss in detail all these fundamental questions.

With kind regards,
Dr Wegman

Dr Bockholt tells me that she has already talked to you regarding the curative eurythmist and has suggested Miss Wegener who could work together with Miss [Maria] Maasberg. I think this might be a good arrangement.

I.W.

Arlesheim, March 8, 1933

Dear Dr König,

Because of the extraordinarily difficult situation it is necessary that those of us who care for the worldwide success of anthroposophical work gather to discuss seriously what steps should be taken and how people can support each other in order to continue this work without disruption. During my visits to England and the Netherlands I could encourage a number of friends to hold regular meetings for discussing the continuation of our work. This is even more necessary because, firstly, in the current situation the relationships within the different countries must be properly upheld, and secondly, because in these difficult times the work in the various activities must be supported by mutual understanding and help. In this difficult time there needs to be intensive mutual support within the various teams and communities. And in order to promote this I have already started approaching some friends to arrange such a meeting. This meeting with those now able to attend will be held in Berlin on April 1 and 2 in the Schillstrasse 11a. As agreed with Mr Dunlop and Dr Zeylmans the following meeting would be in England or Holland and perhaps another meeting in Stuttgart will be needed in between.

I would be a very pleased if you could come to the meeting in Berlin on April 1 and 2 which will also be attended by English friends like Mr Kaufmann, Mrs Merry, friends from Holland like Dr Zeylmans and others.

With kind regards,
Dr Ita Wegman

KLINISCH-THERAPEUTISCHES
INSTITUT
ARLESHEIM

TELEPHON 200

TELEGRAMME:
CLINIC ARLESHEIM

POSTCHECK-KONTO BASEL V 6487
POSTCHECK-KONTO KARLSRUHE 70.104

ARLESHEIM, den 18. März 1933.

Lieber Dr. König!

Es ist jetzt von Kolisko sehr stark der Wunsch - und für Vieles ist es auch gut - in Stuttgart sich zu treffen, weil es ihm ganz unmöglich ist, an diesem Datum von Stuttgart wegzugehen. So habe ich gemeint, dass man einmal zweierlei macht, ein Teil in Stuttgart, mit denen, die da sind und ein Teil in B. Vielleicht sind Sie in Stuttgart und Strohschein in B. Michael Wilson, sowie auch seine Mutter, die eine hervorragende Tätigkeit in Birmingham hat, werden nach B. kommen. Ich habe vorgeschlagen, in Stuttgart 29. und 30. Man kann es auch erst später machen, den 5. Es ist sehr schwer, es so zu dirigieren, dass es zusammenklappt. Meine Frage ist also jetzt: ob 29. und 30. in Stuttgart, was mir und Anderen auch sehr gut passen würde, oder 4./5.? Ich bitte Sie dringlich, über diese Sache nicht zu sprechen, weil doch dieses Zusammenkommen jetzt etwas anderes geworden ist als im Dezember 1932. Ich möchte nicht viel schreiben, möchte lieber mit Ihnen mündlich manches besprechen.

Mit herzlichem Gruss

Arlesheim, March 18, 1933

Dear Dr König,

There is now an urgent request from Kolisko — and this is good in many ways — to meet in Stuttgart because he will be absolutely unable to leave Stuttgart on that date. Therefore I have thought of holding two meetings, one in Stuttgart with those who are there and one in B[erlin]. Michael Wilson and his mother who are doing excellent work in Birmingham will come to B[erlin]. I have suggested [March] 29 and 30 [for the meeting] in Stuttgart. It can also be done later on [April] 5.

It is very difficult to set it up in a way which will work out. So my question now is: [Shall we meet on the] 29th and 30th in Stuttgart which would also suit me and others very well, or the 4th/5th?

I would urgently request you not to talk about this matter because the meeting is now of a different nature than in December 1932. I do not want to put a lot in writing and would prefer speaking to you about some issues.

With kind regards,
Ita Wegman, MD

Arlesheim, July 7, 1933

Dear Dr König,

Returning from my journey I had a meeting with the young doctors about the course that is going to take place with you at the beginning of August. The young doctors are very interested in studying embryology and gaining some clear understanding in terms of *Esoteric Science.* Of course there was a general wish to do this with you. And now I am writing with really very great pleasure because it had been on my mind already for a long time to work on embryology together, and so I would like to ask if you are prepared to come here at the beginning of August to work with us and hold a course for the young doctors on embryology. Afterwards you could, as you mentioned to me, travel to Italy.

We also plan to have a conference after Michaelmas at which we want to work intensely on pastoral medicine — doctors and priests together. We are now thoroughly revising the pastoral-medical course which is, as you probably also know, full of errors. This too, I would like to do together with you while you are here.

The course for young doctors will be of great importance for us because all kinds of decisions will have to be made and therefore it would be good if doctors could be there as well. That the young doctors have without any prompting asked to work with you is, I feel, a guidance from destiny.

I hope you all have arrived home safe and well. Until now there have been no messages from Stuttgart. How are things in Pilgramshain? Please let us know soon so that we can finalize the programmes.

During the course for the young doctors we will also read the Easter course for young doctors. In addition there will be practical work like painting, music, curative eurythmy.

With kind regards,
Ita Wegman, MD

Hondrich bei Spiez, den 14. Juni 1934

Liebe Freunde!

Zur zehnjährigen Geburtstagsfeier von Dr. Steiner's Besuch am Lauenstein möchte ich den Instituten und ihren Führern und Mitarbeitern sagen, dass ich mit warmem Herzen ihrer gedenke. Es ist dieses Mal wohl durch die zehnjährige Wiederkehr ein besonderer Ernst in der Erinnerung an diesen Tag eingetreten. Bis jetzt ist es uns gelungen zusammenzuhalten. Trotz der Differenzierungen innerhalb der Institute, der verschiedenen Art der Charaktere unter den Menschen, gelang es, einheitlich die heilpädagogische Arbeit durchzuführen und bekanntzumachen, und einheitlich höheren Zielen nachzugehen. Diese höheren Ziele lebten in unseren Herzen und wir strebten dahin, sie zu verwirklichen; zu verwirklichen dasjenige, was Rudolf Steiner als das Medizinisch-Esoterische gehalten hat. Das war es, was er als Aufgabe der Medizinischen Sektion auferlegte, nämlich durch die Sektion eine Gemeinschaft von Menschen zu bilden, die für die Heilkunst und die ihr anverwandten Fächer gewillt waren, innerhalb dieser Arbeit sich esoterisch zu vertiefen. Leider musste Dr. Steiner uns allein lassen und so blieb diese heiligste Arbeit in unseren Herzen nur wie eine Sehnsucht, die sich meiner Ansicht nach kundgab darin, dass die Menschen, die sie gefühlt haben, zusammengehalten haben aus dem Tiefsten ihres Wesens heraus.

Jetzt haben wir die zehnte Wiederkehr des Tages und damit kommt meistens eine Entscheidung durch Seelenprüfungen. Deshalb ist dieser Erinnerungstag bedeutungsvoller als vielleicht andere gewesen sind. Werden wir weiter zusammenhalten, nachdem durch die

Gesellschaftskrisis soviel Schwieriges an uns herangekommen ist? Wird durch das Zusammenhalten der Freunde ein Neues anbrechen können und dann der Moment gekommen sein, dass durch eine vertiefte Arbeit in Anthroposophie, Medizin und Heilpädagogik das Medizinisch-Esoterische sich Bahn brechen könnte? Wenn wir diese Vertiefung uns heilig vornehmen wollen, das Zusammenhalten durchführen und den Begriff des höheren Zieles, den Dr. Steiner in die Medizinische Sektion gelegt hat, nicht vergessen, wird sicherlich für uns eine neue fruchtbare Arbeit anbrechen.

Das sind Gedanken, lieber Freunde, die mir in dieser Zeit in Bergeseinsamkeit aufkommen, und obgleich die Welt äusserst düster aussieht, so kann doch mein Herz noch freudig schlagen bei dem Gedanken an die Möglichkeit, dass ich in absehbarer Zeit neu belebt in unseren Kreisen wieder erscheinen kann, um mit Ihnen zu arbeiten und dem Neuen entgegenzutreten und es zu empfangen.

Möge es Ihnen Allen gut gehen!

Mit herzlichem Gruss
gez. Ihre I. Wegman
Dr. Med.

Hondrich near Spies, June 14, 1934

Dear Friends

On the tenth anniversary of Dr Steiner's visit to the Lauenstein, I would like to let the institutes, their leaders and co-workers know that I think of them warmly. With this tenth anniversary a certain seriousness has entered the memories of this day. Until now we succeeded in standing united. Despite the differences between the institutes and the different personalities in them we were able to cultivate a common form of curative education, to represent it and to aspire to common higher goals. These higher goals lived in our hearts and we strove to make them real; making real what Rudolf Steiner considered to be the esoteric medical element. This is what Rudolf Steiner gave as a task for the Medical Section, namely to form a community of people through the Section who, for the sake of the art of healing and its related fields, were willing to go deeper into the esoteric aspect of this work. Sadly Dr Steiner left us on our own and so this most sacred task remained only in our hearts like a longing. In my opinion this longing expressed itself by the people who sensed it standing together out of the greatest depth of their being.

Now this anniversary returns for the tenth time and this is most often an occasion for coming to a decision through trials of the soul. Therefore this day of remembrance is more important than were perhaps others before Will we continue to remain united after the crisis in the [Anthroposophical] Society has brought so many difficulties towards us? Will the loyalty of the friends generate something new and will this be the moment for an esoteric breakthrough facilitated by intensified anthroposophical medical and curative work? If we resolve truly to intensify our work, acting in solidarity, keeping in mind the understanding of the higher goal which Dr Steiner set for the Medical Section, then no doubt we will be able to do new and productive work.

These thoughts have arisen in me, dear friends, in these days of mountain solitude. Although the world outside looks utterly gloomy, my heart beats joyfully at the thought of possibly returning to our circles in the foreseeable future in revived health, to work with you and to meet and embrace what is new.

May all of you be well!

With warm greetings

Yours

Ita Wegman MD

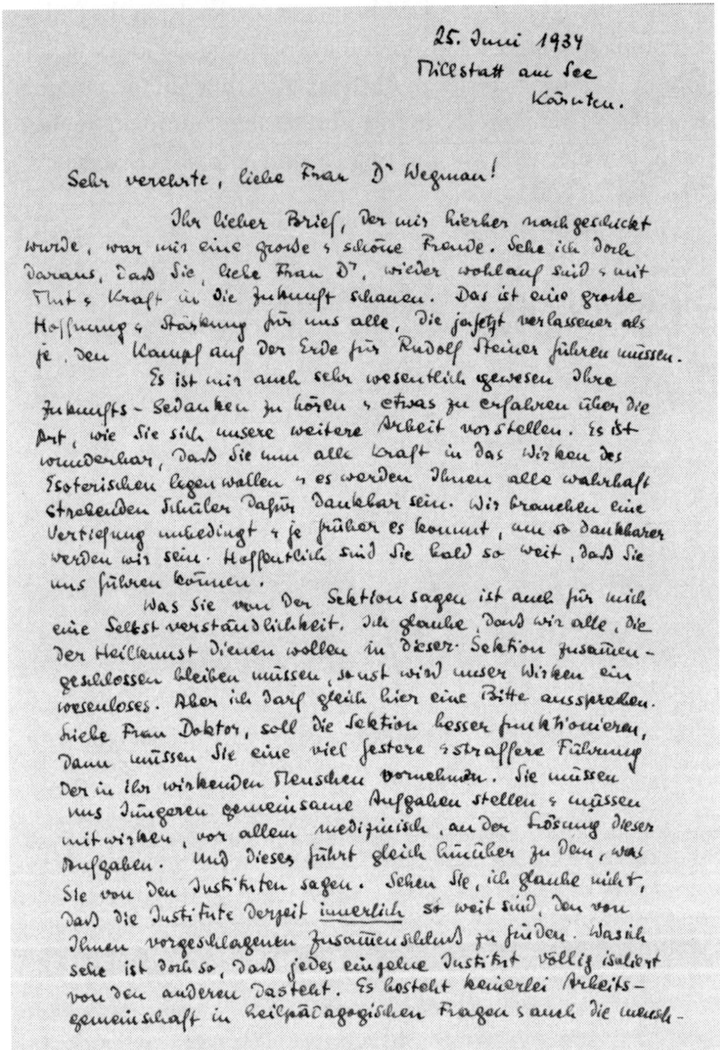

25. Juni 1934
Millstatt am See
Kärnten.

Sehr verehrte, liebe Frau Dr Wegman!

Ihr lieber Brief, der mir hierher nachgeschickt wurde, war mir eine grosse & schöne Freude. Sehe ich doch daraus, dass Sie, liebe Frau Dr, wieder wohlauf sind & mit Mut & Kraft in die Zukunft schauen. Das ist eine grosse Hoffnung & Stärkung für uns alle, die jetzt verlassener als je, den Kampf auf der Erde für Rudolf Steiner führen müssen.

Es ist mir auch sehr wesentlich gewesen Ihre Zukunfts-Gedanken zu hören & etwas zu erfahren über die Art, wie Sie sich unsere weitere Arbeit vorstellen. Es ist wunderbar, dass Sie nun alle Kraft in das Wirken des Esoterischen legen wollen & es werden Ihnen alle wahrhaft strebenden Schüler dafür dankbar sein. Wir brauchen eine Vertiefung unbedingt & je früher es kommt, um so dankbarer werden wir sein. Hoffentlich sind Sie bald so weit, dass Sie uns führen können.

Was Sie von der Sektion sagen ist auch für mich eine Selbstverständlichkeit. Ich glaube, dass wir alle, die der Heilkunst dienen wollen in dieser Sektion zusammengeschlossen bleiben müssen, sonst wird unser Wirken ein wesenloses. Aber ich darf gleich hier eine Bitte aussprechen. Liebe Frau Doktor, soll die Sektion besser funktionieren, dann müssen Sie eine viel festere & straffere Führung der in ihr wirkenden Menschen vornehmen. Sie müssen uns Jüngeren gemeinsame Aufgaben stellen & müssen mitwirken, vor allem medizinisch, an der Lösung dieser Aufgaben. Und dieses führt gleich hinüber zu dem, was Sie von den Instituten sagen. Sehen Sie, ich glaube nicht, dass die Institute derzeit *innerlich* so weit sind, den von Ihnen vorgeschlagenen Zusammenschluss zu finden. Was ich sehe ist doch so, dass jedes einzelne Institut völlig isoliert von den anderen dasteht. Es besteht keinerlei Arbeitsgemeinschaft in heilpädagogischen Fragen & auch die menschlichen Beziehungen sind nicht so gute, wie es notwendig wäre. Eine Änderung können nur *Sie* bringen, mit Ihrer weitausgreifenden Aktivität. Im jetzigen Zeitpunkt wäre ein Zusammenschluss illusorisch. Ich glaube, gerade die Institute könnten eine ausgezeichnete + vorbildliche Arbeitsgemeinschaft bilden, wenn sie wollten. Aber sie wollen noch nicht. Helfen Sie bitte, dass es dazu kommt. Dann werden wir unseren merkurialen Verpflichtungen genügen können.

Den Zusammenschluss der Landesgesellschaften + der Arbeitsgemeinschaft halte ich für notwendig. Wir müssen die Möglichkeit haben Mitglieder aufnehmen zu können + müssen auch einen gemeinsamen Stützpunkt haben, in dem wir uns treffen können. Ich glaube, dass eine solche, erst ganz lose gefügte soziale Gemeinschaft, doch etwas Hervorragendes werden kann, wenn alle freien Kräfte in ihr wirken. Dass gerade Sie + die Sektion daran besonders beteiligt sein müssen ist selbstverständlich.

Liebe Frau Doktor, wenn ich mir vorstelle, dass Sie wieder *neu* in das Leben gestellt, zu arbeiten anfangen, dann sehe ich darin die Hilfe der geistigen Welten + vor allem den Willen, die *wahrhafte* Anthroposophie weiter auf Erden zu wollen. Nicht Resignation, sondern neuer Mut kann daraus hervorgehen. Und *Ihre* eigene Aufgabe sehe ich in zwei Gebieten. Liebe Frau Doktor, fördern Sie die Heilkunst in allen ihren Richtungen; das ist das *Eine*. Und tragen Sie die anthroposophische Esoterik in die neu sich bildenden Arbeitskreise. Das ist das *Andere*. Trennen Sie aber Sektion + Gesellschaft. Die Sektion ist ein esoterisches Wesen, das in alle Arbeitskreise hineinreichen soll, aber sie ist nicht ein Arbeitskreis, sondern ein Wesen, das im *Leib* der Arbeitskreise wirken soll.

In solcher Art sehe ich Ihr künftiges Wirken + bin glücklich, dass es wieder da sein wird. Ich hoffe, dass Sie meiner Treue + Verbundenheit gewiss sind. Verschiedenheiten in einzelnen Dingen haben dabei nichts zu sagen. Ich stehe wie sonst bei Ihrer Persönlichkeit + bei der Aufgabe Ihres Schicksals als freier Diener.

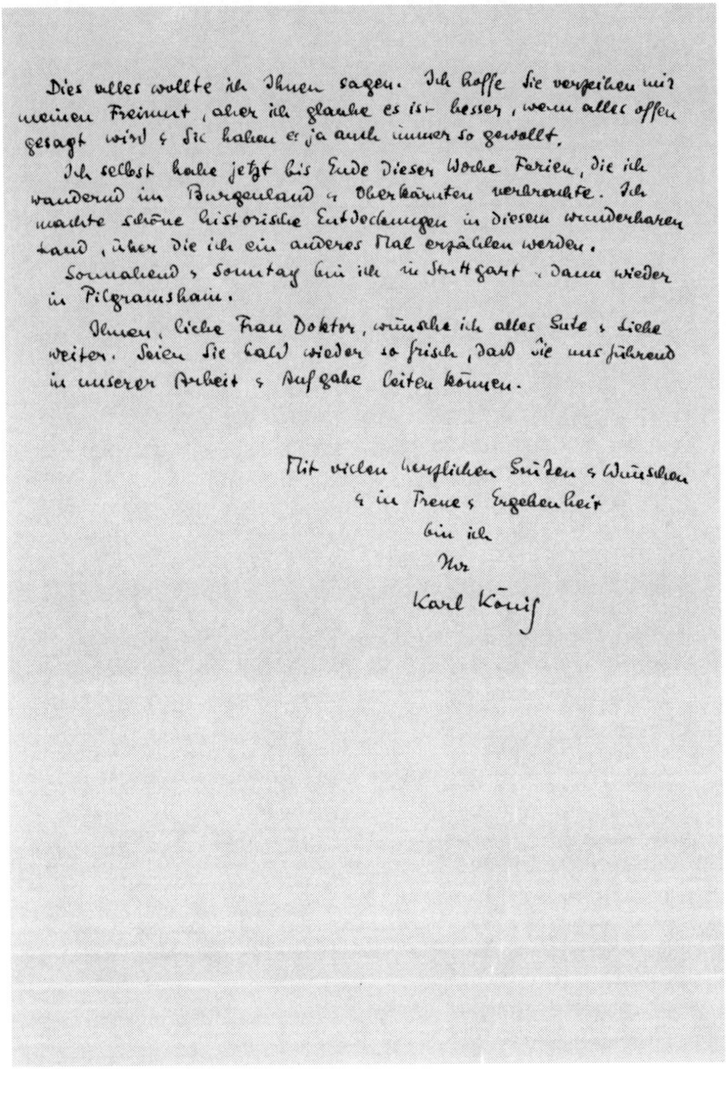

Dies alles wollte ich Ihnen sagen. Ich hoffe Sie verzeihen mir meinen Freimut, aber ich glaube es ist besser, wenn alles offen gesagt wird & Sie haben es ja auch immer so gewollt.

Ich selbst habe jetzt bis Ende dieser Woche Ferien, die ich wandernd im Burgenland & Oberkärnten verbrauchte. Ich machte schöne historische Entdeckungen in diesem wunderbaren Land, über die ich ein anderes Mal erzählen werde.

Sonnabend & Sonntag bin ich in Stuttgart, dann wieder in Pilgramshain.

Ihnen, liebe Frau Doktor, wünsche ich alles Gute & liebe weiter. Seien Sie bald wieder so frisch, daß Sie uns führend in unserer Arbeit & Aufgabe leiten können.

Mit vielen herzlichen Grüßen & Wünschen
& in Treue & Ergebenheit
bin ich
Ihr
Karl König

June 25, 1934
Millstatt am See, Carinthia

Dear Dr Wegman,

Your dear letter which was forwarded to me here gave a deep and great joy. It tells me that you, dear Frau Doctor, are back in good health and are looking ahead with courage and strength. This means real hope and encouragement for all of us who are lonelier than ever in fighting the battle on earth for Rudolf Steiner.

It was also very important for me to read about your ideas for the future and about your plans for our work. It is wonderful that you now want to put all your efforts into the esoteric processes; every truly aspiring student will be very grateful for that. We really need an intensification [of this work] and the sooner this happens the more grateful we will be. Hopefully you will soon be ready to lead us.

What you say about the Section is something I also take for granted. I believe that all of us in the Section who want to serve the art of healing need to stay loyal, otherwise our work will lose its substance. However, at this point I would like to request something. Dear Frau Doctor, for the Section to work better you will have to lead the people in a firmer and stricter way. You need to give us younger colleagues joint tasks and to work with us, particularly medically, in order to tackle them. And this relates to what you say about the institutes. You see, I do not think the institutes are *internally* prepared for the loyalty you suggest. What I see is that each institute stands alone and completely isolated. There is absolutely no cooperation regarding curative educational problems. Personal relationships too are not as good as they should be. Only *you,* with your wide-ranging activities, can bring about change. [Expecting] solidarity at this time would be an illusion. I believe that especially the institutes could form an excellent and exemplary community if they wanted to. But they do not yet want to do this. Please help us make it happen. Then we will be able to meet our Mercurial commitments.

I consider it necessary for the national [Anthroposophical] Societies and the work group [*Arbeitsgemeinschaft*] to join together. We need to have the opportunity to accept members and we also need a base where we can meet. I believe that such a social community, initially loosely interconnected, can grow into something magnificent if energies can act freely within it. Of course particularly you and the Section need to be involved in this.

Dear Frau Doctor, because you, being put *afresh* into this life, are going to resume work I believe that the spiritual world is supporting us and that *true* anthroposophy shall continue on earth. We can take new courage from this rather than feel resignation. And I think that *you* have special responsibilities in two fields. Dear Frau Doctor, the *first* field is the art of healing; support it in all its aspects. The *second* field is esoteric anthroposophy; bring it into the newly forming work groups. But keep Section and Society separate. The Section is an esoteric being which should reach into all work groups, yet it is not a work group itself but a being which should act within the *body* of the work groups.

This is how I see your future work and I am happy that it will be there again. I hope that you trust in my faith and loyalty. Differences in some details do not really matter. As ever I am loyal to you as a person and I support you in your destiny as a servant of my own free will.

All this I wanted to tell you. I hope you forgive my openness but I think it is better if things are openly expressed and you, too, always wanted it that way.

Until the end of this week I am on holiday which I have spent walking in the Burgenland and in Upper Carinthia. In this wonderful country I made some fine discoveries of historical interest which I will tell you about another time. On Saturday and Sunday I shall be in Stuttgart, then again in Pilgramshain.

I wish you, dear Frau Doctor, all the best. Get well soon so that you can lead and guide us in our work and commitment.

With warmest regards and best wishes
I faithfully and loyally remain
yours
Karl König

Striegau-Land, August 10, 1934

Dear Doctor Wegman,

During my holidays I wrote you a long, heartfelt and detailed letter. Up until now I have unfortunately been left without an answer. The questions I sketched out in it, however, are still on my mind, and I would be very grateful if you could let me know what you think about it.

Since I hear that you are in good health I am at the same time taking the liberty to write about a few other issues which are much on my heart and which I would like to discuss with you in writing.

Next week it will six years since I began working here in Pilgramshain and at the same time seven years since I was able to meet you personally and started working actively in the Medical Section. A lot has happened in this time. During the last few weeks I have increasingly felt the need to review my work and to take stock. This was also reflected by my inner experiences, and it happened after a particular night that I woke up in the morning feeling confident that my questions had been answered. The answer was to leave Pilgramshain for about a year and to give my work over to somebody else *only* for that period of time. But there was more in the answer. If my understanding is accurate it means that I should spend that year in Arlesheim helping out there while another doctor should come here to replace me. From Arlesheim I should continue to work for Prague, Vienna and perhaps Paris in order to establish medical work in Vienna and Paris exactly as in Prague.

Dear Frau Doctor, this is *not* a plan I have; it is rather an inner vision which I put forward to you for assessment, asking you what you think about it.

Please write *soon,* of course I would be happy to come to you to discuss these pending issues in conversation.

In the meantime I remain with kindest regards and best wishes for your continued recovery.

Yours faithfully

Karl König

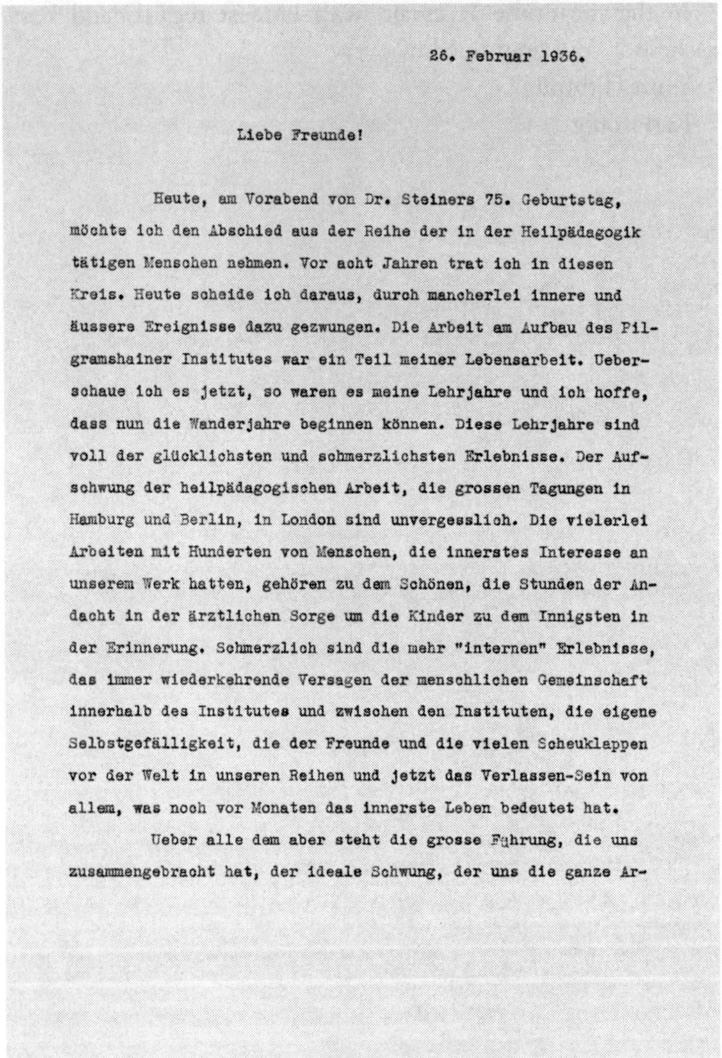

26. Februar 1936.

Liebe Freunde!

Heute, am Vorabend von Dr. Steiners 75. Geburtstag, möchte ich den Abschied aus der Reihe der in der Heilpädagogik tätigen Menschen nehmen. Vor acht Jahren trat ich in diesen Kreis. Heute scheide ich daraus, durch mancherlei innere und äussere Ereignisse dazu gezwungen. Die Arbeit am Aufbau des Pilgramshainer Institutes war ein Teil meiner Lebensarbeit. Ueberschaue ich es jetzt, so waren es meine Lehrjahre und ich hoffe, dass nun die Wanderjahre beginnen können. Diese Lehrjahre sind voll der glücklichsten und schmerzlichsten Erlebnisse. Der Aufschwung der heilpädagogischen Arbeit, die grossen Tagungen in Hamburg und Berlin, in London sind unvergesslich. Die vielerlei Arbeiten mit Hunderten von Menschen, die innerstes Interesse an unserem Werk hatten, gehören zu dem Schönen, die Stunden der Andacht in der ärztlichen Sorge um die Kinder zu dem Innigsten in der Erinnerung. Schmerzlich sind die mehr "internen" Erlebnisse, das immer wiederkehrende Versagen der menschlichen Gemeinschaft innerhalb des Institutes und zwischen den Instituten, die eigene Selbstgefälligkeit, die der Freunde und die vielen Scheuklappen vor der Welt in unseren Reihen und jetzt das Verlassen-Sein von allem, was noch vor Monaten das innerste Leben bedeutet hat.

Ueber alle dem aber steht die grosse Fµhrung, die uns zusammengebracht hat, der ideale Schwung, der uns die ganze Ar-

\- 2 -

beit gründen und weiterfördern liess, und die grossen Durchbrüche, in denen man in der Gemeinschaft der Freunde das Wirken der geistigen Welt unmittelbar erleben durfte. Dieses Wirken bleibt unerschütterlich in unseren Reihen und in unserer Gemeinschaft.

Ich möchte Ihnen noch mitteilen, dass ich zunächst für einige Monate in die Tschechoslovakei gehe, um dort mit einigen Aerzten (etwa 25) intensiv antroposophisch zu arbeiten. Anschliessend daran, am 1. August 1936, werde ich mich in Wien als Arzt niederlassen, um zunächst in aller Stille und Bescheidenheit verschiedene Dinge zu verfolgen, die mir wichtig erscheinen.

Ich werde sehr froh sein, wenn einmal der eine oder der andere von Ihnen sich so an mich erinnert, dass er mich etwas vom Leben in den Instituten wissen lässt.

Ich wünsche allen eine gedeihliche Arbeit und den Segen der göttlichen Mächte!

Dr Karl König

February 26, 1936

Dear Friends,

Today, on the eve of Dr Steiner's seventy-fifth birthday, I want to take my leave from those active in curative education. I joined this circle eight years ago. Today I am leaving, forced by various internal and external events. Building up the institute in Pilgramshain has been part of my life's work. Looking back, these years were my apprenticeship and I hope that I can now move on as a journeyman. These years of apprenticeship were full of the happiest and also most painful experiences. The rise of the curative educational work, the big conferences in Hamburg, Berlin and London are unforgettable. All the activities with hundereds of people who had an innermost interest in our work belong among good memories. The times of devotion when caring medically for the children are the dearest. Painful are the more 'internal' experiences: a repeated failure of community at the institute and between institutes, my own and my friends' complacency and the often blinkered view of the outside world in our ranks. And now the loss of everything that, until a few months ago, was the core of my life.

But above all there is the great leadership that has brought us together, the spiritual momentum which made us start and develop all the work. There are the great breakthroughs shared by a community of friends and giving an immediate experience of the workings of the spiritual world. All this will stay steadfastly with us and in our community.

I would also like to tell you that I will first for a few months go to Czechoslovakia to do intense anthroposophical work with some doctors (about 25). Then, on August 1, 1936, I will open a medical practice in Vienna in order to pursue quietly and in all modesty various things which seem to me important.

I would be very glad if one or other of you would sometimes keep me in mind and tell me about life at the institutes.

I wish you all successful work and God bless you,

Dr Karl König

Arlesheim, June 6, 1936

Dear Doctor König,

I hereby send you the requested reference. I am really sorry that I left it so long and it is always a bit pathetic to say that the reason was a lack of time. And therefore I will not do so now. You know how it can often be at a workplace like ours and with so many unexpected things just recently coming towards us.

You have received my telegram, and Dr Hauschka will travel to Vienna as soon as possible to discuss everything with you in detail, also regarding Miss Förster. The problem is that at the moment neither the clinic nor the laboratory can afford to train new laboratory assistants without receiving payment. If it were up to me I would always agree [to train assistants] and in the past it was also possible to fund the trainings. But this is no longer an option and when I again talked with Mr Rudolf, our administration manager, he had to refuse my suggestion to train Miss Förster, despite his own regrets. But you will be able to discuss all this yourself with Dr Hauschka and I shall hear further about the matter.

I am delighted to hear that you are already busily working. A curative eurythmist, a woman from Holland, has just been here; she has attended courses and received her training here. For the last six months she has worked in Belgrade where she got some doctors and quite a number of people interested in curative eurythmy. We have now received a request to go there and give lectures. And I thought that it would be better if that were done by you. Vienna is not far from Belgrade and perhaps a journey could be arranged. I gave them your address and the doctors in Belgrade will contact you.

I very much hope to gather the doctors for some teamwork in

September, if not in Arlesheim because they might be a bit apprehensive to come here, then in Ticino where we have rented a house.

Is your family now with you?

With kind regards,

Dr I. Wegman

PS: I hope this form in of reference will meet your requirements. If it needs to be more detailed or written in a different way please let me know.

Arlesheim, August 15, 1936

Dear Dr König,

Thank you very much for referring the engineer, Mr Regenstreif to us. He is a nice and likeable person and we were all pleased to have made his aquaintance.

It seems to me as if he has a stomach or even duodenal ulcer. With a strict diet and a lot of rest the pain can be got rid of. But of course he does not want to rest all the time and also is not able to do so and therefore such a treatment is difficult. Antimony is of course here the most effective medication. We have given him antimony injections and stomach packs. We have also given him a powder for internal use, a combination of Tartarus stibiatus, Chamomilla, Belladonna, Wismut (No. 291), further hot packs and, whenever he is in pain, a small amount of fine olive oil which is always of extraordinary alleviating effect. For his liver he got some Hepatodoron. Conchae comp. which you have prescribed is also very good because the Conchae actually removes the pain which is linked to the nerves. However, rest, application of warmth and diet are really important. Mr Regenstreif told me a lot about you but also said that you need some rest.

We are planning now to have a doctors' meeting here during the first week of October, from Friday to Sunday, October 2–4, after the conference in Burghalde. At this meeting we very much want to take up mystery medicine. The correspondence of microcosm to macrocosm plays a big part in this, and on earth this is in practice eurythmy and curative eurythmy. Since curative education has advanced a lot recently and most doctors are not yet quite familiar with this field we wanted to focus this time on the cosmic art of healing. Of course there will be sufficient opportunities to discuss practical issues, too, but we wanted to suggest to the doctors what is mentioned above.

I would now like to visit some institutes in the north like the ones in Iceland and Sweden, and then travel back through

Germany. Then I also have a very great desire soon to come again to Austria, especially now that there are more opportunities in Austria. We also now have another annexe of the clinic in Ticino at Lake Maggiore; I enclose a brochure.

With kind regards, also to your family,

I. Wegman

Arlesheim, December 22, 1936

Dear Dr König,

I must tell you the sad news that our colleague Dr Helene von Grunelius died here in the clinic on December 17. When she returned nine weeks ago from her journey to Italy she was severely ill. Her continuing frail health, the difficulties she had to cope with in Stuttgart, the many and deep disappointments she had experienced gave her such a great shock that she never really recovered. Her old illness flared up again and despite all our efforts we were unable any more to save her. Her heart stopped working properly and perhaps — between ourselves — she did not want to return any more to the old situation, this was quite certainly a deep emotional cause.

We are still feeling the impact of what has happened. Dr von Grunelius was the one who first brought about the young doctors' movement by discussing with Dr Steiner whether it would be possible to bring young doctors together to study medicine in a different way than was until then done by the older generation. So we are all very much struck by this passing just before Christmas. It is not exactly a happy time at the moment and dangers are threatening on all sides.

I hope you are well, dear Dr König. Miss Köhler was here and has been busy painting. She told me she would like to work with you, I really hope this will happen; Miss Köhler is an excellent worker and very talented.

I send my kindest regards to your wife and the children, most of all my godchild. I am sending a picture for Clara Renate which will arrive within the next few days.

With best wishes for a good Christmas season,

Yours I. Wegman

Arlesheim, March 17, 1937

Dear Dr König,

Your kind letter from December still lies here unanswered. Not that I did not want to reply to this letter immediately; but as often happens you leave a letter for a few days, and then a situation arises which makes the time gap even longer and resulting events make letter writing increasingly impossible. I caught flu and went to England before fully recovering, and because of the general flu epidemic there immediately had a relapse. For these reasons many things were left unfinished which I had wanted to get done. But now I do not want to wait any longer to tell you how delighted I was that you are so actively pursuing anthroposophy in Vienna.

It was a great joy to me that you have started a youth group which is doing good work, as you write in your letter. That you are successful and will continue to be, dear Dr König, does not surprise me because there is something about Austria, and you feel the same, which is certainly important for promoting spirituality. That Dr Steiner was born and used to live there, that he felt so close to the Burgenland, is indeed a fact which contributes to the success of spiritual work. The soul-needs and the hardships of everyday life can bring out something which does not arise in life's abundance.

I was pleased to hear that Dr Burmeister will assist you — or perhaps has joined you already. She was in very high regard here and I think your cooperation will be very productive.

Now regarding the other issue you asked me about, dear Dr König, whether it would be a good idea to write a letter to Mr Steffen stating that you want to take back the personal insult. My own opinion of this is actually difficult to put into words because if it is really your view — and the view of your friends — that you personally insulted Mr Steffen then taking the insult back is no longer a matter of course. Your conflict with Mr Steffen needs to be considered differently from a personal insult.

You wanted to defend yourself because you thought you had been treated unfairly by Mr Steffen. Of course it is unfortunate that you made your case against unfair treatment in an inappropriate way. However, you really cannot take back now what you have expressed earlier. Nor can you tell Steffen that you are sticking to what you said but feel that the way you said it was not right because it was insulting to him. You put yourself in a difficult situation when trying to do things so they appear to be right on both sides. Steffen will never accept half an apology only addressing the manner in which you expressed yourself. And surely you cannot, as a man over thirty, change your mind now all of a sudden and have a different opinion than you had three years ago. Doing something just for the sake of pacifying a few people in Austria who otherwise will not want to work with you cannot be right either.

If you ask me what I would do if I were in your place, I think I would just accept that I indeed acted clumsily but that I did so because of my sense of fairness. Of course you have fallen into disgrace and have to deal with some unpleasantness because of this. However, there is nothing else you can do about it than accept this and, for the next time, remember to use your sense of fairness in a way that does not personally offend the other person. Otherwise the person who has acted unfairly can claim to have been deeply insulted; he can pretend that he is completely innocent, that he had been insulted for no reason and that everybody else has made themselves guilty. It is not quite right to support this kind of attitude because everything goes in the wrong direction without proper understanding.

It will be enough if you have a good idea of what happened at that time because you certainly will act differently next time and will still be keen to defend fairness. These things do have an effect in the moral world. We should not care whether others approve or disapprove. Judgment is only done in higher worlds.

If you still wish to write that letter, dear Dr König, then my message should not prevent you from doing so. Deep in your soul, there may still be other reasons urging you to act, reasons which cannot be fully understood by a third party.

I am delighted that you are expecting a fourth child because children want to come down to help bring about the new world order. Please also give my kindest regards to your wife and to Sister Pini.

Perhaps you will still manage to come here for Easter. We have an annexe in Ticino now, and I am sending brochures about it from here. Nearby in Brissago we have a nursery where there is also room to accommodate children in need of curative educational treatment. Perhaps you will consider one or the other when possibilities arise.

With kind regards,

I. Wegman

Cheap accommodation is available in Brissago. Enquiries to Mr Kirchner in Ascona.

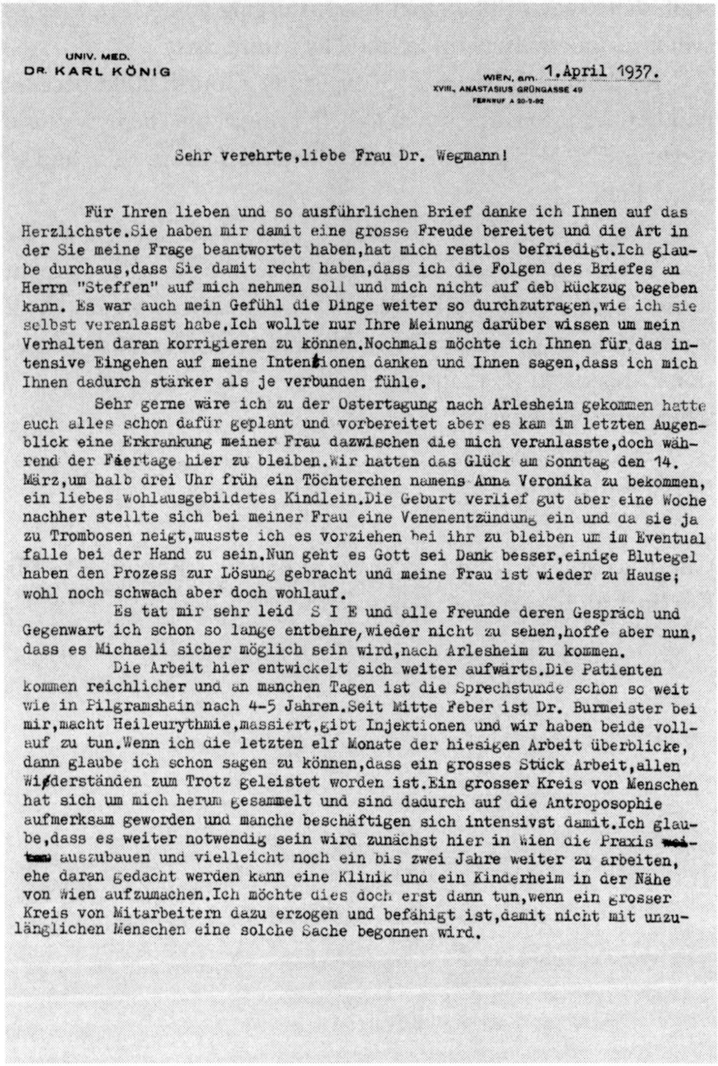

UNIV. MED.
DR. KARL KÖNIG

WIEN, am 1.April 1937.
XVIII., ANASTASIUS GRÜNGASSE 49
FERNRUF A 20-2-92

Sehr verehrte,liebe Frau Dr. Wegmann!

Für Ihren lieben und so ausführlichen Brief danke ich Ihnen auf das Herzlichste.Sie haben mir damit eine grosse Freude bereitet und die Art in der Sie meine Frage beantwortet haben,hat mich restlos befriedigt.Ich glaube durchaus,dass Sie damit recht haben,dass ich die Folgen des Briefes an Herrn "Steffen" auf mich nehmen soll und mich nicht auf deb Rückzug begeben kann. Es war auch mein Gefühl die Dinge weiter so durchzutragen,wie ich sie selbst veranlasst habe.Ich wollte nur Ihre Meinung darüber wissen um mein Verhalten daran korrigieren zu können.Nochmals möchte ich Ihnen für das intensive Eingehen auf meine Intentionen danken und Ihnen sagen,dass ich mich Ihnen dadurch stärker als je verbunden fühle.

Sehr gerne wäre ich zu der Ostertagung nach Arlesheim gekommen hatte auch alles schon dafür geplant und vorbereitet aber es kam im letzten Augenblick eine Erkrankung meiner Frau dazwischen die mich veranlasste,doch während der Feiertage hier zu bleiben.Wir hatten das Glück am Sonntag den 14. März,um halb drei Uhr früh ein Töchterchen namens Anna Veronika zu bekommen, ein liebes wohlausgebildetes Kindlein.Die Geburt verlief gut aber eine Woche nachher stellte sich bei meiner Frau eine Venenentzündung ein und da sie ja zu Trombosen neigt,musste ich es vorziehen bei ihr zu bleiben um im Eventualfalle bei der Hand zu sein.Nun geht es Gott sei Dank besser,einige Blutegel haben den Prozess zur Lösung gebracht und meine Frau ist wieder zu Hause; wohl noch schwach aber doch wohlauf.

Es tat mir sehr leid S I E und alle Freunde deren Gespräch und Gegenwart ich schon so lange entbehre, wieder nicht zu sehen,hoffe aber nun, dass es Michaeli sicher möglich sein wird,nach Arlesheim zu kommen.

Die Arbeit hier entwickelt sich weiter aufwärts.Die Patienten kommen reichlicher und an manchen Tagen ist die Sprechstunde schon so weit wie in Pilgramshain nach 4-5 Jahren.Seit Mitte Feber ist Dr. Burmeister bei mir,macht Heileurythmie,massiert,gibt Injektionen und wir haben beide vollauf zu tun.Wenn ich die letzten elf Monate der hiesigen Arbeit überblicke, dann glaube ich schon sagen zu können,dass ein grosses Stück Arbeit,allen Widerständen zum Trotz geleistet worden ist.Ein grosser Kreis von Menschen hat sich um mich herum gesammelt und sind dadurch auf die Antroposophie aufmerksam geworden und manche beschäftigen sich intensivst damit.Ich glaube,dass es weiter notwendig sein wird zunächst hier in Wien die Praxis auszubauen und vielleicht noch ein bis zwei Jahre weiter zu arbeiten, ehe daran gedacht werden kann eine Klinik und ein Kinderheim in der Nähe von Wien aufzumachen.Ich möchte dies doch erst dann tun,wenn ein grosser Kreis von Mitarbeitern dazu erzogen und befähigt ist,damit nicht mit unzulänglichen Menschen eine solche Sache begonnen wird.

erledigt

Die Arbeit der Jugendgruppe geht gut weiter,es sind jetzt meistens 20 junge Menschen die mitarbeiten,ausserdem ein Kreis von 10 Ärzten die jede Woche bei mir zur Arbeit zusammenkommen.

Nun hätte ich eine Frage die ich Sie bitte mir recht umgehend zu beantworten.Es hat sich seit Herbst vorigen Jahres ein junger Arzt in die Jugendgruppe gefunden der mit allen Segeln in die antroposophische Medizin hineingekommen ist und nun nichts sehnlicher wünscht als so bald als möglich bei Ihnen arbeiten zu können.Er ist meiner Meinung nach ausserordentlich begabt,sehr frisch und jugendlich und mit viel Enthuasiasmus bei der Sache. Klinisch ist er sehr gut vorgebildet und nur dadurch,dass er recht radikale politische Ansichten hatte(die aber jetzt völlig vorbei sind) in seinem ganzen Gehaben vielleicht noch ein wenig ungehobelt aber nicht auffällig. Nun wollte ich Sie fragen ob es möglich wäre,dass dieser junge Arzt,er heisst Weissberg nach Arlesheim kommen könnte um dort bei Ihnen zu arbeiten und zu lernen.Wenn das möglich wäre hätten wir für die hier zu beginnende Arbeit ~~ei~~ eines Kinderheimes eine vorzügliche Hilfe und ich wäre Ihnen schon sehr dankbar wenn Sie ihm diese Möglichkeit geben könnten wie Sie Sie genau vor 10 Jahren mir gegeben haben.Allerdings befindet er sich materiell in den gleichen Verhältnissen wie damals ich und könnte sich bestenfalls die Reise nach A. ~~sich~~ ermöglichen.Aber ich glaube,dass er einen solchen Ausnahmefall bedeutet ,dass es eben wirklich gut wäre ihm die Klinik mit ihrer ausgebreiteten Arbeit erleben zu lassen.Ich weiss nicht wie ich ihn sonst so führen soll,dass er uns ein gesunder Mitarbeiter wird.

Ausserordentlich viel hätte ich auf medizinischem Gebiete zu erzählen aber das kann leider nicht brieflich geschehen.Ich wollte Sie nur fragen,ob es Ihnen lieb wäre,wenn ich jetzt einen grösseren Aufsatz über die sieben Planetenmetalle Ihnen zuschicken würde,da ich gerade in der letzten Zeit viel darüber gesprochen und gearbeitet habe.Zum Schluss wünsche ich Ihnen von Herzen alles Gute,vor allem Gesundheit und Kraft zur Arbeit.

Ich bin in tiefer Ergebenheit und Verbundenheit

Ihr

Dr Karl König

Vienna, April 1, 1937

Dear Dr Wegmann,

Warmest thanks for your kind and detailed letter. I was much delighted by it and completely satisfied with the way you answered my question. I definitely think you are right in saying that I have to accept the consequences of my letter to Mr Steffen and that I cannot now go back. I also felt that I have to continue the matter in the same way as I myself brought it about. I just wanted to hear your opinion so that I could correct my attitude. Again I want to thank you for going so intensively into my intentions and would like to state that as a result I feel closer to you than ever.

I really would have liked to come to Arlesheim for the Easter conference and had already planned and organized everything for this, but at the last moment my wife fell ill, so I decided to stay here over the holidays. On Sunday March 14 at half past two in the morning we were happy to have a little daughter named Anna Veronika, a lovely, well developed baby. The delivery went well, but a week later my wife fell ill with phlebitis, and because she has a tendency towards thrombosis I had to stay with her in order to be there just in case. Thank God things are better now, a few leeches have helped solve the problem and my wife is back home, still weak but well.

I was very sorry not to see YOU and all the friends whose company and conversation I have been missing for so long, but now hope it will be possible to come to Arlesheim at Michaelmas.

Work here is progressing further. More patients come to see me and there are days when my surgery is as busy as it has been in Pilgramshain after 4–5 years. Since mid February Dr Burmeister is working with me, doing curative eurythmy, massaging, giving injections and we are both working busily. Looking back at the last eleven months of work here I think it is safe to say that a great deal of work has been achieved despite all difficulties. A large circle of people has gathered around me and as a result come to know anthroposophy, and some of them study it most intensively. I think it will still be necessary first to build up the practice in Vienna and keep working for another year or two before we can think of opening a clinic and a children's home near Vienna. I only want to do this when a substantial group of assistants has been trained and qualified for this work in order to avoid starting such a project with inedaquately trained people.

Work in the youth group is progressing well, usually there are now twenty young people taking part, and in addition there is a group of ten doctors coming to my home once a week to study.

Now I have a question and I would ask you to reply to it as soon as possible. In autumn last year a young doctor joined the group of young people and has avidly taken on board anthroposophical medicine. Now it is his most earnest wish to work at your clinic as soon as possible. In my opinion he is extraordinarily talented, very brisk, youthful and full of enthusiasm. Clinically he is *very* well trained, but because he had rather extreme political views (which are now completely over) he may still be somewhat blunt in his manners, but not exceptionally so. Now I would like to ask you if it would be possible for this young doctor, called Weissberg, to come to Arlesheim to learn and work at your clinic. If this was an option we would have excellent help when starting work here for a children's home, and I would be really grateful if you could give him this opportunity just as you gave it to me exactly ten years ago. Mind you, financially he is in the same situation as I was at that time and could afford no more than the journey to A. But I believe his case is so exceptional that it would be really good to give him full experience of the work at your clinic. I cannot think of another way of developing him into a strong and capable colleague.

There are lots of medical issues I would like to tell you about but unfortunately I cannot do this in writing. I just wanted to ask if you would like me now to send you a longer essay about the seven planetary metals, because I have been studying and lecturing on them quite a lot recently. Finally, I sincerely wish you all the best, most of all good health and strength for your work.

Yours respectfully and faithfully

Dr Karl König

Arlesheim, July 23, 1937

Dear Dr König,

Many thanks for your letter of July 11. Meanwhile your patient Mrs Gericke from Neisse arrived here. I think it very good that she can breath some different air. She really needs good care and lots of fresh air because I think her lungs are not quite healthy either.

It is a pity you did not take a quick trip to us while you were on your way from London. It has been a long time since we spoke to each other but perhaps there will be an opportunity sometime soon. I still want to visit Austria again but have not yet had a chance to do so. At the moment a medical student, Mr Schauder, is on the curative educational seminar here at the Sonnenhof. I was very pleased to see him again because I thought he had already given up medical studies as Miss Förster has done.

I can see from your letter that you have already arranged things with Dr Weissberg. Otherwise I would still have asked you to send him to us. As you know, Dr Bockholt has been unwell since May, suffering from heart complaints and general tiredness. The cause is probably a mild myocarditis to which she certainly has not paid enough attention because for some time already her heart has not felt well. We feel that Dr Bockholt's absence has a very strong impact. And Dr Leroi must go on holiday because he really needs to. So Dr van Deventer and I are on our own here at the clinic and given its size it is quite a lot of work.

Mrs Gericke had no problems getting foreign currency so one has the impression it is easier now for patients wanting to travel into Switzerland to leave their country.

I hope your wife and the children are well. I send you, dear Dr König, kindest regards.

Yours

I. Wegman

PS: Of course young doctors need to come here for training and we definitely would like to arrange that. But I do think it can only be done if others share the burden with us. If, as you say, you want to start a fund for this purpose together with the engineer, Mr Meisel, I very much welcome this. In such cases a stay here can be charged at cost price.

I.W.

UNIV. MED.
DR. KARL KÖNIG

WIEN, am 9.August 1937.
XVIII., ANASTASIUS GRÜNGASSE 49
FERNRUF A 20-2-99

Sehr geehrte Frau Dr. Wegmann!

Für Ihren lieben Brief danke ich Ihnen sehr herzlich und bin froh,dass Frau Gericke nunmehr bei Ihnen gelandet ist und wie ich auch hoffe dort Heilung finden kann.

In den nächsten Tagen wird sich eine Patientin aus Wien bei Ihnen vorstellen und ich bitte Sie,ihr ein ausführliches Gespräch und eine gründliche Untersuchung zu gewähren.Es ist Frau Lilly Gorge aus Wien,die seit einem Jahr in meiner Behandlung steht.Es ist eine recht komplitzierte Patientin,dadurch,dass allerverschiedenste Dinge in ihr zusammenwirken.Vor einigen Jahren wurde ihr die linke Niere wegen TBC herausgenommen.Dann verlor sie ihren Mann,der einer der angesehensten Architekten in Wien war und lebt nun als Witwe allein mit ihren 3 Kindern.Vor etwa 2 Jahren fand sie zur Antroposophie und versucht nun allmählich in die Geisteswissenschaft hineinzukommen.Da sie Jüdin ist, und das Judentum in einer stark prononzierten Art in sich trägt,fällt ihr diese nicht leicht und man muss dauernd versuchen, sie vor Übertreibungen zu behüten.Seit dem Tode ihres Mannes leidet sie an schwersten Migräneanfällen,die besonders zur Zeit der Periode auftreten und ihr für 3-4-5 Tage das Arbeiten unmöglich machen.Es liegt sicher dabei eine ovarielle Störung vor,ausserdem aber ein gestörter Stoffwechsel im Leber-Gallegebiet und schwere psychotische Erscheinungen die sich oft im kramfhaften Weinen zu lösen versuchen.Durch die ganze Persönlichkeit geht ein manisch-depressiver Zug,den man immer wieder beobachten kann.Ich wäre Ihnen sehr dankbar wenn Sie Frau Gorge genau untersuchen würden und ihr einige Medikamente verordneten.Ich habe alles mögliche versucht und ~~sie~~ in der erzählten Führung sie psychisch ins Gleichgewicht gebracht aber die Migränen zu bannen ist mir noch nicht gelungen.Desshalb bitte ich sehr um Ihre Hilfe. Wichtig wäre noch zu erwähnen,dass Frau Gorge derzeit Eurythmie treibt mit der Absicht im nächsten Jahr,Ihre oft starken Energien der Heileurythmie zur Verfügung zu stellen.

Ferner möchte ich für den 23.August eine Patientin anmelden,die ich gerne für 4 Wochen in der Klinik untergebracht hätte.Es ist die Frau eines Kollegen,Frau Dr. Galatzer.Der Kollege lebt in Wr.Neustadt und ist ein Mensch der es in seinem Streben ausserordentlich weit gebracht hat.Er ist Homöopath aber mit einer seelischen Verinnerlichung die ich kaum jemals bei einem Arzt gefunden habe.Eine starke mystische Natur die heute so weit ist, dass sie nichts anderes mehr liest als das Evangelium und dem es gelingt durch inneren Zuspruch und Aussprache,viele Menschen zu heilen.Daneben steht nun seine Frau,die dem Streben des Mannes nicht nachgekommen ist und darunter bis ins körperliche hinein krank geworden ist.Sie leidet an einer kaum bezähmbaren Trägheit,ausserdem erscheint mir der ganze Fettstoffwechsel und damit der gesamte Mars-Prozess vollständig gestört zu sein.Ich glaube ausserdem,dass am rechten Oberarm Entzündungserscheinungen vorliegen die besonders zur Zeit der Periode zu Temperatursteigerungen führen und dadurch den Zustand des Krankseins noch verstärken.Das Wichtigste bei dieser Patientin scheint mir,sie seelisch so zu führen,dass sie allmählich zu sich slbst zurückfindet.Ihr Mann legt grossen Wert darauf,dass arbeitstherapeuthisch viel mit ihr getan wird und so denk ich,dass sie vielleicht in den ersten 2 Wochen ihres Dortseins,vor allem mit Malen und Plastizieren beschäftigt wird und nachher vielleicht auch im Laboratorium von Dr. Hauschka einiges Handwerkliches, helfend tun kann.Medikamentös werden Sie ja selbst am besten finden was zu tun ist.Bisher hat :"Graphit,Stibium und Calicum carbonicum" Gutes geleistet.Ich möchte Sie bitten umgehend an Frau Dr. Galatzer direkt zu schreiben ob sie zum bezeichneten Termin nach Arlesheim kommen kann.Da ich Ende dieser Woche in Urlaub gehe,bitte ich die Antwort direkt an die Patientin zu richten.Ihre Adresse ist Fr. Dr. Galatzer,Wiener-Neustadt, Beethovengasse 14.

Mit grosser Erschütterung vernahm ich die Kunde vom Tode des Herrn Dr. Greil.Es ist der zweite Freund,der in kurzer Zeit von unsgenommen wurde.

Ich hoffe sehr zu Michaeli bei der Ärztetagung sein zu können und freue mich,Sie,wieder zu sehen.Ich bitte Sie,mir sowohl über Frau Gorge,als auch über Frau Galatzer zu schreiben und verbleibe inzwischen mit vielen

herzlichen Grüssen

Ihr

Dr Karl König

Vienna, August 9, 1937

Dear Dr Wegmann,

Many thanks for your kind letter. I am glad Mrs Gericke has now arrived at your clinic and hope she will make a full recovery there.

Within the next few days a patient from Vienna will come to see you and I would ask you to give her a thorough consultation and examination. It is Mrs Lilly Gorge from Vienna who has been my patient for a year. She is a rather complicated patient because the most diverse processes are working together within her. A few years ago her left kidney was removed because of tuberculosis. Then she lost her husband who was one of the most distinguished architects in Vienna, and she now lives alone as a widow with her three children. About two years ago she came into contact with anthroposophy and is now slowly trying to gain more understanding of spiritual science. Because she is a Jew and takes her Jewishness very seriously, anthroposophy does not come easily to her and you must always try to protect her from exaggeration. Since her husband died she has suffered from most severe migraine attacks which occur especially during menstruation and make it impossible for her to work for 3, 4 or 5 days. There is certainly a dysfunction of the ovaries as well as of the metabolism in the liver and gall bladder area and severe psychotic conditions often expressed by fits of crying. Her whole personality shows signs of manic depression which can be observed frequently. I would be very grateful if you could examine Mrs Gorge thoroughly and prescribe some medication. I have tried everything possible and by guiding her in the way mentioned above could stabilize her emotional condition, but have not yet managed to control the migraine. So I am very much asking for your help. It is also important to let you know that Mrs Gorge is currently doing eurythmy with the intention next year to direct her often powerful energy into curative eurythmy.

I would also like to make an appointment for a patient on August 23 whom I would like to refer to your clinic for a four weeks stay. It is Mrs Galatzer, from in Wiener-Neustadt, who is the wife of a colleague, Dr Galatzer. He is a person who has got exceptionally far in his endeavours. He is a homeopath and yet with an inwardness of soul to a degree I have hardly ever seen in a doctor. He has a strong mystic nature which is now so advanced that he reads nothing but the Bible, and is able to cure many people through encouragement and speaking with them. At his side his wife could not keep up with her husband's aspirations and consequently has become physically ill. She suffers from an almost uncontrollable lethargy, and apart from that the whole lipometabolism and thus the whole Mars processes seem to be in complete disarray. I also believe there is inflammation in her right upper arm which causes increases in body temperature especially during the period and therefore increases the condition of illness. The most important thing for this patient seems to me to be emotional guidance of such a kind that she can gradually reclaim her own self. Her husband emphasizes that she needs to receive a lot of occupational therapy. Therefore I think that during the first two weeks at the clinic she should perhaps do painting and sculpture. Later on she could perhaps also do some practical work and help in Dr Hauschka's laboratory. Regarding medication you will best find out yourself what to do. Until now 'Graphite, Stibium and Calcium carbonicum' have worked well. I would ask you to write *immediately* directly to Mrs Galatzer whether she can come to Arlesheim on the date mentioned above. Please send the reply direct to the patient since I am going on holiday at the end of this week. Her address is: Mrs Galatzer, Wiener-Neustadt, Beethovengasse 14.

It was a real shock for me to hear that Dr Greil has died. This is the second friend who has recently been taken away from us.

I really hope to be able to attend the doctors' conference at Michaelmas and look forward to seeing you again. Please write to me concerning Mrs Gorge and Mrs Galatzer. In the meantime I remain, with kind regards,

Yours

Dr Karl König

Arlesheim, August 19, 1937

Dear Dr König,

I have received your last letter and thank you very much for it. Mrs Gorge has been here already. I believe her stay here in Dornach and everything spiritual she could experience through the mystery plays and eurythmy has done her a lot of good. She got over her migraine and was quite well when she came to see me. I think how you treated her was the right way. As a preventative when a migraine attack approaches, or at the very start of a migraine, we often inject Quartz D20 with Arnica WA D15. This combination works exceptionally well. Mrs Gorge could help herself with washings whenever her feet got cold and her head hot and a migraine was impending. Perhaps she will have to continue doing this. Of course it is vital to keep her enthusiasm for anthroposophy going which will help her to get over various things.

When the other patient arrives on August 25 I shall still be in England where I am going now for the summer school conference; but I shall be back on August 30.

Mrs Gericke is making extraordinary progress. She is gaining weight, sleeping well and is very happy and in her element here because she has opportunity to study anthroposophy busily and take curative eurythmy and painting lessons. Dr Helmi Burmeister, who already had a relationship to her through yourself, will take care of her during my absence.

I would be delighted if you came to the doctors' conference. I also would like to draw your attention to a lung remedy made from Petasites which, according to the results we have, should have a good effect. Perhaps you might try it too. We prepare Petasites in two ways: firstly following Dr Hauschka's WA D3 method using the whole plant and secondly an alcoholic extract which is not like our Hauschka remedies but still works well in certain cases. The latter shows good results in cases when tuberculosis has to be combated by the metabolism, the first one is good in cases when tuberculosis affects the head, therefore in more hardened cases. It seems as if the alcoholic essence very strongly draws out certain substances which have this particular effect on the metabolism. The experiments on this are not yet complete and I want to ask our medical examiners also to get involved in working with this remedy.* It would be wonderful if the outcome was something effective in combating tuberculosis. For this reason too a meeting of doctors is already needed to discuss these things in detail.

With kind regards also to your wife,

I. Wegman

* But I ask you to keep this quiet and regard it just as confidential information. We call this medicine Pneumonion.

den 8. November 1937.

Lieber Dr. König!

Für Ihren Brief danke ich sehr. Es war schade, dass Sie zur Aerzte-Zusammenkunft nicht kommen konnten. Wir konnten sehr schön miteinander arbeiten. Es war auch aus dem Grunde schade, dass Sie nicht da waren, weil Sie gewiss noch manches uns hätten sagen können. Manche Dinge sind bei uns doch ein wenig liegen geblieben durch die viele Arbeit, die wir immer hatten, auch dadurch, ass einige unserer Aerzte (durch die Verhältnisse verursacht) von uns haben weggehen müssen und neue nicht kommen konnten, sodass wir einen Mangel an Arbeitskräften hier haben. Momentan sind wir wieder sehr stark beschäftigt mit der Ausarbeitung des Krebsproblems und auch mit dem, was die Maschine noch für Geheimnisse in sich birgt. Es sind dabei schon sehr schöne Resultate herausgekommen, die wenn sie sich bewahrheiten, auch manchen Gebieten, hauptsächlich was die Wirkung auf das Pflanzenwachstum betrifft, von Bedeutung sein werden. Ueber diese Dinge wird jetzt viel gearbeitet. Ein abschliessendes Urteil kann darüber noch nicht da sein.

Dass Sie so schön arbeiten mit jungen Aerzten, freut mich ausserordentlich. Sie haben ja viel, wenn Sie alles das tun, was Sie mir in dem Brief geschrieben haben.

Mrs. Ronals ist schon einige Zeit hier und scheint sich gut bei uns einzuleben. Dass sie immer klagt, ist ja wohl wahr, aber das hängt ja sicher auch viel zusammen mit den Stauungen, die sie vom Bein aus hat, und so glaube ich doch, dass ich ihr allmählich auch das beibringen kann, was für sie wichtig ist.

Wie geht es Ihrer Frau und den Kindern? Ich hoffe gut.

Seien Sie mit Ihrer Familie herzlich gegrüsst

Ihre I. Wegman.

Arlesheim, November 8, 1937

Dear Dr König,

Thank you very much for your letter. It was a pity you could not come the doctors' meeting. We did some very good work together. It was also a pity you were not there because you could certainly have told us a few things. Some issues have been neglected a bit because of all the work we always had to do, also because some of our doctors (due to circumstances) had to leave us and new ones were not available so that there is a lack of colleagues here. At the moment we are again very busy studying the problem of cancer and also figuring out the workings of the machine [for mistletoe extracts]. We have already had very good results which, if they prove to be right, will be of importance for some areas, mainly regarding the effects on plant growth. A lot of work is now being done on these things. At this stage it is still too early for conclusions.

I am hugely delighted that you are working so well with young doctors. You will be really busy if you are doing everything you wrote about in your letter.

Mrs Ronals has been here quite a while now and seems to adjust well. It is true that she is always complaining but this surely also has a lot to do with the oedema in her leg, and so I am confident that I will be able to familiarize her with spirituality, which is important for her.

How are your wife and the children? I hope they are well.

Kindest regards to you and your family,

I. Wegman

Arlesheim, February 17, 1938

Dear Dr König,

Since it will soon again be spring I would like to remind you about our annexe in Ticino. It is beautiful weather there and soon the mimosas and camellias will also be in bloom again. We are sending you brochures of the annexes of our clinic and I would ask you to put them out in your waiting-room or hand them to this or that suitable patient. Within the short time we have been sending patients there, there has been a considerable rate of successful recoveries. As you know, the climate in Ticino is particularly healthy due to the combination of southern sun and quartz ground, the terrain there being outliers of Mount Gotthard.

Casa Andrea Cristoforo in Ascona is beautifully located, very well furnished and equipped and suitable for those who like a little comfort and who also need care. La Motta Farm in Brissago is much plainer yet homely, also very beautifully located and offers a wide range of opportunities for recreation and holidays. Both half-board and self-catering accommodation are available at La Motta Farm; fruit and vegetables can be bought at the big biodynamic garden on the premises. There is also a section for children who need recuperation or have developmental deficiencies. Dr Rudersdorff is the doctor there, he lives in Brissago on La Motta Farm and from there frequently visits Ascona.

I would also like to recommend our clinic and I would ask you to keep it in mind whenever you have patients in need of extensive treatment, occupational therapy, curative eurythmy, etc. It is such a pity that people from Germany are no longer able to come here for treatment.

You might also be interested to hear that there is now another annexe of our children's home in France. This was necessary because too many children were recently registered for whom there was not enough room in the Rue de l'Assomption. We also need suitable staff. So, if you know interested people who would want to be trained for this kind of work it would be good to do it now because times are getting ever more difficult, yet despite everything there are still some opportunities in France.

I hope your wife and the children are well! We had a good Christmas and the days after January 6 were also very good and inspiring.

With kind regards to you and your family

I. Wegman, MD

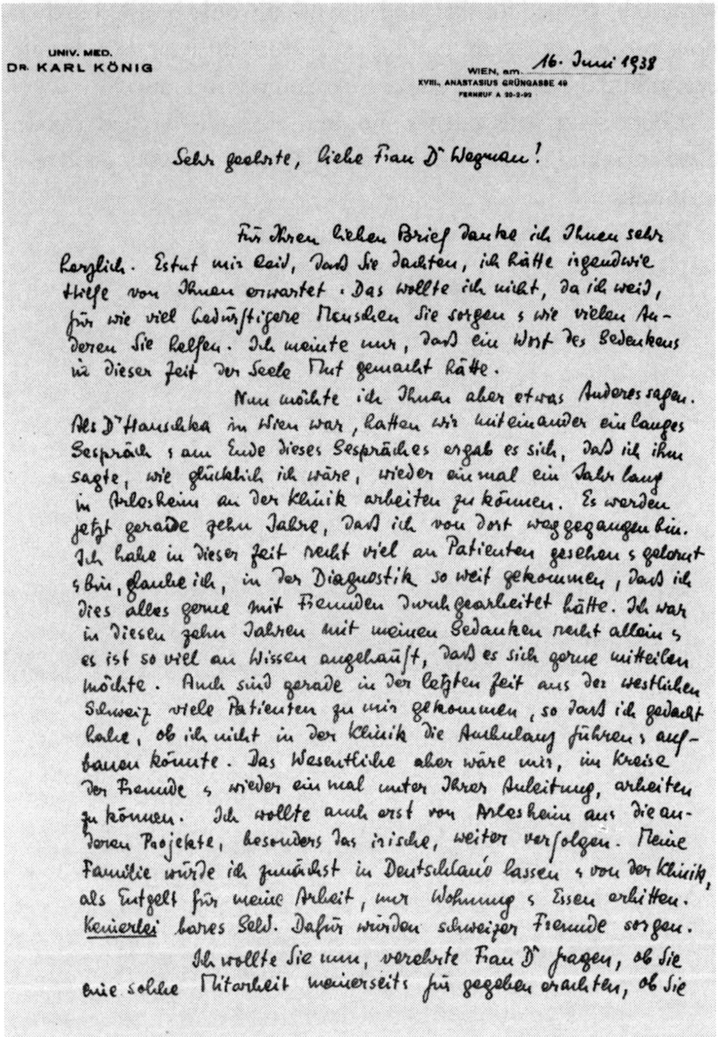

UNIV. MED.
DR. KARL KÖNIG

WIEN, am 16. Juni 1938
XVIII., ANASTASIUS GRÜNGASSE 40
FERNRUF A 20-2-92

Sehr geehrte, liebe Frau Dr Wegman!

Für Ihren lieben Brief danke ich Ihnen sehr herzlich. Es tut mir leid, daß Sie dachten, ich hätte irgendwie Hilfe von Ihnen erwartet. Das wollte ich nicht, da ich weiß, für wie viel bedürftigere Menschen Sie sorgen & wie vielen Anderen Sie helfen. Ich meinte nur, daß ein Wort des Gedenkens in dieser Zeit der Seele Mut gemacht hätte.

Nun möchte ich Ihnen aber etwas Anderes sagen. Als Dr Hauschka in Wien war, hatten wir miteinander ein langes Gespräch & am Ende dieses Gespräches ergab es sich, daß ich ihm sagte, wie glücklich ich wäre, wieder einmal ein Jahr lang in Arlesheim an der Klinik arbeiten zu können. Es werden jetzt gerade zehn Jahre, daß ich von dort weggegangen bin. Ich habe in dieser Zeit recht viel an Patienten gesehen & gelernt & bin, glaube ich, in der Diagnostik so weit gekommen, daß ich dies alles gerne mit Freunden durchgearbeitet hätte. Ich war in diesen zehn Jahren mit meinen Gedanken recht allein & es ist so viel an Wissen angehäuft, daß es sich gerne mitteilen möchte. Auch sind gerade in der letzten Zeit aus der westlichen Schweiz viele Patienten zu mir gekommen, so daß ich gedacht habe, ob ich nicht in der Klinik die Ambulanz führen & aufbauen könnte. Das Wesentliche aber wäre mir, im Kreise der Freunde & wieder einmal unter Ihrer Anleitung, arbeiten zu können. Ich wollte auch erst von Arlesheim aus die anderen Projekte, besonders das irische, weiter verfolgen. Meine Familie würde ich zunächst in Deutschland lassen & von der Klinik, als Entgelt für meine Arbeit, nur Wohnung & Essen erbitten. Keinerlei bares Geld. Dafür würden Schweizer Freunde sorgen.

Ich wollte Sie nun, verehrte Frau Dr fragen, ob Sie eine solche Mitarbeit meinerseits für gegeben erachten, ob Sie

Erledigt!

glauben, daß es gut wäre, mich für einige Zeit wieder in den Verband der Klinik aufzunehmen. Ich hätte schon sehr den Wunsch, ein Jahr lang ruhige Arbeit leisten zu können, vieles von dem, was in mir lebt mitzuteilen, vieles auch aufzuschreiben.

Falls Sie diesen Plan für gut halten, möchte ich ihn _bald_ zur Durchführung bringen, müßte Sie bitten, bei der Berner Fremdenpolizei für mich vorzusprechen. Näheres darüber steht in einem Brief an Dr Hauschka.

Ich wäre Ihnen für eine baldige Mitteilung Ihrer Stellungnahme dankbar

und verbleibe mit herzlichen Grüßen,

Ihr sehr ergebener

Dr Karl König

Vienna, June 16, 1938

Dear Dr Wegman,

Thank you very much for your kind letter. I am sorry you thought I somehow expected help from you. This was not my intention because I know how many people with much greater needs you care for and how many others you help. All I meant was that a word of sympathy in these times would have been encouraging.

But now I want to tell you something else. When Dr Hauschka was in Vienna we had a long conversation together and at the end of this conversation I happened to tell him how happy I would be if I could work again at the clinic in Arlesheim for a year. It is now ten years since I left that place. During this time I have seen many patients and have learnt quite a lot and I think I have reached a certain standard in diagnostics: I would like to discuss all this in depth with friends. During these ten years I have been rather alone with my ideas and have gathered so much knowledge that I would like to share this with others. In addition a lot of patients have recently come to me from west Switzerland, so that I have thought perhaps I could oversee and develop the outpatients' department of the clinic. It would be most important for me, however, to work once again with the friends and under your guidance. I would also like to watch from Arlesheim how the other projects are doing, particularly the one in Ireland. I would leave my family in Germany for the time being and in return for my work would ask the clinic only for accommodation and food. *No* cash. Swiss friends will take care of that.

I wanted to ask you now, dear Frau Doctor, if you think that there is such an opportunity, if you consider it a good idea to include me again for a while in the clinic community. I really would like to work for a year in peace and to write down and communicate much of what is on my mind.

If you approve of this idea I would like to turn it into reality *soon* and would need to ask you to speak to the immigration authorities in Berne on my behalf. There is more about this in a letter to Dr Hauschka.

I would be very grateful if you could tell me your opinion soon and remain with kind regards,

Yours faithfully

Dr Karl König

Arlesheim, den 12. Juli 1938.

Lieber Dr. König!

Ich habe durch Dr. Hauschka gehört und auch in Ihrem Brief sprechen Sie davon, dass Sie gern hierher zu uns kommen möchten. Da wir nur eine bestimmte Anzahl Aerzte hier haben können, weil das jetzt alles behördlich festgelegt ist, müsste ich natürlich Ihren Fall – so wie Sie vorschlagen, dass Sie ein halbes Jahr oder ein Jahr lang mit uns hier arbeiten wollen – den Behörden in Bern bekanntgeben. Dafür wird unser Rechtsanwalt Dr. Löw, der immer für uns diese Sachen regelt, bei den Behörden anfragen. Es ist dieses auch nur möglich, wenn wir Lösungen gefunden haben für Dr. Glas und Frau. Wenn dieses klargestellt werden kann den Behörden gegenüber, wird es wahrscheinlich keine grossen Schwierigkeiten geben, für Sie die Erlaubnis zu bekommen, hier eine Weile zu arbeiten, hauptsächlich wenn wir erklären können, dass Sie als wissenschaftlicher Mitarbeiter kommen wollen. Wir sind wirklich sehr daran, die Verhältnisse von Herrn und Frau Dr. Glas zu regeln, es wird uns dieses vielleicht auch gelingen. Die Schwierigkeit ist, dass Frau Dr. Glas selber noch nicht ganz geheilt ist und immer noch krank darniederliegt. Herr Dr. Elbogen ist jetzt mit Arbeitserlaubnis in England und die Schwester Clara Woedtke in Amerika, und diese werden schon Menschen wieder anziehen. Wir können nur soviel tun, wie uns behördlich erlaubt ist, auch ist es nur möglich, als vorübergehender Gast hier zu sein.

Ich schreibe Ihnen sofort wieder, sobald wir Nachricht haben. Sollte dieses so möglich sein, dann werden wir uns alle freuen, Sie wieder einmal in unserer Mitte zu haben.

Mit recht freundlichem Gruss

gez. Ihre I. Wegman
dr. med.

Arlesheim, July 12, 1938

Dear Dr König,

I have heard from Dr Hauschka and you too tell me in your letter that you would like to come here. As we can only have a certain number of doctors here because everything is now officially regulated I would of course have to notify the authorities in Berne of your case -- that you suggest working with us here for half a year or a year. Regarding this our lawyer Dr Löw who deals with these issues on our behalf will make enquiries with the authorities. Additionally it will only be possible if we find a solution for Dr Glas and his wife. If this issue can be clarified with the authorities there are unlikely to be any major problems getting permission for you to work here for a while, especially if we can make it clear that you want to come as a scientific colleague. We are really trying very hard to sort out Mr and Mrs Glas's situation which perhaps we will manage to do. The problem is that Dr [Maria] Glas is not yet back to full health and still lying ill. Dr Elbogen is now in England with a work permit; Sister Clara Woedtke in America, and I am sure they will again attract people. We can only do as much as the authorities allow us; in any case, you can only come here as a temporary guest.

I shall write to you as soon as we know. Should it be possible we shall all be very pleased for you to rejoin us.

With kind regards,

I. Wegman, MD

Arlesheim, November 28, 1938

Dear Dr König,

I have not received any news from you for a long time. It seems as if your stay in Paris is not going as smoothly as we all assumed. If you still do not have your *Carte d'Identité* I would ask you to try to see the journalist Jules Sauerwein. According to what I have heard and what I personally know about him this Jules Sauerwein seems to be a friend of the French Foreign Minister Bonnet. I have now written a letter to Jules Sauerwein, with whom I am on good terms, asking him if he could do something for you. If I am not mistaken you once told me that Baroness von Bonstetten also knows Foreign Minister Bonnet and this way had secured a visa for you. Perhaps these two connections, Jules Sauerwein and Bonstetten, can help you obtain permission via Bonnet. So, find out if Jules Sauerwein is around and if he can see you. His private address is Paris, rue Jean Goujon 24; and if he is not there — you should try in the morning or in the evening — then he will be in his office at *Paris Soir,* I think the telephone number is Elysée 70 03, but you can probably find out there.

Yesterday George Kaufmann was here and perhaps you talked to him there as well. He wanted to try talking in Paris to Mr Salomon, who has connections to Montpellier, to see if it would be possible to let some refugees stay there. And there is also an urgent request from the engineer Mr Regenstreif; Kaufmann visited him in Vienna and of course he is very much in danger too. There is an astrological society in France, unfortunately I do not have the address but perhaps Alexander Noir's father — Sister Vala knows who that is — knows something and can provide some information.

I am very keen to hear Dr van Deventer's news when she comes home tomorrow. You wrote that you were a bit disappointed with the French. This is a valid point of view but it would be a pity if spiritual work could not be carried out in

France. In that case the situation in France would deteriorate rapidly and Europe too will perish because I have no trust — although George Kaufmann said something different — that England will then help Europe. I rather have the feeling that a close alliance between England and America will form, and that this will be the end of Europe.

With kind regards,

I. Wegman

Arlesheim, January 11, 1939

Dear Dr König,

Many thanks for your long and interesting letter. I have read it all with great interest and think that it is definitely the right thing to do, the way you want to go about it now. Since the Haughtons take so much interest in medicine and have shown so much good will you should not reject this course of destiny. I have seen the house next to the church myself, it certainly has potential for something good. Hopefully you will find enough young people for the work because of course this is what needs to be done first.

Of course I feel very sorry that you cannot commit yourself to the project in Paris, but after all people in Paris are becoming increasingly narrow-minded and nobody knows what will happen there, whereas Scotland's island location provides more safety. Given the circumstances, whether the house at the Rue de l'Assomption can be kept is of course a question which I cannot answer straight away. It is a financial problem and because no-one in France can raise money and because the house cannot be kept, the work will one day have to change; instead of the house at the Rue de l'Assomption a small studio could be rented and turned into a small centre for curative education with lodgings so that Courcelles is not left completely on its own. Time will slowly tell how these things need to be taken further.

That you are going to come to Paris in February and also here will give us great joy. I can well imagine that the projects in Scotland and in France can support each other effectively but I do think that you need to pass the exam before you set about this grand plan. Again and again I see how serious are the consequences of Dr Nunhöfer and also Dr Engel not having passed the exam; Nunhöfer because he tried many times and always failed and Engel because he does not have the financial means, and also because people thought that Nunhöfer should do it first. For this reason Kent Terrace is now represented by doctors who in the long run will not be regarded as qualified because they have not passed the English exam. I could so well experience this when an English doctor, Dr Ellis, came here recently and discussed the situation with me. English doctors are a bit petty because they fear for their reputation — you can be struck off the list right away if you work with unapproved doctors — yet this is a fact we need to keep in mind. The future of these two gentlemen is thus a concern for them and activities in Kent Terrace are also at risk. But perhaps your activities can bring many things back to life and your powerful energies also inspire others to work harder. Most often the cause for failure is a lack of effort.

I am pleased that your wife and your children are in England already, that is one big concern off your mind.

We had a good Christmas here. We are doing well although there is a strong sense of restriction because people are not free to go where they want. At Christmas a few German friends were here but not nearly enough, there is too much fear.

With kind regards also to your wife, and to Mr and Mrs Haughton when you go there and to the Glas's when you are in London.

Yours,

I. Wegman

Arlesheim, August 19, 1939

Dear Dr König,

We were all very pleased that the friends finally got their official permission to go to Scotland. Now Miss Blau and Miss Potlitzer will leave from here soon — I have already informed Mr Haughton in writing. Miss Blau is very able as a curative education assistant; Miss Potlitzer is capable in every way and will be a good support for all initial work. Regarding Miss Lissau we have done the following. When her residence permit came to an end and her situation became desperate we did everything to help her extend it. She has not yet completed her training, especially in music which is her main field. So we offered the authorities a surety of 3000 Swiss francs to keep her here, and this, we have been told, will probably be approved. And since Miss Lissau herself would first like to finish her training we would really appreciate it if she could stay here for the time being. We can always see later what will be done about her because we do not know whether this residence permit is valid indefinitely or only for a certain period of time.

Mr Schauder, as you probably know, became ill again, he is in Ascona and I believe already getting better. He is frail, but will possibly be healthier when he can live in a more settled situation and without worry about his future and when the separation from Miss Schwab is also over. Mr Amann is in Paris and is very capable, I think he will also be a great help to you. I do not know much about the others on your list.

I hope, dear Dr König, that you and your family are well. I have heard about you from time to time and was hoping to see you at the summer school. Unfortunately something happened I had not thought of. Because the summer school started so early the two Swiss doctors, Dr Kaelin and Dr Marti, were still on holiday; so I could not leave because complications might have arisen which were better avoided.

At the moment Dr Ungar, who also wants to leave Vienna, is

here too; and at any time we are expecting Mr Regenstreif who will probably also go to England. So one by one you will have all your old friends in England.

On my journey to the East — I went to the Black Sea — I passed through Vienna. This Vienna was a very sorry sight to see. It was as if people were unable to recover from the blow they had been dealt. The people on the street did not seem to be quite there and those who were a bit more cheerful were foreigners or Germans. On the whole you had the impression of a culture that was already dead, independently of what Hitler had done.

Further East it was a different picture. There was a sense of something youthful, vigorous, which had not yet taken shape. How important it would be to bring anthroposophy to these places in the East and to empower people there. Just now they are looking around, at one time they believe that strength and support will come from England, another time they desperately look towards Germany or Russia, or even Turkey, because they do not feel spiritually strong enough to withstand the brunt of those forces.

Yugoslavia is mostly Roman Catholic and Bulgaria is mostly Greek Catholic [Orthodox]. The latter has something of Russia, of Russian spirituality I mean, very appealing and very spiritual. At the Black Sea I could experience much of importance, giving me a clear idea of historical events which took place there. Visiting historical sites definitely helps one to understand many things which happened in the past.

I was also in Germany, and something strange is going on there: a decline and at the same time a steep rise in spirituality. Many people are ready for anthroposophy and actively involved in it. There is a lot of understanding for spirituality, yet not a calm, contemplative understanding. It is rather reckless and thrives on demolishing and knocking over everything, although there are no achievements of their own whatsoever. They demonstrate their powers by pushing over everything, knocking down many buildings and replacing them with new ones which are no different; they are not built in a new architectural style which would indicate some progress. Nothing changes but there is a lot of stir, and this stir is expressed by the demolishing of whole streets and quarters. You can talk to some of them and point out to them the effects of spirituality which can be found everywhere; then they might listen, agree to some points and demonstrate briskness and a thirst for action. What is overly structured in England is still completely lacking in shape in the East; and in Central Europe they are breaking the old structures without having anything new to build.

That is how the world looks. If the leading powers were any wiser they would understand it and would reach out to each other and a lot would happen for the benefit of mankind. Unfortunately ignorance prevails, not the intention to be a bit more tolerant towards others. As a result we are in a very difficult situation, and any moment this tension can trigger an outburst. Europe will then be lost. Even so I am still hopeful that it will not come to that. England should be very watchful and look eastwards because the greatest danger will certainly come from there. If they do not succeed in sorting out the East, it will act as a bridge for the Mongols coming over to Europe; this again will be another, perhaps equally great danger.

Well, in Scotland perhaps you will be able to work in peace. Mr and Mrs Haughton have always said that if there is any war it will not reach the North of Britain. So now you have the opportunity to work intensively and constructively. I hear you are already studying. When will you pass the exam?

I would be really glad if you could write to me, if you have the time. Now that things are taking shape you perhaps also have something to write about which might be of interest for me as well.

Kind regards to you, your wife and the children,

I. Wegman

Arlesheim, January 18, 1940

Dear Dr König,

I was really glad about the letter you wrote to me on December 31. What you have achieved over the last year is already a lot and certainly gives reason to be very pleased. You also write that you want to leave Kirkton House because there is no electric light. Have you found a suitable home yet? I hope you will find something good. Certainly it is more convenient if you do not live too far away from each other. I really hope there will be no breakup with Williamston, that would a be real pity because we rely on each other for our progress.

Liesel Schwalb and Dr Schauder will also be able to leave Ticino soon. Both have recovered well, and he has got much stronger than he was. Miss Lissau whom you would like to have in Scotland has still not received her visa for France, this has become extraordinarily difficult recently, but it will come one day if she is just patient enough. We are really sorry to lose Miss Lissau, she is excellent at music, but for her future it is better that she moves to Scotland.

For the year 1940 I wish you and everyone in Kirkton House and the convalescent home all the best. I hope your wife and the children are well. Mr and Mr Haughton too are always asking me if I could once again come to Scotland, and I hope to do so as soon as an opportunity again arises. Even people from neutral countries cannot now get visas except for family circumstances or in case of an emergency for which you need to give reasons. So we just need to wait quietly until the war is over.

You ask about our work and how I am doing personally. The work continues despite the difficulties but of course there are a lot of restrictions. Especially Arlesheim experienced this because the inflow of foreigners came to a stop. In many ways we had to cut back on things. To some extent this was of benefit for the work, because it was easier for us to oversee what needed to be done; this had often been difficult recently with everything developing more and more. But something else became evident, namely that in the south, in Ascona and Brissago, things got livelier because the climate and the beautiful location attracts a lot of people. On the whole we are still complete, only a few friends have left. Personally I am well, although still affected by my accident — a complicated fracture of my left arm. I still do not have full movement of the arm and it may never come back completely. After the wire that kept the bones in place was removed the bones moved apart again, and I was where I had been before the operation; this makes the healing of the fracture very difficult. I was in Ascona for a longer time, and will also go back because work is easier there, while here I am always very much caught up in duties. I am convinced that here in Switzerland we will be able to continue working well.

It is a question whether America at the present time stands open to us; I do not think that this is the case. It is also the human issue which plays a part. Kolisko's death has left a huge gap because I always hoped he would be the right person for America. I do not see real opportunities in America, although I have some friends there who would gladly help if something could be done. I have also often thought of British Columbia, I even had a kind of vision of the actual house (a nice clinic on a hill). But that may have been pure imagination.

You accuse me of not sending any messages or advice or instructions for the hard work you are doing there. But dear Dr König, how could I possibly do so? That is something which cannot be done from here. In new situations like this when you have to build relationships with people you do not know very well, things keep changing rapidly. The situation today can have completely changed by tomorrow. I rather had the feeling that you should be left to get on with things because you have always been considerate and tactful enough to solve any difficult situations. So please do not begrudge me for not having written very often. Be assured that I will always remain connected to your work. I am also very closely connected to everyone who is with you now. The clinic is also very connected with you and the work you are doing over there.

Kind regards to you and please give my regards also to your wife, my godchild Renate and the other children as well.

Yours,

I. Wegman

14.April 1940.

Sehr geehrte Frau Dr.Wegmann!

Anbei übersende ich Ihnen einen Brief, den ich vor zwei Tagen von Frl.Lissau bekommen habe. Ich muss sagen, dass ich mehr als erstaunt bin, dass nach monatelangem Warten Frl.Lissau plötzlich die Idee bekommt, nicht mehr zu kommen, mit dem Hinweis, dass Sie dafür waren, jetzt Leierkonzerte zu geben und dass Sie das für wichtiger halten, als die Heileurythmie für die kranken Kinder. Wir haben durch die Güte eines englischen Vaters, ein sehr grosses Haus in der Nähe von Aberdeen zur Verfügung gestellt bekommen und übersiedeln Ende Mai dorthin. Wir beginnen unsere Arbeit dort mit zwölf Kindern und ich habe absolut sicher mit dem Kommen von Frl.Lissau gerechnet. Sie wissen genau, oder können es sich vielleicht vorstellen, welche Mühe und Not uns die Beschaffung des Permits gekostet hat. Wir brauchen dringenst eine Heileurythmistin und Sie wissen, wie ~~dringend~~ notwendig die Heileurythmie für die Heilpädagogik ist. Ich habe keine Lust es hier so wie in Clent zu machen, wo seit Jahren ohne Heileurythmie gearbeitet wird. Die Beschaffung des französischen Durchreisevisums wäre bestimmt möglich gewesen, wenn Frl.Lissau sich genügend darum bemüht hätte; scheinbar glaubte sie damit das Kommen nach Schottland unmöglich zu machen. Ich möchte nun Sie sehr dringend bitten, uns einen Ersatz zu geben. Es ist so, dass uns nun von allen Seiten und speziell von den öffentlichen Behörden und Universitäten ausserordentlich entgegengekommen wird und unserer Arbeit viel Interesse entgegengebracht wird und es ist deshalb notwendig, dass wir diese Arbeit in einem vollen und zufrieden-stellenden Masse ausführen. Dazu ist die Heileurythmie und die am Sonnenhof entwickelte Musik notwendig. Ich kann nicht verstehen, dass man uns in dieser Hinsicht so in Stich lässt und ich appelliere hiemit an Sie, diese Situation in irgendeiner Art zu klären.

Ich habe Ihnen noch für Ihren lieben Brief vom Januar zu danken. In der letzten Woche ist der Kaufvertrag geschlossen worden und wir werden Ende Mai ~~dorthin~~ übersiedeln. Es ist ein grosses Haus mit zwei Kleineren, mit je vier Zimmern, inmitten eines 22 acres grossen Garten, mit einem schönem Gemüse- und Obstgarten, zwei Feldern und vielen Ställen und Nebengebäuden, in denen alles das, was wir zur Arbeit brauchen, auf das vorzüglichste entwickelt werden kann. Ich bin sehr froh, dass innerhalb eines Jahres dieser Fortschritt schon gelungen ist und es ist für mich ganz erstaunlich, welches Interesse, wie ich schon erwähnte, uns gerade von offizieller Seite entgegengebracht wird. Deshalb sind die Möglichkeiten ausserordentliche, aber die Anforderungen auf der anderen Seite sind ebenso grosse und ich möchte in dieser Hinsicht nichts versäumen. Ich ersuche Sie nocheinmal, uns mit der Heileurythmie nicht in Stich zu lassen und hoffe, dass es Ihnen gelingen wird, einen Ersatz zu finden.

Ich hoffe, dass es Ihnen gut geht und dass Ihr Arm allmählich verheilt ist.

Mit vielen herzlichen Grüssen
bin ich Ihr sehr ergebener

Karl König

April 14, 1940

Dear Dr Wegman,

I enclose for you a letter from Miss Lissau which I received two days ago. I have to say that I find it more than astonishing that after months of waiting it suddenly occurs to Miss Lissau not to come any more, and that she refers to your approval of now giving lyre concerts and that you think this more important than curative eurythmy for ill children. Due to the kindness of an British father, a very big house near Aberdeen has been made available for us und we will move there at the end of May. We will start work there with twelve children and I was absolutely confident that Miss Lissau would come. You know very well or can perhaps imagine how difficult it was for us to get the permit. We are in most urgent need of a curative eurythmist, and you know how vital curative eurythmy is for curative education. I am not keen on doing things like in Clent where they have been working year after year without curative eurythmy. Miss Lissau could certainly have obtained a French transit visa if her efforts had been serious enough; she seemingly believed that this would make it impossible to come to Scotland. I would now ask you urgently to send us a replacement. The fact is that there is extraordinary good will towards us from all sides, especially from the authorities and the universities, and our work is met with a lot of interest. We therefore need to do this work to a full and satisfactory extent. Curative eurythmy and the music developed at the Sonnenhof is necessary for this. I cannot understand that we are being let down so much in this respect and I appeal to you in some way to clarify the situation.

I must still thank you for your kind letter from January. Last week the purchase contract was signed and we will move at the end of May. It is a big house and two smaller ones with four rooms each in the middle of 22-acre grounds with a beautiful fruit and vegetable garden, two fields and a number of stables and outhouses. They are ideal for setting up everything we need for our work. I am really glad that this progress could be made within a year and am quite surprised — as I mentioned before — about the interest which even the authorities are taking in our work. That means there are excellent opportunities and on the other hand equally great challenges, and in this regard I do not want to miss anything. Regarding curative eurythmy I would ask you again not to leave us out in the cold, and hope you will be able to find a replacement.

I hope you are well and that your arm has gradually healed.

With kind regards I remain

yours faithfully

Dr Karl König

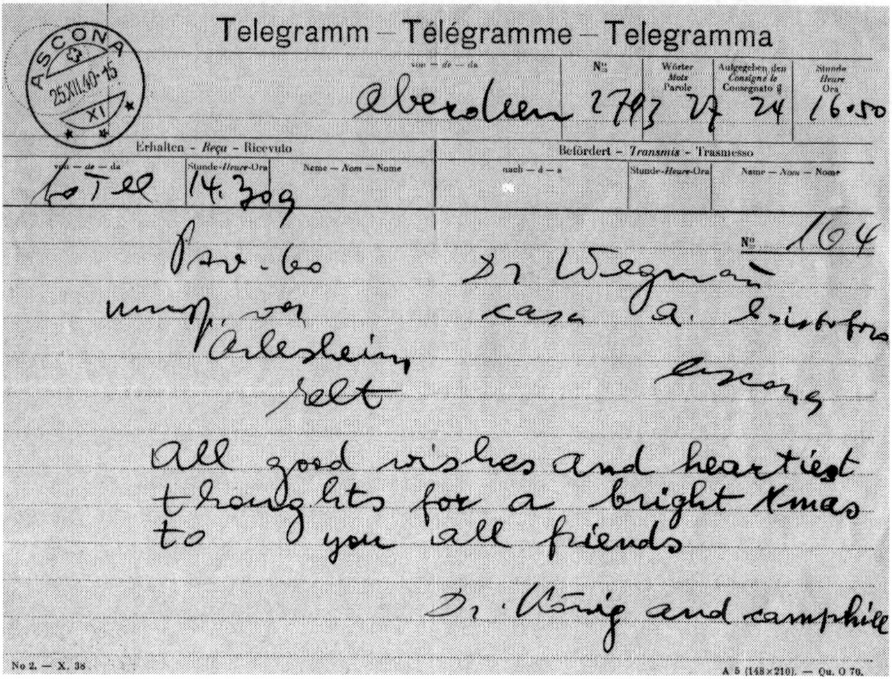

Telegramm – Télégramme – Telegramma

ASCONA 25.XII.40-15 XI

von – de – da: Aberdeen | Nº 2793 | Wörter – Mots – Parole: 27 | Aufgegeben den – Consigné le – Consegnato il: 24 | Stunde – Heure – Ora: 16.50

Erhalten – Reçu – Ricevuto | Befördert – Transmis – Trasmesso

Nº 164

Dr Wegman
casa S. Cristoforo
Ascona

All good wishes and heartiest
thoughts for a bright Xmas
to you all friends

Dr. König and camphill

No 2. — X. 38 A 5 (148×210). — Qu. O 70.

Telegram

Aberdeen, No. 2793, 27 words, sent 24 [Dec 1940] 16.50 hours

Dr Wegman, Casa A. Cristoforo, Ascona

All good wishes and heartiest thoughts for a bright Xmas to you all friends

Dr König and Camphill

9th. June, 1941.

Dear Dr. König,

It is quite a long time since I heard from you though I see by the News Sheet that the Home and lectures go on quite actively, but I am always glad to hear and should like also to know if Lehrs and Roeschl are both with you? It is difficult to make a true picture of the work for oneself when letters and news are so scarce. The News Sheet speaks of the work but cannot of course give the details one would so gladly hear and in any case it is not possible in these times to write of those things which lie deep at heart. So you must understand in the same way when you do not hear so often from me for it does not in any way mean that you are not, all of you, frequently in my thoughts, and I long for the time when all the present time barriers are away and we may again have free intercourse with each other.

How is your wife and family? I am especially curious to know how my god-child   is developing and whether she goes to an English school? How are all the former students and workers from the Clinic and Sonnenhof at Arlesheim? Potlitzer, Blau and others.

I am glad to be able to say that up to the present the work here goes on. We have reduced the Clinic and Sonnenhof and have our Dépendance in the South and there I mainly carry on the work though now and again goin between the two. The climate suits me much better and that is one reason why we decided to have some doctors at Arlesheim and somemaere. here. Then there are quite a good number of children at Brissago.

Please remember me kindly to all our friends when and where you may meet them and assure them of our constant remembrances and hopes for their welfare. With heartiest greetings to yourself and family,

Yours sincerely,

June 9, 1941

Dear Dr König,

It is quite a long time since I heard from you though I see by the News Sheet that the Home and lectures go on quite actively, but I am always glad to hear and should like also to know if Lehrs and Roeschl are both with you? It is difficult to make a true picture of the work for oneself when letters and news are so scarce. The News Sheet speaks of the work but cannot of course give the details one would so gladly hear and in any case it is not possible in these times to write of those things which lie deep at heart. So you must understand in the same way when you do not hear so often from me for it does not in any way mean that you are not, all of you, frequently in my thoughts, and I long for the time when all the present[-]time barriers are away and we may again have free intercourse with each other.

How is your wife and family? I am especially curious to know how my god-child is developing and whether she goes to an English school? How are all the former students and workers from the Clinic and Sonnenhof at Arlesheim? Potlitzer, Blau and others.

I am glad to be able to say that up to the present the work here goes on. We have reduced the Clinic at Sonnenhof and have our Dépendance [annexe] in the South and there I mainly carry on the work though now and again going between the two. The climate suits me much better and that is one reason why we decided to have some doctors at Arlesheim and some here. Then there are quite a good number of children at Brissago.

Please remember me kindly to all our friends when and where you may meet them and assure them of our constant remembrances and hopes for their welfare. With heartiest greetings to yourself and family,

Yours sincerely

Ita Wegman

TEL. CULTER 214.

CAMPHILL,
MILLTIMBER,
ABERDEENSHIRE.

July 15th,1941

Dear Dr. Wegman,

you can hardly imagine what joy we all felt when your letter arrived. I had just returned from London where I attended the General Meeting and gave two lectures. There I heard that everything is going well, but it was back here in Camphill where I received your letter that I felt relief. I was so glad that you were able to take over a second house and that things are developing in spite of the grave times.

We have now been in Camphill a year. It is a beautiful estate 7 miles from Aberdeen in a wonderful river valley. We have three houses, one big and two small. The Community is working the land and the garden and everything which makes us more or less self-supporting. We now have about 20 children of various types. They are not very backward and through this, our work is extremely satisfactory. Our connection with the outer world is a strong one. We had a very good Whitsuntide Conference here with 130 people in the lectures which were held by Dr. and Mrs. Lehrs and myself. The Lehrs are now in Aberdeen where they have opened up a centre with lectures and classes. We are also in close touch with the Educational Department which shows great interest in our work, and hardly a day passes without visitors who are impressed by our methods and especially the manner of our Community living.

I am glad to say that my family is very well. Renate is developing wonderfully. She does a lot of painting and drawing and is especially gifted in that way. The others are also very well and Mrs. König acts as matron and does a lot of wonderful work. All my helpers are full of enthusiasm. Miss Blau married Mr. Amann three weeks ago. Miss Potlitzer works in our guest-house 2 miles from Camphill. This house will, in Autumn, be turned into a home for difficult and backward girls over 14 years of age.

Because of all the work there is to do, I was until now not able to sit my examinations but think I shall start them in October.

I was very glad to hear that you are better and that the climate in Ascona suits you more that it does in Arlesheim. Please give our kindest regards to all your friends and helpers, and we all send you our love and confidence and inmost feeling with you and your work.

With heartiest greetings,

I am,

yours ever,

Karl König

Camphill, July 15, 1941

Dear Dr Wegman,

you can hardly imagine what joy we all felt when your letter arrived. I had just returned from London where I attended the [Annual] General Meeting and gave two lectures. There I heard that everything is going well, but it was back here in Camphill where I received your letter that I felt relief. I was so glad that you were able to take over a second house and that things are developing in spite of the grave times.

We have now been in Camphill a year. It is a beautiful estate 7 miles from Aberdeen in a wonderful river valley. We have three houses, one big and two small. The Community is working the land and the garden and everything which makes us more or less self-supporting. We now have about 20 children of various types. They are not very backward and through this, our work is extremely satisfactory. Our connection with the outer world is a strong one. We had a very good Whitsuntide Conference here with 130 people in the lectures which were held by Dr and Mrs Lehrs and myself. The Lehrs are now in Aberdeen where they have opened up a centre with lectures and classes. We are also in close touch with the Educational Department which shows great interest in our work, and hardly a day passes without visitors who are impressed by our methods and especially the manner of our Community living.

I am glad to say that my family is very well. Renate is developing wonderfully. She does a lot of painting and drawing and is especially gifted in that way. The others are also very well and Mrs König acts as matron and does a lot of wonderful work. All my helpers are full of enthusiasm. Miss Blau married Mr Amann three weeks ago, Miss Potlitzer works in our guest-house 2 miles from Camphill. This house will, in Autumn, be turned into a home for difficult and backward girls over 14 years of age.

Because of all the work there is to do, I was until now not able to sit my examinations but think I shall start them in October.

I was very glad to hear that you are better and that the climate in Ascona suits you more than it does in Arlesheim. Please give our kindest regards to all your friends and helpers, and we all send you our love and confidence and inmost feeling with you and your work.

With heartiest greetings,
I am, yours ever,
Karl König

3

Karl König: Memories of Ita Wegman

March 17, 1960[1]

She was queenly, and yet she radiated a deep brotherliness.

Ita Wegman, Sonnenhof in 1927

Do not assume that she was intelligent, she was wise.

It is a great privilege to have the opportunity after so many years to say a few words about Ita Wegman. Tomorrow it will be seventeen years since she passed through the gateway of death. It happened during the Second World War und those who could be with her during her last days of her life have described how deeply affected and worried she was almost until her last hours about what was going on in the world at this time. She was always concerned about the historical aspects of her time and she was a person who immersed herself into the events around her regardless whether she was immediately affected or not. She was of a strikingly open-hearted nature.

It is not difficult to describe Ita Wegman, especially if, like me, one had the privilege of meeting her in person, of travelling with her, of talking to her and of living near her. Of course you can look at a person from many angles. But what strikes me today as most exceptional when I try to remember some of the more important experiences of her, is that I can only say I never met a person who was so queenlike. She had a really queenly character! That does not mean that she was unapproachable, distanced or indifferent to the needs and the events of her time. She was queenly, and yet she radiated a deep brotherliness. As far as she was concerned everyone was equal. Whether she was occupied with a handicapped child, a screaming lunatic, a Prussian general or an English earl, a young doctor or a medical student, a nurse, a gardener or a beggar — to everyone she spoke in the same way: like a sister to her brother. And yet she was queenly and lived with a certain style.

I well remember the day on which I met her for the first time. It was an evening in September 1927 in Vienna when she arrived at the station to attend the funeral of Rudolf Steiner's sister. On the platform there was a group of doctors and very distinguished anthroposophists to welcome her (at this time she was still a member of the Executive Board of the Anthroposophical Society), and then she stepped off the train — in my mind's eye I can still see her: tall and with a powerful radiance. I think four or five people were in her company. She had style, you know, but it was a beautifully plain and natural style. Wherever she went she was naturally the focus of attention. For example, whenever she was in a restaurant in the company of other people, the waiter, without knowing anybody, always addressed her first. It was always like that.

I mention this because I feel that we need to understand this first before we can form an initial idea of the special nature of this person who was so natural, so straightforward and utterly kind to everyone. She radiated brotherliness, but in herself she was really a 'queen' — but a very kind queen. Every time I met her the words *homo sum* came to my mind; because this feeling emanated from her and one could experience it. She could be affectionate, full of love and devotion and concerned for everyone who was in trouble. She would listen to everybody who told her of their problems. When she listened she put aside everything she had on her mind before or after; she was completely there for that single person. But she could also become very angry, she could scream and cry in desperation. *Homo sum* — the essence of being human — queenly and at the same time brotherly to everyone.

The Clinical Therapeutic Institute in Arlesheim was not particularly striking nor notably big. But when you entered it and lived there for months and years, as I had the opportunity to do, you felt like at a prince's court. Hundreds of people came and went, there were telephone calls from all over the world, telegrams, letters, patients, attachés, attendants. It was very lively with comings and goings, but permeated by a deep sense of humanity. As a young person you were trustingly included, and you felt accepted as a friend.

Never will I forget my first Christmas at Arlesheim in 1927. A few weeks before Christmas Ita Wegman came to me and said, 'König, I think you should hold a keynote lecture at the Goetheanum.'

I replied, 'But Frau Doctor, I have never held a lecture before.'

And she said, 'But you will be able to do it, you will be able to do it.'

And that's what happened. She told me, 'I will accompany you to the lecture, take you to the room, show you the lectern from where you will speak and will sit in front of you, and everything will be fine.'

And with the protection of her presence it all went very well.

This spirit of brotherliness which she extended to all people also influenced her therapeutic work. This [work] was outstanding as she was without doubt the best doctor I have ever met. Do not assume that she was intelligent, she was wise. In one or other way she used everything in order to heal; a medicine, a strong phrase, a loving glance, a piece of music, a painting, a walk in the countryside, she made use of whatever was available. She was not like those doctors who use a medication and perhaps an ointment and nothing else, because their understanding of medicine has become so narrow. They have forgotten that the whole world, if you have the right attitude towards it, is therapeutic. Ita Wegman saw the same spirit of brotherliness in everything that was alive, that had a soul and a spirit — and she made use of it in order to heal.

She had a remarkable life. She was born in Java [now Indonesia] in 1876, her parents were Dutch. She grew up in affluence, in freedom, amid the wonders of tropical nature — certainly this was one of the reasons for her queenlike appearance. For six months she lived very close to Rudolf Steiner: during his illness from September 28, 1924 until his death on March 30, 1925. She was his personal physician and companion, she cared for him. And yet for her it was a matter of course to live during this time in a wooden hut, utterly without comfort, with just an iron bedstead.

After Rudolf Steiner's death her qualities unfolded in the most amazing way; it was as if a flower opened and blossomed. Yet she encountered a lot of misunderstandings, misjudgments and ill will which were the cause for her gradual withdrawal from what was going on within the Anthroposophical Society. But again she withdrew in style: an example to everyone around her, how she tried to resolve all grievances. To be able to see what is positive in those who had hurt her so much was always her greatest wish.

She died — for someone as queenly as her — in utter solitude, only a few people kept her company. Her true friends in Germany, the Netherlands, America and England could not be with her because of the war. Thus she was completely isolated. Yet — according to the friends who were with her — at the other side of the gateway she was surrounded by many and received into the light of the Spirit-Sun.

Appendix

Karl König's Letter to Thomas Weihs
October 24, 1940

Camphill-House
Milltimber
Aberdeenshire
24. Oktober 1940

Mein lieber Thomas!

Es ist lange, daß ich nicht an Euch alle geschrieben habe, aber es ist die Zeit so kurz für alle Arbeit, die zu tun ist, daß es wirklich schwer fällt, eine ruhige Stunde zu finden.

Vor allem: Ich bin sehr glücklich über das, was sich mit Ihnen vollzogen hat. Der Tag, an dem ich ihren Brief bekommen habe, war ein von Sonne & Glück überstrahlter, weil ich es lange nicht zu hoffen wagte & dann hat es sich <u>doch</u> vollzogen! So ist es mir, wie auch Ihnen eine Art Schicksals-Krönung, die zum Guten führen soll. Zum Guten für Sie & auch für unsere Gemeinschaft, die jetzt fester gebaut ist, seit nicht nur Hans & Peter, sondern nun auch Sie diesen klaren Entschluß zu einem bestimmten Weg gefaßt haben. So umarme ich Sie & begrüße Sie neu mit aller Liebe & Freundschaft.

Ich versuche Tag um Tag mit Euch zu leben & Euch bei aller Arbeit, die hier geschieht, dabei zu haben. Die Hauptarbeit ist jetzt im Garten & draußen überhaupt. Ich bin jetzt

vor allem Gartenarbeiter, Knecht & Haus-
diener. Vor allem habe ich die von Mr. Gill
abundant vorhandenen Misthaufen auf-
geräumt, habe mit den Kindern viel Holz
gesammelt & für den Winter vorbereitet.
Dann sind im Garten viele Beete nicht nur
umzugraben, sondern auch zu roden, da
vieles seit Jahren vernachlässigt war. Ich
habe viel Bäume & Sträucher herausge-
nommen, die alt & unbrauchbar waren,
habe die Geräte halbwegs in Ordnung ge-
bracht & manches im Haus getan.

Jetzt ist auch die Zentralheizung in
Gang gebracht, der Keller geordnet, Kohle
& Anthrazit gesondert & hergerichtet.
Heute sind auch die Stiegen & Gang-
teppiche gelegt worden & gestern das Lino-
leum im Cottage. Dort sieht es schon sehr
schön aus. Sagen Sie Peter, daß ich seine
Bücher geordnet habe & daß sie sehr auf
ihn warten.

Am Montag haben wir Kartoffel-Ernte
gehabt & alles in einem Tag hereingebracht.
In der Frühdämmerung um 7h standen die
Pferde vom Farmer am Pflug, dampfend im
zarten Nebel & wir alle waren mit den Kin-
dern draußen & haben Furche auf Furche
ausgenommen. Das obere Feld hat einen
recht guten Ertrag gegeben, das untere
fast gar keinen. Dieses Feld muß vollständig

umgearbeitet & reichlich gedüngt werden für das nächste Jahr.

Daneben läuft alles andere, die Verhandlungen mit dem Comité in Aberdeen & die vielen Versuche für Eure release. Morgen geht endlich das Gesuch für Sie & Peter zu Miss Mackinnon & zu Miss Osmond & ich hoffe, dass es sehr schnell zur Erledigung kommen wird. Es sind so viel als möglich Beilagen & Zertifikate & ich bin eigentlich ganz überzeugt, dass es günstig entschieden wird! Bitte seid in dieser Beziehung ganz ruhig.

Vor zwei Wochen, Thomas, war ich bei Henny & Cheilin. Es war sehr schön & gut. Cheilin sieht ganz entzückend & lieb aus; mit dunklen, langen Haaren & strahlenden Augen, sehr zufrieden & behaglich. Sie hat ein kleines Strohkörblein & ich habe Henny sehr zugeredet, es dem Kind so warm als möglich zu machen; ich glaube sie tut es auch. Henny sieht gut aus & hat viel Freude mit dem Kind. Auch alle die Tiere sehen gut aus & der Esel ist ein lieber Bursche. Das Pony hat keinen Stall & das wird schwer für es im Winter werden. Gestern sah ich Henny in Aberdeen & sie sagte wieder, dass alles gut geht.

Vom Besuch der Universität bin ich befreit! Das ist eine grosse Hilfe. Ich habe die Erlaubnis bekommen, für mich zu studieren & die Prüfungen zu machen, wann ich will. So ist viel Zeit & Geld & überflüssige Not gespart.

Vorige Woche waren Reporter hier & haben mich interviewt & photographiert, das Resultat findet ihr beiliegend.

3 oder 4 Kinder werden auch in der nächsten Zeit kommen. Ich verhandle jetzt darüber. Die Vorträge in Heathcot, das gut besetzt ist habe ich gestern abends begonnen. Ich werde jetzt jeden Mittwoch über Fixsterne & Planeten, in ihrer Beziehung zum Menschen dort sprechen. Jeden 2. Sonntag-Nachmittag spreche ich ab Anfang Dezember in Gilhobley's Haus in Aberdeen über anthroposophische Menschenkunde. Wenn ich die polizeiliche Erlaubnis bekomme, werde ich vom 4.-8. November, die schon lange geplante Missionswoche mit George Macleod in Edinburgh halten & zu 50-60 Studenten ein bis zweimal täglich über: „Wissenschaft & Evangelium" sprechen. Am 17. & 18. bin ich nach Glasgow eingeladen um vor den Pfarrern über „New understanding of the gospels" zu sprechen.

So seht Ihr, dass manches schon geschehen ist & hoffentlich folgt bald mehr.

Aber zwischen aller Arbeit überfällt mich immer wieder der Gedanke, dass Ihr noch dort im Haus № 6 seid, in den kalten Zimmern, in der Sinnlosigkeit & dann ist es schwer, das zu tragen.

Die Frauen arbeiten alle sehr lieb u. brav, aber es waren die langen Monate Alleinsein irgendwo zu viel u. sie brauchen Hilfe u. Hilfe u. Liebe u. Fürsorge. Und ich bin nicht stark genug, um allem gerecht zu werden. Aber ich versuche es jeden Tag neu.

Ännchen ist die weitaus Tapferste, unermüdlich, ganz ausdauernd u. kräftig. Sie erstaunt mich jeden Tag neu. Suchi ist schon ganz in ihr Kommendes hinein versunken u. lieb u. findet jeden Tag einen neuen Schritt näher zum Geist. Trude u. Liesl arbeiten treu gut, sind aber versorgt. (Hansen's Application geht morgen früh ab!). Alix u. Marie sind brav.

Seltsam ist es für mich, nun ganz unter Frauen zu leben u. diesen grandiosen Gegensatz zu dem vorhergehenden Männer-Dasein zu erfahren! Wie neu muss ich diese andere Welt verstehen u. begreifen lernen; aber es ist eine gute Schule. Es geht alles sehr in Liebe u. Güte u. sehr selten kommt es noch, dass der Löwe brüllen muss. Und nachher tut es ihm sehr leid.

Den Brief von Dr Lehrs habe ich erhalten. Ich grüsse ihn sehr schön u. schreibe ihm am Sonntag. Hoffentlich ist Sucher wieder gesund. Auf Hans warten wir täglich u. hoffen sehr, dass er bald kommt.

Bitte grüßen Sie Rhode & Römer, Herrn Staude & alle andern! Besonders Herrn Broder, Stern & Rodern. Ich hoffe, dass es allen erträglich geht!

Peter, Hans, Lehrs, Sucher umarme ich & grüße ganz, ganz herzlich, so stark ich nur kann.

Ihnen liebe Thomas, alles Gute. Und viel Kraft & Mut & Frömmigkeit.

Ich bin in aller Liebe

Ihr

K König

Camphill-House
Milltimber
Aberdeenshire

October 24, 1940

My dear Thomas,

I have not written to all of you for ages, but there is so little time for all the work which needs to be done that it is really difficult to find an hour in peace and quiet.

Above all: I am very happy with what has taken place within you, Thomas. The day I received your letter was bright with sunlight and happiness because for a long while it seemed to be too much to hope for and then it *did* take place! So it is for me as for you a a kind of crowning of destiny for the best. The best for you and also for our community which is now more firmly established since not only Hans [Schauder] and Peter [Roth] but now you too have taken this clear decision for a particular path. So I embrace you and welcome you anew in all love and friendship.

Day after day I try to include you in my life and in all the work being done here. The main work is now in the garden and outside in general. I am now mostly gardener, farm labourer and servant. Most of all I have tidied away the dung heaps which had still been on the estate in abundance since Mr Gill's times; together with the children I have collected a lot of wood and prepared it for the winter. Then there are many beds in the garden which need to be dug up and even cleared because much had been neglected for years. I have taken out many trees and shrubs which were old and useless, have to some extent fixed the tools and have done a few things in the house.

The central heating is now up and running, the basement is tidy, the coal and anthracite are sorted and ready for use. Today the stairs and the rugs in the corridors have been put in and yesterday the linoleum in the cottage has been laid. It is already looking very nice there. Tell Peter that I have sorted his books and that they are very much waiting for him.

On Monday we harvested the potatoes and brought them all in. About 4 AM at break of dawn the farmer's horses were harnessed to the plough, steaming in the hazy mist, and all of us were out with the children collecting the potatoes furrow by furrow. The upper field yielded quite a good crop, the lower field almost none at all. This field needs to be completely dug up and thoroughly manured for next year.

At the same time everything else goes on, the negotiations with the committee in Aberdeen and the many efforts for your release. Tomorrow the application for yourself and Peter will finally go off to Miss Mackinnon and Miss Osmond and I hope that it will be dealt with quickly. There are as many attachments and certificates as possible and I am actually quite confident that it will be approved. In this respect please stay calm.

Two weeks ago, Thomas, I went to see Henny [Thomas's wife] and Cheilin . It was a very good and pleasant visit. Cheilin looks *really* nice and lovely; with dark, long hair and bright eyes, very content and snug. She has a little basket made of straw and I encouraged Henny to keep the child as warm as possible; I am sure she is doing so. Henny looks well and much enjoys being with the child. All the animals look good too, and the donkey is a nice fellow. The pony has no stable and this will be difficult in the winter. Yesterday I saw Henny in Aberdeen and she said again that everything is fine.

I have been exempted from attending university. This is a great help. I have got permission to study on my own and take the exam whenever it suits me. This way we shall save a lot of time and money and unnecessary hardship.

Last week reporters were here and interviewed me and took photos, you may find the results enclosed.

Three or four children are soon due to arrive. I am now in negotiations about this. Yesterday evening I have the lectures in Heathcot, which is fully occupied. I will now be lecturing there every Wednesday on the fixed stars and planets in connection to man. From the beginning of December I will speak every second Sunday afternoon in Gilhodley's house in Aberdeen about anthroposophical study of the human being. If I get permission from the authorities I will hold the long planned mission week together with George Macleoud [MacLeod] in Edinburgh from November 4 to 8, and will speak once or twice a day to fifty or sixty students about 'Science and the Gospel.' On the 17th and 18th I am invited to Glasgow to speak to ministers about 'New Understanding of the Gospels.'

So you see that quite a few things have already happened here und hopefully it will be more from now on.

But amongst all the work the thought repeatedly comes to me that you are still in House No. 6, in those cold rooms, in that pointless situation, which is then hard to bear.

The women are all working very hard and with good will but the long months on their own were somehow almost too much for them and they need support, love and care. And I am not strong enough to cope with everything. But I am trying again every day.

Ännchen [Anke Weihs] is by far the most intrepid, untiring, very tough and strong. She amazes me again every day. Gucki [Thomas's sister Karin Gretton] is already immersed in what is coming and gentle, every day taking another step closer to the spirit. Trude [Amann] and Liesl [Schauder] are working well and faithfully, but they are looked after. (Hans's application will go off away tomorrow morning!) Alix [Roth] and Marie [Korach] are very good.

It is strange for me to be now living solely among women and to experience this grandiose contrast to the previous male existence! I need to make a completely new start in understanding and grasping this different world; but it is a good learning experience. Everything goes on in love and kindness and only very rarely does the lion still have to roar. And he is very sorry afterwards.

I have received Dr Lehrs's letter. I send him kindest regards and will write to him on Sunday. Hopefully [Willi] Sucher is back to health. We expect Hans any day und much hope that he will soon arrive.

Please give my regards to Rhode and Römer, Mr Staude and everyone else! Especially Mr Broder, Stern and Modern. I hope you are all bearing up!

I embrace Peter, Hans, Lehrs and Sucher and send my kindest, kindest regards with all my heart.

I wish you, dear Thomas, all the best and much strength and courage and godliness.

With all my love

Yours,

Dr König

Notes

HMW is Hans Müller-Wiedemann, *Karl König, a Central European Biography of the Twentieth Century.*

IWA is Ita Wegman Archive, Arlesheim, Switzerland.

KKA is Karl König Archive, Camphill, Scotland. All König's surviving diaries are here.

Preface

1 Peter Selg, *The Angel over the Lauenstein,* p. 57.

2 The surviving correspondence contains references to letters no longer extant. A substantial part of Ita Wegman's correspondence with Karl König – an estimated third of all letters – is lost. Ita Wegman's letter of April 27, 1929, the only surviving original document written by Wegman, is in KKA. Carbon copies of a large number of other letters written by Ita Wegman together with 20 of Karl König's original letters are at IWA.

3 Steiner, *Mysterienwahrheiten und Weihnachtsimpulse,* pp. 22ff, lecture of December 23, 1917.

Chapter 1

1 Letter written by Ita Wegman to the curative educational institutes, June 14, 1934.

2 Steiner, *Das Zusammenwirken von Ärzten und Seelsorgern,* p. 165.

3 Hans Müller-Wiedemann summarized König's inner and social situation as a student (HMW, p. 39):

> Despite intense human encounters with his peers, König remained a solitary soul during his studies; he was strongly open to the impressions of what went on around him and what he was concerned with, but then became reserved to the point of spurning approaches in a way that people found hard to accept.

4 Diary, May 1922, quoted in HMW, p. 51.
5 Diary, quoted in HMW, p. 56.
6 König, *My Task,* p. 21.
7 Karl König did not join the Anthroposophical Society on March 30, the day of Rudolf Steiner's death, as Hans Müller-Wiedemann mistakenly assumed (HMW p. 50). A few days after König joined the Anthroposophical Society Norbert Glas wrote a letter to Margarete Bockholt asking with concern about Rudolf Steiner's state of health and noting about König: 'A doctor, Karl König, joined last week. I had a great deal to do with him but now he is firmly established with us and in a while will be able to do much work.' (Undated, around March 29, 1925, IWA.)
8 König, *My Task,* p. 22.
9 The correspondence between Ita Wegman and Karl König quoted in this chapter is not separately referenced; all letters are quoted in full in Chapter 2.
10 For Norbert Glas and the Esoteric Core of the Medical Section see Selg, *Die Briefkorrespondenz der 'jungen Mediziner,'* pp. 145ff.
11 Schickler's letter to Norbert Glas, May 13, 1925, IWA.
12 'That I, ... a city dweller and a Jew too, had found my home ...' (September 5, 1925, quotation in HMW, pp. 522f). And König, *My Task,* p. 20.
13 See Selg, *Die Briefkorrespondenz der 'jungen Mediziner,'* pp. 152f.
14 Letter of February 16, 1926, IWA.
15 Margarete Bockholt's letter to Karl König, May 20, 1926 (IWA):

> Dear Mr König,
>
> In reply to your letter of May 5, I can inform you on behalf of Dr Wegman that she hopes soon to use the article you sent, *Über die ätherischen Bildekräfte, welche die Nase des Menschen bilden,* [On the etheric formative forces shaping the human nose] in a medical publication and therefore has not given it to Dr Wachsmuth.
>
> We would be pleased to receive more of your work.
>
> With best regards
>
> Doctor Bockholt

16 For the concept and aims of the Medical Section at the Goetheanum in Rudolf Steiner's time, see Selg, *Die Medizin muss Ernst machen mit dem geistigen Leben,* Chapters 1, 2 and 5.
17 See Selg, *Anfänge anthroposophischer Heilkunst,* pp. 105ff.
18 As can be seen from the correspondence between Karl König and Ita Wegman, in some autobiographical contributions König obviously was mistaken about the date of his first encounter with Wegman in Vienna which he put as having taken place in 'September' *(Der Kreis der zwölf Sinne und die sieben Lebensprozesse,* p. 108), or 'October' 1927

(My Task, p. 25). Hans Müller-Wiedemann, too, who did not know Karl König's letters to Ita Wegman, was led to wrong assumptions regarding the date and context of this encounter in Vienna and wrote (HMW p. 521):

> Possibly Ita Wegman was passing through in order to see Rudolf Steiner's seriously ill sister before her death. Since König actually began his work at the Therapeutic Institute in Arlesheim on 7 November, it is also probable that the meeting with Dr Wegman took place at the end of September (as König reports in another memoir), as at the Vienna meeting a period of refers to 'about a couple of weeks' was mentioned.

19 König, 'The Candle on the Hill,' in HMW, p. 65.
20 König, 'The Candle on the Hill,' in HMW, pp. 65f.
21 König, *My Task,* p. 26. In a later reference Ita Wegman herself dated König's work in Arlesheim from November 1.
22 Chapter 3.
23 Ita Wegman's letter of November 29, 1927 (IWA) asked for his article *'Wirkung homöopathisierter Metallsalzlösungen auf Entwicklung und Wachstum von Kaulquappen'* (the effects of homeopathically processed metal salt solutions on development and growth of tadpoles).
24 See Husemann, *Der Heilpädagoge Karl König,* pp. 50ff.
25 König, *My Task,* pp. 27f.
26 See Selg, *Die Kultur der Selbstlosigkeit,* p. 59.
27 König, *My Task,* p. 28.
28 Chapter 3.
29 Chapter 3.
30 In *My Task* (pp. 28f) Karl König describes:

> I walked around 'pregnant' with the lecture content during all of Advent. I intended to speak about human embryo sheaths and to describe how their process of development parallelled the six days of creation in Genesis. My preparation was accompanied by the image of Raphael's Sistine Madonna – in her I saw an artistic enhancement of the human embryo sheaths. The Jesus child in her arms carried the imprint of the incarnating soul that is striving towards the earth.

31 See Fritz Götte, 'Nachruf auf Karl König' in *Mitteilungen aus der anthroposophischen Arbeit in Deutschland,* St John's Tide 1966, reprinted in Selg *Anthroposophische Ärzte,* pp. 286ff.
32 Ita Wegman's letter to Rhoda Alexander, January 5, 1928, IWA.
33 HMW, p. 99. In a letter of May 20, 1928 to Tilla Maasberg (KKA) Karl König wrote how he had experienced spiritual support from Ita Wegman in a decisive situation which was crucial for his life:

> About four weeks ago, when again I was torn and troubled by a destiny I went to sleep addressing the question to the spiritual

> world what I should do. I no longer knew what the right action was, so entwined were evil and truth. I got the answer: In my dream Doctor Wegman gave me a ring with alchemical signets. That was sufficient for me because thus I knew that currently I should not become engaged with anybody else than the Divine Wisdom (Isis-Sophia).

34 Letter to Hans Mothes, April 7, 1928 (IWA). According to Zeylmans (*Wer war Ita Wegman,* Vol. 2, p. 58), during their first meeting in Vienna Ita Wegman already offered Karl König the post of medical director at the convalescent home in Gnadenwald: 'When he refused she invited him to Arlesheim.' This astonishing statement is however not verifiable by the archive material available (including König's self-portrayal). Also Zeylmans's subsequent statement, 'König also refused Friedrich Husemann's offer of work at the Sanatorium in Wiesneck' is – with this emphasis – not sustainable, as shown by König's relevant letter to Wegman.

35 HMW, p. 70.

36 According to Zeylmans's – in all likelihood wrong – assumption Karl König went *at Ita Wegman's request* to Pilgramshain: 'Encouraged by Ita Wegman he joined the new institute in Pilgramshain a year later [1928]' (*Wer war Ita Wegman,* Vol. 2, p. 58.)

37 HMW, p. 99.

38 In a reference (written eight years later) Ita Wegman wrote about Karl König's work in Arlesheim (IWA):

> Dr Karl König worked with us as an assistant doctor at the Clinical Therapeutic Institute and in our children's home Sonnenhof in Arlesheim from November 1, 1927 to August 1, 1928. He took the opportunity to study extensively the diagnostic and therapeutic methods of the anthroposophical medicine which are especially used at our Institute. Also at the Sonnenhof Institute, where children in need of soul care are treated medically and with curative education according to the same methods, Dr König engaged in studies as well as in practical medical work.

39 Letter to Albert Steffen of Oct 25, 1928 (IWA).

40 For Albrecht Strohschein's life, the time he spent together with Karl König in Pilgramshain and his somewhat complicated relationship to König, see Afred Kon's description, *Gründerschicksale der Heilpädagogik.*

After Strohschein's death on October 1, 1962 König wrote in his diary: 'In the late afternoon a telegram arrives [with the message] that Albrecht Strohschein has died in the morning. And now I remember that I woke up at 5 o'clock in the morning all of a sudden seeing his signature and I asked myself what that could mean. But I forgot about it because other thoughts were rushing into my mind. Strange that he has gone now.' A day later, on October 2, 1962, König wrote: 'Strohschein's death is constantly present in my mind. There are moments when it feels as if I look back at life together with him. Spiritually we are so close but in this incarnation his earthly being was still strange and distant.' (KKA).

41 Letter to Miss Bauer, November 7, 1928 (IWA).

42 Ita Wegman's letter to Eugen Kolisko, January 22, 1929 (IWA)

43 Letter to Werner Pache, March 5, 1929 (IWA).

44 In his letter of August 12, 1928 (KKA) Gerhard Suchantke wrote from Arlesheim to Karl König:

> It is Frau Doctor's explicit wish that some time in autumn Schickler or I hold a public lecture in Berlin about carcinoma. I said that this could be done as part of the lecture series which you have arranged. Then Frau Doctor said that she would like to know what plans you really have for Berlin because it is unlikely that arrangements have already been made. I think it would be a good idea if you gave her some information about this in writing.

45 Gerhard Suchantke's letter to Karl König, August 12, 1928 (KKA).

46 Letter to Siegfried Palmer, July 5, 1929 (IWA).

47 König's Pilgramshain notebooks (KKA).

48 Ita Wegman's letter to Erich Trummler, June 13, 1929 (IWA).

49 For Ita Wegman's struggle about the overall medical responsibility for training in curative eurythmy and her conflict with Marie Steiner regarding this matter see Wegman's relevant letters, in Wegman, *Die Zivilisationsaufgabe der Anthroposophie und das Schicksal der Anthroposophischen Gesellschaft.*

50 Wegman's letter to Heinrich Hardt, January 31, 1933 (IWA).

51 See Selg, *Geistiger Widerstand und Überwindung,* pp. 22ff.

52 Erich Kirchner's letter to Wegman, June 20, 1933 (IWA), see also facsimile of page 1 of this letter in Selg, *Geistiger Widerstand und Überwindung,* p. 33.

53 Wegman's letter to Madeleine van Deventer, November 8, 1933 (IWA). Ita Wegman Archive, Arlesheim.

54 Wegman's letter to König, January 6, 1930 states:

> Of course it is very positive that people in Prague gradually show interest in the work of curative education. But it is still too early to start an institute because we do not have enough people available who are able to carry the curative educational work. We will otherwise not actually get the results Dr Steiner intended. You cannot have people working at the institutes who have not undergone training here; only if they have been taught the theory here and have afterwards been working at one of the

institutes for a year or two, can you talk of an appropriate training. Otherwise you get a badly watered down version for which I cannot take responsibility. We simply cannot think about new foundations in the near future until enough people have been properly trained. There is a general lack of the right people. But I fully agree with you that in the future a fertile ground for curative education will certainly arise in Prague.

During an extensive biographical review in his memorial address for Eberhard Schickler on September 20, 1963 in Camphill, König himself referred to the premature dimension of many endeavours during the twenties and thirties and said:

I had opportunity to meet Dr Schickler already in 1928 – thirty-five years ago. At that time there was immense enthusiasm among young doctors. They were trying to put Rudolf Steiner's indications into practice. *Often far too hastily, far too superficially.* The problem of cancer was addressed as well as curative education, medical practice, and work as a school doctor. There was not much time. Eight years passed from Rudolf Steiner's death until Hitler's takeover. (KKA, Selg's italics).

55 Letter to Margarete Bockholt, January 12, 1934 (IWA). See also Selg, *Geistiger Widerstand und Überwindung,* pp. 53ff.

56 The minutes of the Annual General Meeting of March 27/28, 1934, (p. 115, Goetheanum archive) report Hans Jenny saying:

For example Dr König's articles about embryology, published years ago, in which the ideas of anthroposophy were used in a purely dogmatic and arbitrary way and superimposed onto the details of embryology, ... in a wild, almost crazy fantasy, apostles and amnions and planets and corneas were lumped together.

As the Annual General Meeting continued Dr Jenny reported further that, during a Section meeting three years earlier (1931) and in the presence of the doctors Friedrich Husemann, Richard Schubert, Julius Solti and Jenny himself, Ita Wegman had steadfastly refused even to acknowledge that there was a problem with Karl König's cognitional method: 'The only answer given by the head of the Medical Section – and I have to say this although Dr Wegman is not here – her only answer to this central cognitional problem was: "these are mere linguistic misunderstandings".'

During the Annual General Meeting Jenny further referred to Ita Wegman, Karl König and the 'spirit' of the Medical Section:

It came to light that there was a complete lack of awareness of this actual problem of a cognitional system. Dr König did not then write anything for some time. After a while he started again with a number of articles entitled 'Contributions on Pure Anatomy' – the same ado began all over again, just in different

> terms. Nothing had changed. It was now concerned with Goethe, and in the most outlandish manner and completely arbitrarily he cobbled the idea of metamorphosis onto the concepts and understanding of nature. ... Get the volumes of *Natura* for yourselves, peruse the lectures, read them; it does not matter that these are specialized scientific questions, instead it needs to be observed that there is a dogmatic approach at work, that Rudolf Steiner's ideas are being devalued and played around with in the most trivial way. This dogmatism on one side produces a corresponding mindset on the other, in every sphere of human expression. And this is what matters, to make apparent, to illustrate that the human being actually is a whole, that if a person makes a start at one point this has the same effect at every other point, that within the sphere of will, power politics and desire for power emerge. Therefore instead of a sense of community, sectarianism; instead of truth, error, dishonesty, delusions. By using this example first and briefly mentioning Dr König's examples I wanted to describe this continuity. (Minutes of AGM, p. 116).

After Hans Jenny's speech Eugen Kolisko defended himself against fierce attacks and then referred Karl König:

> I also disagree with many things friends of mine have published, but have to say that I do prefer to work with friends who develop teething troubles – and every one of us develops such teething troubles – and rely on friendly understanding for their correction rather than to expose every single thing which appears to a sarcastic polemic down to the last detail which in the end disparages the character of the person concerned! We must also have the opportunity to shape something out of our imperfections. By this I do not want to give a *carte blanche* for imperfection, but somehow imperfections should be tolerated without being disparaged for decades. (Minutes of AGM, p. 121).

During the Annual General Meeting Kolisko also referred to the detrimental effects of such internal anthroposophical annihilation to the outside world ('souls who come into contact with our movement will not understand it. Those souls cannot cope with, cannot understand this criticism, this demolishing of people trying to do something'). Friedrich Husemann again emphasized Karl König's scientific carelessness, a behaviour supported by Ita Wegman – and again recalled the Section meeting in 1931 discussed by Jenny:

> Dr König had written these essays. Myself and others then speaking up, and a few more, regarded these essays as having insufficient methodic foundation. We pointed out these deficits

> and there was a discussion about whether they were methodically based or not. Opinions differed, and I then said there should be a chance of voicing fair criticism where those essays had been published, therefore in *Natura.* I asked Dr Wegman to give Dr Jenny, who already then had strongly opposed the essays, the opportunity to critically review the essays published in *Natura* and thus say in a factual way what he thought necessary. Dr Wegman refused. I then asked her whether *Natura* was not claiming to be a scientific journal. This was denied, I do not exactly remember in what form; anyway, it was denied that *Natura* was a scientific publication. This prompted me to say, 'Then I am not interested in it any more!' (Minutes of AGM, p. 124).

Finally Margarete Bockholt also gave a speech at the Annual General Meeting spoke and in looking back at the *Natura* discussion and Karl König's controversial studies said:

> I remember very well that Dr Wegman did not deny that *Natura* was meant to be a scientific publication; instead, in my view, it was stated ... that *Natura* was addressing the general public ... And it is always possible, and no anthroposophist can deny this, to view an issue from quite different angles. At this time the opportunity for Dr Jenny to write a critical review for *Natura* was refused. Dr Husemann suggested that it would increase the publicity of *Natura* – and this we also refused – if there was criticism and counter-criticism, it would catch people's interest ... Dr Jenny was given the opportunity to describe the same topic from his own point of view which could then be published – therefore not to write a critical review but to describe it from his standpoint. Apart from this I would like to say with regard to Dr König's article that the lecture about amnions and apostles was not published in *Natura,* and that we, too, did not exactly like it. (Minutes of AGM, p. 127).

57 IWA.

58 See the extensive report by Herbert Korach in *Korrespondenz der Anthroposophischen Arbeitsgemeinschaft,* July 1934, Vol. 3, No. 10, pp. 18–20.

59 Karl König was one of the Ita Wegman's colleagues who strongly supported her 'removal.' On April 30, 1934, just less than two weeks before Wegman was brought to Lake Thun, he wrote to Margarete Bockholt in Arlesheim: 'I think this is a very fortunate solution so that at last she can escape the bad atmosphere in Dornach.' (In the same letter König notified Bockholt of the forthcoming Whitsun conference in Pilgramshain. IWA.)

60 See Selg, *Geistiger Widerstand und Überwindung,* pp. 99ff.

61 On June 12, 1934 König had written from Vienna to Madeleine van Deventer in Arlesheim asking that study material for his work group in Prague be sent to him quickly:

Dear Dr Deventer,

The medical work in Prague is progressing very well. I have now gathered 14 new doctors including two lecturers from the university. These doctors are now planning intensive studies and together want to build up an anthroposophical library. For a start *all* volumes and issues of *Natura.* Please send them to Dr Ctibor Bezděk, Prague II, Drevna ulica 2.

Furthermore I would ask you to send the First Course for Doctors of March/April 1920 to the following: 1) Dr Souček, Prague II, Špalena 53. He is a dentist actively supporting us. 2) Dr Zdenka Tillova, Prague II, Karlova naměsti 9. She has already stayed in Pilgramshain for two weeks and in Arlesheim as well. 3) Dr Kamil Jedlička, Prague XII, Bělohdradská 13. Dr Kaelin is in contact with him and he will come to Arlesheim in August. Please ensure that these are sent *immediately,* it is very important.

I hope that otherwise you are all well. Please give my regards to all the friends.

With kind regards, yours Dr Karl König.

Madeleine van Deventer then arranged for the requested material to be sent promptly to König by Wegman's secretary, Else Koch. 'I am immensely delighted that in Prague there is such an active medical work. The course material and *Natura* will be sent immediately.' (June 16, 1934, IWA.)

62 On August 12, 1934 Ita Wegman wrote from Champex, Switzerland, to Madeleine van Deventer replying in detail to some queries she had received:

Dr König enquired if he could come to work in Arlesheim for a year and thereby assist us. From Arlesheim he would like to establish groups in Prague and Paris and start medical work there. This question too needs soon to be answered because he wants soon to have my opinion. I would agree to it, but perhaps it would be more appropriate if he did relief work first so you and Bockholt could take your holidays. How about asking him to come on August 20 and stay for September and October, he could then work with Dr Simonis as well. He should not leave Pilgramshain for too long; or are you aware that he is having difficulties?' (IWA.)

63 From Elisabeth Dank's letter to Wegman, January 5, 1935 (IWA): 'Dr König told us about your lectures and I was especially delighted with what he said about [the evangelist] Matthew.'

64 Wegman's letter to Gerhard Suchantke, March 19, 1935 (IWA):

> In Pilgramshain I got a very good impression of the work there. This institute will definitely do well despite all the difficulties within the [Anthroposophical] Society. König managed to build up a group of patients who do not have a lot to do with the Society, and the children there too have come through contacts outside the Society.

65 In her introduction to Rudolf Steiner's lecture series *Egyptian Myths and Mysteries,* also printed in the *Mitteilungsblatt* of November 30, 1930, Marie Steiner had at first severely criticized König's lectures and essays on aspects of embryology in connection to the Sistine Madonna : 'Is it necessary that this infinite chastity and purity, speaking to us from the Isis-Maria image like a bright spell from spiritual worlds of spring, be dragged down into the sphere of ordinariness and of anatomical concepts as has been done in an anthroposophical youth publication?' She had also referred strongly to the risks attached to such a course of action:

> In a movement like the anthroposophical one, the greatest gifts are given and the greatest risks prowl around beside them. Not just those risks coming from the hearts of striving individuals and which, as Rudolf Steiner so often tells us, bring the worst – that otherwise remains dormant – out of people if there is only a one-sided drive for spiritual experience without sufficient moral discipline; there are also dangers coming from those spiritual powers which want to drive us even deeper into materialism, to transform the spiritually uplifiting forces into forces which draw people down. These forces are active and what they can grab from Rudolf Steiner's gifts for their own purposes they will try to get with great cunning and persuasiveness. Things will emerge to captivate people, to impress their prevailing taste, and many get their heads caught in the net. Let us pay attention to seemingly insignificant symptoms. They can be of great consequence and might arise from a highly purposeful will which wants to take advantage of our blindness. Let us remember the warning words of our teacher who time and again reminded us of such things. We must preserve the purity of his work and protect his legacy.

Immediately after the publication of this essay Karl König wrote a letter to Marie Steiner (December 1, 1930), 'in which I tried to clarify what seemingly has been misunderstood or taken in a different way than it was meant' and sent a copy of his letter to the Executive Board of the Anthroposophical Society *('In eigener Sache').* After the programme of Karl König's and Emil Bock's course on pastoral-medical problems and issues of current interest had been published in the

Mitteilungsblatt in January 1931 it was in part fiercely criticized. 'A conference at which lectures were held exclusively on topics such as sexual life, crime, drugs, etc.' Zeylmans, *Wer war Ita Wegman,* Vol. 3, p. 316). Marie Steiner again had her say in the *Nachrichtenblatt* of February 15, 1931 and once more criticized König's essays and lectures:

> In a lecture which I listened to myself ... not only the Gospel according to John but also [Rudolf Steiner's] lectures on the Fifth Gospel, which by the way have *not* been made available [by Steiner] for use in lectures and writings, was in many ways brought into connection with embryological expositions. We experienced how the calling of the first two disciples was compared with the allantois, the calling of another one with the egg yolk, and so on. These revelations were presented with a certain solemn mood and with the pretension of occult intuitions; they thus had a suggestive effect and were received by many with devout reverence, others of course rejecting them with indignation. They inaugurated a kind of movement within our Society.

In his reply, *'In eigener Sache,'* which again was sent to all members of the Executive Board, König went into details of his Whitsun lecture in 1928, to which Marie Steiner had referred, and explained once more (as in his previous letter of December 1, 1928) in what way he had drawn connections and also quoted the shorthand notes of his lecture. However, he denied any pretence of 'occult intuition.'

> I firmly reject this statement as I never dared to make this claim. In introducing the lecture I also explained in detail why I came to the given suppositions and emphasized several times that these were 'suppositions.' This can also be seen from the shorthand notes of the lecture and was also described in the essay, *'Das logogenetische Grundgesetz'* published in *Natura* (Vol. 3, No. 6).

König stressed that he had no knowledge of any 'movements' inaugurated by him: 'In this regard I would also like to state that nothing of this kind of movement is known to me.'

66 König reacted in his open letter (written in the context of the long lasting conflicts within the Anthroposophical Society and movement) to Curt Englert-Faye's article *'Juvenilitis typica – oder ein Träger des anthroposophischen Jugendimpulses'* [Juvenilitis typica, or a carrier of the anthroposophical youth impulse] in the same journal edited by Albert Steffen. In his article Englert-Faye had vehemently attacked Ernst Lehrs in a way that, in König's view, Steffen should have stopped. 'Your approval makes it possible for people to be slandered by a really boundless flood of dirt and meanness. I must ask you, Mr Steffen,

whether – in face of this article – all your observance of human dignity and respect for human existence have died out?' Englert-Faye had also quoted out of context in a way that distorted from Rudolf Steiner's Pastoral-Medical Course and Curative Educational Course; at that time these unpublished lectures were strictly only available to the appropriate professional groups (to which Englert-Faye did not belong). Consequently König wrote to Steffen:

> You, as a member of the Executive Board, participated in this [pastoral-medical] course and I hope you still remember how Dr Steiner pointed out that precisely these passages should not be made accessible to the general public but remain the spiritual property of doctors and priests. As you are aware of this, you have allowed a theft of spiritual property .... Not only have you permitted this unauthorised usage but you have promoted the circulation of this stolen property. You should acknowledge your guilt.

At the end of his letter to Albert Steffen, König as it were forced its publication, concluding with these sentences:

> That is my opinion which I wanted to tell you. If you have integrity and honesty you will also publish this opinion in the *Mitteilungsblatt* which is supposed to be open to *every* member. But I assume you will not do so, because for years in this journal you have only allowed room for publications suiting yourself, but no space for free and honest words coming from another side.
>
> Do what you think is right. I know that in this particular matter I cannot remain silent any longer, according to the true call of my conscience. (*Nachrichtenblatt* Vo. 12, No. 7, Feb 17, 1935, pp. 27ff.)

The printing of this letter was followed by a commentary from Marie Steiner and Guenther Wachsmuth concluding with the words: 'The president cannot be expected to defend himself against such attacks on this level. The Society must protect him and itself.'

See also Karl König's letters to Albert Steffen of January 20 and November 26, 1932 regarding the problem of the controversial cancer research group in Switzerland and also König's anthroposophical work in Silesia (Anthroposophical Group Liegnitz); they also refer to the reproach by Albert Steffen and Guenther Wachsmuth that König misused his medical work for anthroposophical activities and groupings critical of the Society (Dornach). Steffen and Wachsmuth had outlined this in a letter to Albrecht Strohschein signed in the name of 'the Executive Board at the Goetheanum.' At the end of November 1932 König commented in detail on this issue and again sent a copy to *every* member of the Executive Board, writing:

> First and foremost I firmly reject the allegation that I use my medical work for anything other than healing patients as best I can. I would like to emphasize that I explicitly forbid everyone to speak in this manner about my medical work because I find it slanderous; and I would like to ask you, dear Mr Steffen, in your role as president of the Anthroposophical Society, to refrain from using such terms against a member of the General Anthroposophical Society, especially in a letter to a third party. ... I have neither taken part in an Annual General Meeting in recent years nor felt a desire to interfere in these matters in any way. The only reason why I do not hold my lectures here in Silesia within the existing branches is that the existing branches do not want my lectures. On the other hand, however, there is a large group of people at various places in Silesia who are especially interested in those anthroposophical issues which I can treat in my lectures. In doing so I am solely guided by Rudolf Steiner's words which he once used in a lecture at Dornach on April 7, 1920 (*Physiologisch-Therapeutisches auf Grundlage der Geisteswissenschaft*): 'If someone who promotes teaching about mankind, teaching about health and illness in the human being, even someone who specializes as a medical doctor is placed with such knowledge into society, he will then be in a position to enlighten that society, for he will find understanding. The connection of a doctor to society does not just consist in one going up to his house … and calling him out when something hurts or a leg is broken. The connection to a doctor will rather consist in the doctor being a continuous teacher who gives instruction in prophylactic healthcare. Continuous intervention by a doctor consists not only in healing a person whose illness goes so far that he notices it, but in keeping people healthy, as far as this is feasible. A living social interaction will take place between a doctor and all the rest of mankind. The healthiness of such knowedge will then radiate onto medicine itself.'
>
> It is only in this sense that I understand my lecturing activity and I trust and hope that the General Anthroposophical Society is open and generous enough not only to acknowledge such activity but to appreciate it too. I hope you see from this that my activity is by no means aiming at 'creating new entities which practice tasks within the Society.' (IWA).

Emanuel Zeylmans van Emmichoven studied the lives of Wegman and König extensively. On him König's experience of segregation and emigration as a Jew had a deep impact as well as the fact that König repeatedly suffered fierce attacks from anthroposophical circles not only because of the characteristic style of his lectures, but because of his Jewish background and the social orientation of his work ('a conference at which lectures were held exclusively on topics such as sexual life, crime, drugs etc.'). Zeylmans wrote (*Wer war Ita Wegman,* Vol. 2, p.253):

> In the anthroposophical historic record (as far as its existence is recognized) the fact that the activities of people like Karl König had already since 1931 been openly attacked and denounced is concealed by the coming to power in 1933 of the National Socialists in Germany with their terror regime, as well as the start of the Second World War and the resulting chaos in Europe after 1939. (See for instance, Marie Steiner's essay *'Meine Erwiderung'* [my reply] in the *Nachrichtenblatt* of February 15, 1931, Vol. 8, No. 7, pp. 27ff and her essays of March 22 and 29, 1931 in the same publication, pp. 49ff and 53ff.) The fierce argument between Karl König and Albert Steffen in the *Nachrichtenblatt* of February 17, 1935 (Vol. 12, No. 7, pp. 27ff) which led to König's exclusion from the Anthroposophical Society (see *Nachrichtenblatt* of May 19, 1935, pp. 82ff) can be regarded as the aftermath of long-lasting attacks on König. In my view it is time that these things were historically accounted for in detail, because otherwise it will never be known how these devastating political events were preceded by a macabre prelude within the Anthroposophical Society itself. It will also become more understandable why when Ita Wegman died (March 4, 1943), König could see a link between her and Kaspar Hauser. I only learned about König's diaries through Müller-Wiedemann's biography. König's 'Requiem for Ita Wegman' (March 8, 1943) is very worthy of consideration. Until then, while studying Ita Wegman's biography, I rather associated her with the destiny of Joan of Arc.

67 In Karl Day's indirect and condensed report of the Annual General Meeting published in *Was in der Anthroposophischen Gesellschaft* on May 12 and 19, 1935, Brabínek's proposal was commented as follows:

> Brabínek, Prague, does not want to back Dr König's letter but for personal considerations does not approve of an exclusion. Dr König is intensely involved in activities with doctors in Prague and freely admits that he owes his success to Dr Steiner and anthroposophy. It is easy to condemn a person but not easy to create such intense activity as carried out by Dr König. The motion to exclude him should be opposed. (Zeylmans, *Wer war Ita Wegman,* Vol. 2, pp. 348ff.)

68 At the beginning of May Dr Dostal, a doctor in Prague, had obviously informed Ita Wegman that the Anthroposophical Society in Czechoslovakia had discredited Karl König in a medical journal and had

caused severe damage to his public medical work. He had asked Wegman if she could formally protest against this on behalf of the Medical Section at the Goetheanum. Dostal's letter does not exist any more but Ita Wegman's reply of May 10, 1935 still exists, where she wrote:

> I have read your letter with interest. The way the Anthroposophical Society in Czechoslovakia has acted in regard of Dr König is downright outrageous. Of course it is incredible that the Anthroposophical Society has taken this judgment upon itself in medical journals. You ask me if I can intervene in this matter. I do not think that will be of much use because I am no longer a member of the Executive Board. Furthermore the Med. Section cannot operate without further ado unless it is connected to the Executive Board as Rudolf Steiner intended. In any case I will, of course, continue to work on the tasks given to me by Rudolf Steiner; but the work of the Med. Section has been made very difficult by these remarkable machinations within the Society. One again sees from its way of opposing Dr König how far the Anthroposophical Society has lost the ability to preserve its dignity before the public. I think it is best if you, dear Mr Dostal, brought your friends – preferably doctors – together in order to guard against this course of action, to protest against it on the basis of the medical work you did together in Prague; eventually you can perhaps also unite with Czechs in Bohemia, like Brabínek and a few others who had anyway opposed this plotting against Dr König, and, if possible, publish something in support of Dr König in the same journal. I do not mean a correction but a positive comment on Dr König, for instance expressing that Dr König's work is highly valued. If negative things are being printed in specialist journals, perhaps appreciative comments can also be included in the same publications. At the same time it could be the best possible advertisement for Dr König if a group of people wrote in this specialist journal that, for instance, they have complete trust in Dr König. Then Weleda, Mr Brabínek and Dr Heinitz should protest in strongest terms against the damage caused to their business, since it is Dr König who is of vital importance for Weleda. I do not think it would be good to let things slide, and I am convinced that you would get the best possible support by conferring with Brabínek and Dr Heinitz on how to deal with the situation.
>
> As said before it would not help a lot if people here, from the Med. Section, put in a veto since this Med. Section is still left somewhat hanging in the air because I am out of the Executive Board. That does not mean that I will not work with all my

> strength to pursue within the Section the tasks which Rudolf Steiner has given me. They still need to be pursued outside the Goetheanum. The work as such will remain the same. The decisions of the Annual General Meeting are indeed irrelevant to our activity. Accordingly Dr König's expulsion also does not really affect his activity. Of course, public attacks causing damage to the work need to be fended off. It really is a shame that things are being taken that far.
>
> Thank you for your report. I wish you all the best, and I believe that if we keep faithfully to the medical principles Rudolf Steiner gave us we will still achieve something in this world.
>
> With very kind regards
>
> Yours, Ita Wegman (IWA)

69 IWA.

70 König, *My Task,* p. 36.

71 'I did not have enough time, peace and quiet or the possibility for the intensity of effort which would be necessary to deepen and thoroughly work through the images that had come to me regarding the different human conditions.' According to König's self-critical review of his time in Pilgramshain and the curative educational work there 'I did not engage with this task to the fullest possible extent at the time.' (*My Task,* pp. 36f.)

72 For König's motivation to leave see also the diary entry of May 13, 1936, Note 75 below.

73 Ita Wegman's letter to Sister Gertrud Pini, March 23, 1936 (IWA).

74 Letter to Gertrud Pini, March 23, 1937 (IWA). Regarding Ita Wegman's motif of expanding her activities towards Eastern Europe, see in particular her essays of July 1925. There she states that in future the work of Michael will be orientated mainly towards the north-east ('Michael's main direction, especially in the future, will be the north-east. And Michael will be followed by those individualities who have worked earlier within the Aristotelian and Alexandrian stream and the Arthurian stream.'). Wegman continued in this context:

> If one considers the undermining forces which keep pressing forward from the East towards the West and are already evident in the most recent world affairs, then one can imagine how hugely important the north-east orientation will become, and what immense responsibility will be placed on the centres which are already in the East and bringing anthroposophy eastwards like a wall of light. In last period of his life Rudolf Steiner often warned that we are on a volcano which can erupt at any moment if it is not prevented by sufficient spiritual forces on the earth. *(An die Freunde,* pp. 53f.)

Four months later and following a visit to Prague to found an Anthroposophical Society in Bohemia, Ita Wegman wrote in another essay *(An die Freunde,* p. 121): 'If you think how the East-West issue is continuously gaining in significance then you understand why Dr Steiner, despite the distance, visited Prague so frequently and with so much affection. The light of anthroposophy needs to be brought to the East by the Czechs, he said.'

Karl König's bonds with Eastern Europe were deep and played a part in his destiny (see HMW, p. 81), and he felt quite affected by what happened there because of his Viennese birth and his family background. 'My father was of Burgenland descent and my mother came from Moravia' *(My Task,* p. 17). Ita Wegman from the start welcomed König's intention to work in Eastern Europe; she wanted him to take the post of medical director of the Gnadenwald Institute and develop it further, 'in order from there to open the way towards the East' (Wegman's letter to Georg Moritz, Prince of Sachsen-Altenburg, January 15, 1941, IWA).

In 1939 she wrote an extensive report to König about her journey to the Balkans (see page 81), because she knew about his own travels there two years earlier. A more important reason was his historical consciousness and willingness to act. But like Ita Wegman Karl König could no longer pursue his course towards Eastern Europe before his death. In 1966 he died while planning to start projects there. On March 21, 1966, just a few days before his death, he wrote to Margit Engel: 'Many more journeys lie before me now, above all a visit to East Germany, whither I have now been officially invited by Leipzig University to give lectures about Camphill. From there I shall go to Dresden, Prague, Budapest and Vienna so that the advance towards the East is really beginning.' (HMW, p. 549.)

75 On May 13, 1936, two weeks after arriving in Vienna, König again summarized his decision:

> We have now made the steps which have changed the course of our destiny and led us back to my native home. It is a year ago now since I returned from Greece and since then I have been planning and thinking about giving up the work which has been done in Germany for the last seven years, and returning to Vienna. There were external as well as personal reasons for this. The decision was increasingly shaped by various considerations, phantasms, ideologies and also realities.
>
> The work in Pilgramshain had come to a certain conclusion. Being together with the friends was no longer inspired by the flame of enthusiasm which had shone brightly at the start. The immediate work with the children started to become a matter of routine which compromised the healing effect, because the

divine flame of help was obscured by the smoke of many misunderstandings and sometimes a sense of resignation. The number of patients had grown to such an extent that it was not possible any more to attend to each one with accuracy and thoroughness. As a result the work became rushed and left a sense of dissatisfaction which again restricted what help I could give.

Another aspect was that I felt tied to community forms. There seemed to be too little freedom. People only came on search and with requests, and rarely with an understanding which during conversation could be expected to be on an equal level. As a result I needed to give and give all the time. Receiving something back was reduced to such a degree that I gradually felt like a well drying up. Even though, while working, the source of vitalizing energy repeatedly kept flowing into me, this condition became ever more rare, so that my strength began to fade away. Added to this were the external events. We so-called non-Aryans increasingly found ourselves being officially defamed and with no rights. Everyone with the wish to do so was allowed to insult us. And although this hardly once occured to me, the uncertainty, the shame of degradation and the feeling of being powerless, unable to speak up in the name of truth, weighed on us ever more heavily. I still remember how, three years ago around this time, I had to give up all lecturing because it would put the audience in danger; how the patients, although they intrepidly stayed with me, nevertheless became cautious, and how eventually even my friends considered our work to be at risk if I was with them any longer.' (KKA).

76 König, *My Task,* p. 40.

77 'Quite some time passed before the first patients arrived and sometimes I did not know where the money would come from for our daily needs; yet we seldom went hungry. For many months, however, only the essentials of daily life were available to us.' König, *My Task,* p. 40.

78 Steiner, *Das Zusammenwirken von Ärzten und Seelsorgern,* p. 165.

79 Certificate of baptism (KKA). Hans Müller-Wiedemann mistakenly gave 1927 as the date of Karl König's baptism, writing: 'Before König received Christian baptism in the Christian Community in 1927, he had been baptized through his spiritual encounters with Rudolf Steiner.' (HMW, p. 61.)

80 König thanked Ita Wegman for this advice and felt that it was correct and helpful at that time. But eleven years later, on June 9, 1948 – five years after Ita Wegman's death and in different historical circumstances – he wrote during a visit to Arlesheim (using the Camphill letterhead, yet writing from 'Arlesheim near Basle') to Albert Steffen:

Dear Mr Steffen,

For the last three years I have more and more been feeling that I should write a letter to you. All I want to say is that what I wrote to you in 1935 for me no longer stands justified; this means that I have meanwhile accepted that the manner of my action at that time was not only hasty but also irresponsible.

When I then was expelled from the Anthroposophical Society it was at first not fully clear to me what that meant. I have come to the conclusion that I was banned and I have tried to cope with it as best I could.

In this letter I want to tell you personally that the insults I inflicted on you by writing that letter were severe and that, for many years, it has been painful for me to know that I did such a thing. Perhaps I had to feel that pain personally and this is what I wanted you to know.

I am prepared to do everything in order not to cause any problem or obstacle regarding a readmission.

Most sincerely yours Dr Karl König.

(Goetheanum Archive, Dornach.)

Just two days later Albert Steffen replied from Dornach:

Dear Mr König!

I was most happy to receive your letter. The matter which you refer to is, as far as I am concerned, already long since closed. Perhaps you remember that already in 1935 I spoke against expulsion. The Annual General Meeting has now decided – as you have been told already – that you are readmitted. Therefore I have the pleasure to welcome you as a member.

With all best wishes Albert Steffen.

Dornach, June 11, 1948. (Goetheanum Archive, Dornach.)

81 See König, *My Task,* pp. 40f. HMW, pp. 108f, and Bock, *The Builders of Camphill.*

82 IWA.

83 See König, *My Task,* pp. 47ff:

We had firm faith in our [shared curative educational] idea and most of us were absolutely determined to follow it through to its practical realization somewhere in Europe. And so the group devised the following plan: Each one of us would make an independent attempt to escape entrapment in Austria; we would do everything to keep strong and true bonds to each other; and the first of us to discover a situation where we could potentially realize our plans would inform the others. This is how we ensured a common path of action. Perhaps the old strategic law of 'March alone; fight united' was behind our plan. The friends' gradual exodus from Vienna began in early summer. One went

> to Paris; another to Prague; a small group was given permission to stay in Basle temporarily. The others fled to Milan, Zagreb, London and Zurich. It was comforting to know that nearly everyone had already left Vienna well before I could consider leaving the city.

84 On July 15, 1938 Ita Wegman wrote to a former colleague in her clinic about a possible 'affidavit' for König to England; Norbert und Maria Glas who, like König, were of Jewish origin, had stayed in Arlesheim before moving to England with Ita Wegman's support in autumn 1939.

85 'The Party and the authorities soon began to pressurize me and I knew that I would have to act quickly if I was to escape the Gestapo's web vanishing without a trace.' (König, *My Task,* p. 49.)

86 König, *My Task,* pp. 50f.

87 A letter from Gerhard Suchantke to Ita Wegman of February 22, 1935 shows how the doctors and curative teachers around Ita Wegman had reacted at that time to König's open letter to Albert Steffen. Suchantke, who had initially been much in favour of König, wrote:

> Finally there is the matter of König's letter. Everyone here [in Berlin] feels that this letter, the factual aspects of which are none too bad, is a big blow for all of us. And König should go out of his way to make clear that this is solely his private business. Whoever I spoke to was appalled. König always talks about friendship and cooperation but then he acts like this. Other usually very reasonable people are also beside themselves because of the tone he strikes. Even doctors wrote to us hoping that König would not join our conference because they feel this is a big problem for the whole cause and for their own person. In one stroke König has put himself into a completely isolated position, and that is the saddest thing about the matter. (IWA.)

At the beginning of March 1935 the curative teachers around Ita Wegman met with her in Berlin to discuss König's letter and its consequences in detail, 'to talk about what has happened through König' (Wegman's letter to Suchantke, March 19, 1935, IWA). Even Hilma Walter who lived far away at Clent in England and used to stay out of all debates concerning the Society had written to Ita Wegman on February 20, 1934, two days before Gerhard Suchantke:

> König's letter which I read today in the *Mitteilungsblatt* will also not make the situation any easier. I feel so infinitely sorry that this has happened. I just cannot understand how somebody can do a thing like that. All this will now reflect badly on himself and his friends, even if the latter inwardly reject the action.' (IWA.)

For the way König's early lectures and *Natura* essays were discussed see Note 56.

88 HMW, p. 124.
89 HMW, p.125.
90 König, *My Task,* p. 53.
91 König, *My Task,* p. 51:

> In mid-October a letter arrived from the British Consulate in Berne. I was one of fifty Austrian doctors who had been given the permission of His Majesty's Government to study medicine and work as a doctor in Britain.

König received this letter on October 12; on October 16 he wrote to Barbara Lipsker in Vienna: 'Four days ago a permit suddenly arrived for me which is also valid for my wife and children, and I do not know how or from what source.' (HMW, p. 126.)

92 On November 28 König wrote from Courcelles to Barbara Lipsker that he would after all now have to go to England and at least for the time being abandon France: 'I hope that we shall see one another in London. It is now so difficult here that my residence permit has been revoked and I must go to London at the beginning of December. I think this is a good thing, for in this way France is making its will not to receive us outwardly apparent.' (HMW, p. 126.)
93 See Selg, *Marie Steiner-von Sivers,* pp. 192ff.
94 König wrote in retrospect on August 14, 1948 about his thoughts and feelings before going to Scotland – after Ita Wegman had firmly encouraged him – and about his first negotiations with the authorities:

> At that time I did not say much [with reference to Wegman's words] because Scotland was far away and I could not imagine myself setting foot in that strange and distant country; I knew little about this country and could hardly imagine that there could be a possible base for a curative educational project.
>
> Two months later [in January 1939] in Edinburgh I was sitting opposite the secretary of the Board of Control, that is the authority which oversees curative educational institutes, and tried – in clumsy English – to explain my plans to him. The friends Dr Wegman had mentioned had made a small house north of Aberdeen available for me, and there I wanted to start a modest institute. While talking I was thinking that this man would soon tell me with a smile that the door on my right through which I had entered the room was also there for vacating it. But he then said something different: 'For ten years we have been waiting for someone who would like to open a private institute for children with developmental deficiencies; so give it a try.' And so I tried. (Manuscript; KKA.)

95 'The house could not be enlarged, the living conditions – paraffin lamps and open fireplaces – were not acceptable to the authorities

(they endangered the handicapped children), and the work was being brought increasingly under the thumb of the owners of Kirkton House.' (HMW, p. 151.)

In an autobiographic reminiscence from 1961 (HMW, p. 157) König dated the growing problems with the Haughtons back to just a few days after the start of the war:

> To begin with, life and work continued in their familiar ways. However, a few days after war broke out a letter arrived from Mr Haughton on 7th September in which he placed some pressing demands on us. His requirement was that from now on he would be obliged to take over the running of the financial affairs of our growing enterprise; that he alone would deal with the relevant officials and that his wife would now have the oversight of our educational and curative-educational affairs. If we were not to accept, he would no longer be able to shield us from the authorities. What choice did we have but to accept? At the same time, nevertheless, we resolved to leave Kirkton House as soon as possible and find another place for our work. Having to bow to this supreme authority brought with it the seeds of rebellion.

96 See also HMW (p. 174 et. seq.) for König's intense efforts to adjust from the start to British culture, to speak the language of his host country within the community and to appreciate his environment gratefully and openly. Already at the opening of Kirkton House on May 28, 1939 König not only expressed his heartfelt thanks to Mr and Mrs Haughton but also stated in principle:

> If one travels through the countryside here, one can have the impression that Christianity must be brought back and that this is possible in a transformed way through anthroposophy.
>
> We must understand this rightly. It is not that we should see ourselves as the bearers of a mission, but that we should try to bring about a meeting with the English spirit and the spirit of Central European, a meeting between everything that has been dreamt and thought by the German spirit and that which the English spirit can accomplish by way of deeds. We should promise one another not to create an island of Central European here but to try as well as we can to act for the good of this land. (HMW, p 449.)

97 On April 2, 1940 Susanne Lissau, who later became Hans Müller-Wiedemann's wife, wrote to Karl König:

> Dear Dr König,
>
> Please accept my apologies for not having contacted you for such a long time. But now, after going through a deep inner conflict, I have decided to stay here. I find it really very difficult to tell

you this because you have been waiting for my arrival for long enough. Had I quickly received my French visa, going to Scotland would clearly have been the right thing for me to do.

But when it did not arrive, the possibility arose that I would have to stay here anyway. In the meantime the situation here has stabilized again and Dr Wegman strongly wished that the four of us – Pracht, Miss Loudon, Miss Russ and myself – should engage ourselves in publicly promoting the lyre by organizing concerts, etc.

All this and my old desire to work and learn here for longer have finally led me to my decision. Perhaps you can also understand how difficult this is for me, because working in Scotland rather appealed to me. In addition I have for the time being to go without seeing my parents and siblings.

I really hope that I have not caused you too much inconvenience and that you will soon find someone else as a replacement. Please do not be too angry with me, I am really sorry to have caused you so much trouble. With kindest regards

Yours, Susanne Lissau. (IWA)

98 Letter of December 28, 1940 (IWA).

99 About these days and his own feelings König wrote further in his diary:

The day before yesterday [March 3, 1943], in the morning before waking up, all of a sudden Dr Bockholt was there. So kind and gentle as I have never seen her before; she tried to say something but I could not understand her. I think she came to prepare me, but I did not hear or understand what she said.

Who will lead us now? Does it not seem as if everything within our movement has gone to pieces?

Who will carry the chalice when Doctor Wegman is not there any more?

She will now be lying in state, in one of her long dresses, in silent beauty and in patient calm. On her delicate fingers the rings designed for her by Rudolf Steiner.

And he will receive her, welcome her, upraise her. But we are alone, alone, alone. *Where is the help?*' (KKA.)

100 The theme of Kaspar Hauser had been on Karl König's mind for many years. In February 1935 König's friend Eugen Kolisko had held a Medical Section lecture at the Goetheanum about the enigma of Kaspar Hauser. In Stuttgart he had also spoken together with Caroline von Heydebrand about Kaspar Hauser's destiny. During his visits to Pilgramshain, too, König and Kolisko repeatedly discussed Hauser; in 1934 König stated in his diary: 'From conv. with Dr Kolisko. *Kaspar Hauser:* He is a personality who has never been

incarnated before. The child of Europe. Put into this world as a Mercury impulse against the Mars impulse of Napoleon. Incarnated through Napoleon's genetic line in Baden. Murdered, probably by the same person who brought him up. – Puts the impulse of curative education into the world.'

On February 25, 1940, before moving to Camphill, König held a lecture at Heathcot (at that time a guest house where the parents of Alix and Peter Roth lived) focusing on Kaspar Hauser and anthroposophical curative education. In spring 1943 König gave a lecture in Camphill on Kaspar Hauser and Jakob Wassermann. His memorial text for Ita Wegman related to his previous studies: 'As a kind of requiem for Doctor Wegman I would like to write down everything which *for the past few months has been in my soul and feels close to the being of Kaspar Hauser.*' (Diary, KKA. Selg's italics.)

Also at the beginning of 1943, König had made an intensive study of Rudolf Steiner's Curative Educational Course and had held a lecture on this for his friends (see diary entries and notes about the structure of the Curative Educational Course in König, *Vorträge zum Heilpädagogischen Kurs,* pp. 191 ff). There he spoke about the 'being of the course' which came about not only through Rudolf Steiner and Ita Wegman but also through the existence of the 'handicapped child' and Kaspar Hauser. (See also Selg, *Der Engel über dem Lauenstein.)*

101 HMW, p. 207.

102 For Karl König's diary notes, the greater part of which were burnt in Camphill decades after his death, see Selg, *Karl König's Path into Anthroposophy,* pp. 9ff.

103 Diary entry of January 3, 1946. For this Ephesus dimension of König's destiny, see the diary entries of May 28, 1953, in Selg, *Karl König's Path into Anthroposophy,* pp. 53f.

On board a ship in the South Atlantic on his way to South Africa, König wrote to Eberhard Schickler on March 1, 1961: 'On March 4, Frau Doctor [Wegman's] death day, I shall arrive in South Africa. *I hope to be able to work there in her spirit.*' (KKA, Selg's italics.)

104 König's letter to Erika von Arnim, June 29, 1964, KKA.

105 KKA.

106 See Selg, *Ita Wegman und Arlesheim,* pp. 33f.

107 Wegman's letter to Joseph van Leer, December 23, 1933.

Chapter 2

1 Diary (KKA).

Chapter 3

1 König's memories of March 17, 1960 were part of his lectures held on March 3, 10 and 17, 1960 in Newton Dee. 'Seven years ago curative educational diagnostics of the twelve senses was introduced in Camphill. We have now made the first steps in curative educational diagnostics of the seven life processes. That I was able to do this so to speak in Dr Ita Wegman's presence and to offer it to her eternal being was for me a great honour.' (König, *Der Kreis der zwölf Sinne,* p. 149.) For Ita Wegman's relationship to the world of the etheric, see Selg, 'Vom Umgang mit dem Tod.'

Appendix

König's letter to Thomas Weihs, KKA.

Bibliography

Bock, Friedwart (Ed.) *The Builders of Camphill. Lives and Destinies of the Founders*, Edinburgh 2004.

Brons, Michael and Müller, Georg (eds.), *Anthroposophische Heilpädagogik und Sozialtherapie in der Schweiz. Ein Almanach* [Anthroposophical curative education and social therapy], Dornach 2006.

Husemann, Godhard M. *Der Heilpädagoge Karl König* [The remedial teacher Karl König], Stuttgart 1971.

Kon, Alfred, *Gründerschicksale der Heilpädagogik – Albrecht Strohschein und sein Lebensumkreis* [Lives of founders in remedial-pedagogics; Albrecht Strohschein and his life and times], Paderborn 2004.

König, Karl, 'In eigener Sache' [on my own account], typescript with signature, no date [1931] IWA.

—, *Der Kreis der zwölf Sinne und die sieben Lebensprozesse* [The cycle of the twelve senses and the seven life processes], Stuttgart 1999.

—, *My Task. Autobiography and Biographies,* Edinburgh 2008.

—, *Vorträge zum Heilpädagogischen Kurs Rudolf Steiners* [Lectures on Rudolf Steiner's Curative Educational Course], Stuttgart 2000.

Müller-Wiedemann, Hans, *Karl König, A Central-European Biography in the Twentieth Century,* Camphill Press 1996.

Selg, Peter, *Anfänge anthroposophischer Heilkunst* [Beginnings of the anthroposophical art of healing], Dornach 2000.

—, (ed.), *Anthroposophische Ärzte. Lebens- und Arbeitswege im 20. Jahrhundert* [Anthroposophical doctors; life and work]. Dornach 2000.

—, *Die Briefkorrespondenz der 'jungen Mediziner.' Eine dokumentarische Studie zur Rezeption von Rudolf Steiners 'Jungmediziner'-Kursen* [The correspondence of the young doctors. A documentary study on the reception of Rudolf Steiner's young doctors courses], Dornach 2005.

—, *Edith Maryon, Rudolf Steiner und die Dornacher Christus-Plastik* [Edith Maryon, Rudolf Steiner and the Christ sculpture in Dornach], Dornach 2006.

—, *Der Engel über dem Lauenstein. Siegfried Pickert, Ita Wegman und die anthroposophische Heilpädagogik* [The angel over the Lauenstein. Siegfried Pickert, Ita Wegman and anthroposophical curative education], Dornach 2004.

—, *Geistiger Widerstand und Überwindung. Ita Wegman 1933–1935* [Spiritual resistance and overcoming. Ita Wegman 1933–35], Dornach 2005.

—, *Helene von Grunelius und Rudolf Steiners Kurse für junge Mediziner. Eine biographische Studie* [Helene von Grunelius and Rudolf Steiner's courses for young doctors. A biography] Dornach 2003.

—, *'Ich bin für Fortschreiten,' Ita Wegman und die Medizinische Sektion* ['I am for progress,' Ita Wegman and the Medical Section], Dornach 2004.

—, *Ita Wegman und Arlesheim,* Dornach 2006.

—, 'Ita Wegman und der Aufbau der anthroposophischen Heilpädagogik' [Ita Wegman and the development of anthroposophical curative education] in Brons & Müller, *Anthroposophische Heilpädagogik und Sozialtherapie in der Schweiz.*

—, *Karl König's Path into Anthroposophy, Reflections from his Diaries,* Edinburgh 2008.

—, *Die Kultur der Selbstlosigkeit. Rudolf Steiner, das Fünfte Evangelium und das Zeitalter der Extreme* [The culture of altruism. Rudolf Steiner, the Fifth Gospel and the era of extremes], Dornach 2006.

—, *Die letzten drei Jahre. Ita Wegman in Ascona 1940–1943* [The last three years. Ita Wegman in Ascona 1940–43], Dornach 2006.

—, *Marie Steiner-von Sivers. Aufbau und Zukunft des Werkes von Rudolf Steiner* [Marie Steiner-von Sivers. Development and future of Rudolf Steiner's work], Dornach 2006.

—, *Die Medizin muss Ernst machen mit dem geistigen Leben. Rudolf Steiners Hochschulkurs für die 'jungen Mediziner'* [Medicine needs to be serious about spiritual life. Rudolf Steiner's course for young doctors], Dornach 2006.

—, 'Vom Umgang mit dem Tod. Ein Beitrag zur ärztlichen Gesinnung Ita Wegmans' [How to deal with death: a contribution on Ita Wegman's medical ethics], in *Der Merkurstab,* 2006, No. 1, pp. 3–7.

Steiner, Rudolf, *Physiologisch-Therapeutisches auf Grundlage der Geisteswissenschaft. Zur Therapie und Hygiene,* GA 314, Dornach 1989.

—, *Mysterienwahrheiten und Weihnachtsimpulse*, GA 180, Dornach 1980.

—, *Das Zusammenwirken von Ärzten und Seelsorgern. Pastoral-medizinischer Kurs,* GA 318, Dornach 1994.

Wegman, Ita, *An die Freunde* [To the friends], Arlesheim 1986.

—, *Die Zivilisationsaufgabe der Anthroposophie und das Schicksal der Anthroposophischen Gesellschaft. Ausgewählte Briefe* [The civilizing mission of anthroposophy and the destiny of the Anthroposophical Society. Selected correspondence] (in preparation).

Zeylmans van Emmichoven, Emanuel, *Wer war Ita Wegman. Eine Dokumentation* (3 volumes), 2nd ed, Dornach 2000 (in English: *Who was Ita Wegman?* Spring Valley 1995.

Index

Karl König's collected works are being published in English by Floris Books, Edinburgh and in German by Verlag Freies Geistesleben, Stuttgart. They are issued by the Karl König Archive, Aberdeen in co-operation with the Ita Wegman Institute for Basic Research into Anthroposophy, Arlesheim. They seek to encompass the entire, wide-ranging literary estate of Karl König, including his books, essays, manuscripts, lectures, diaries, notebooks, his extensive correspondence and his artistic works. The publications will fall into twelve subjects.

The aim is to open up König's work in a systematic way and make it accessible. This work is supported by many people in different countries.

Overview of Karl König Archive subjects

Medicine and study of the human being
Curative education and social therapy
Psychology and education
Agriculture and science
Social questions
The Camphill movement
Christianity and the festivals
Anthroposophy
Spiritual development
History and biographies
Artistic and literary works
Karl König's biography

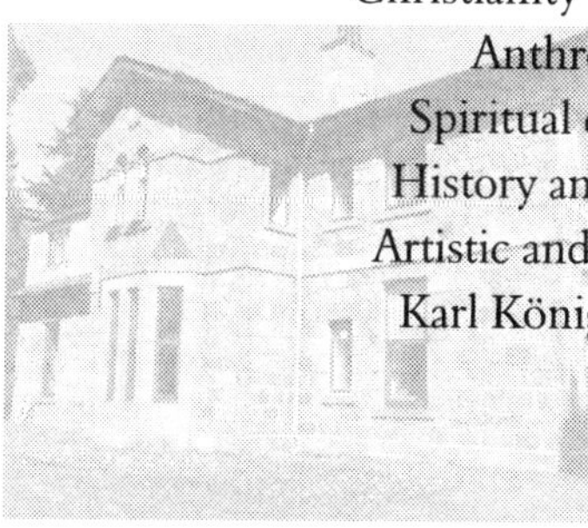

Karl König Archive
Camphill House
Milltimber
Aberdeen AB13 0AN
United Kingdom
www.karl-koenig-archive.net
kk.archive@camphill.net

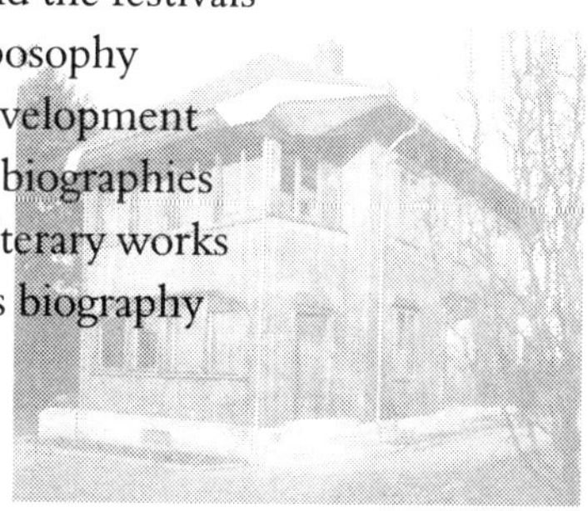

Ita Wegman Institute for Basic
Research into Anthroposophy
Pfeffingerweg 1a
4144 Arlesheim
Switzerland
www.wegmaninstitut.ch
koenigarchiv@wegmaninstitut.ch